## The Four Pillars of NLP

- **Setting your goal.** Know exactly what you want, in any situation. Once you have outcomes you stop thinking about the problems to overcome and focus on the future.

- **Using your senses.** Pay close attention to the world around you. As you develop your sensory awareness find out much more about how you and others act and react – and make productive change.

- **Behaving flexibly.** Keep on changing what you do until you get what you want, and remember, the path that leads to realising your goals is not always a straight one.

- **Building relationships.** Others contribute to you achieving what you want in life. As you learn how to create and deepen rapport you'll discover even more success.

## NLP Principles

- The map is not the territory.

- People respond as a result of their maps.

- Every behaviour has a positive intention.

- There is no failure, only feedback.

- The meaning of the communication is the response it gets.

- You cannot not communicate.

- People have all the resources they need.

- If what you are doing is not working, do something different.

- In any system the person with the most flexibility controls the system.

- Choice is better than no choice.

## Logical Levels of Change

Change can happen at one or more of six levels:

- **The environment level** describes the situation. This level answers the questions *where? when?* and *with whom?*

- **The behaviour level** refers to what people say and do within the environment. It answers the question *what?*

- **The capabilities level** includes the skills and knowledge that direct people's behaviour in the environment. This answers the question *how?*

- **The beliefs and values level** encompasses those things that are true and important to people within the situation. It answers the question *why?*

- **The identity level** is people's sense of self or their roles. It answers the question *who?*

- **The purpose level** is about how people connect to something bigger than themselves. It answers the question *what for?*

*For Dummies: Bestselling Book Series for Beginners*

# Business NLP For Dummies®

**Cheat Sheet**

## Well-formed Outcomes

Achieve more with well-formed outcomes for different areas of business including:

- **Selling:** Helping customers work out what they want.
- **Negotiating:** Ensuring you have a realistic outcome.
- **Influencing:** Getting what you want from a conversation or meeting.
- **Coaching:** Helping others to improve their performance.
- **Relating:** Building important relationships and networks.
- **Recruiting:** Knowing exactly what kind of people you need.
- **Setting targets:** Determining goals for sales, costs, productivity, or efficiency.

## Action Planning

- What needs to happen for [outcome]?
- Is there anything else that needs to happen for [outcome]?

  *Keep on asking this question until the answer is 'No'.*
- What needs to happen first?
- Can you [do first thing]?

## The Characteristics of a Well-formed Outcome

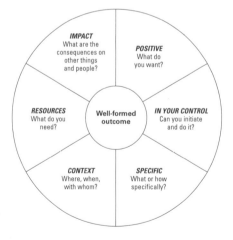

*For Dummies: Bestselling Book Series for Beginners*

# Business NLP
## FOR
# DUMMIES®

A John Wiley and Sons, Ltd, Publication

# Business NLP

## FOR

# DUMMIES®

by Lynne Cooper

A John Wiley and Sons, Ltd, Publication

**Business NLP For Dummies**©

Published by
John Wiley & Sons, Ltd
The Atrium
Southern Gate
Chichester
West Sussex
PO19 8SQ
England

E-mail (for orders and customer service enquires): cs-books@wiley.co.uk

Visit our Home Page on www.wiley.com

For general information on our other products and services, please contact our Customer Care Department within the U.S. at 800-762-2974, outside the U.S. at 317-572-3993, or fax 317-572-4002.

For technical support, please visit www.wiley.com/techsupport.

Wiley also publishes its books in a variety of electronic formats. Some content that appears in print may not be available in electronic books.

British Library Cataloguing in Publication Data: A catalogue record for this book is available from the British Library

ISBN-13: 978-0-470-69757-3 (P/B)

Printed and bound in Great Britain by Bell & Bain Ltd., Glasgow

10 9 8 7 6 5 4 3 2

WILEY

# About the Author

**Lynne Cooper** facilitates organisational change and leadership development. With extensive business and management experience, she uses NLP to help business leaders bring about fast and sustainable change for themselves and their organisations. Lynne specialises in developing leadership skills and improving team working to maximise performance, working one-to-one, and with groups. Lynne is an NLP Master Practitioner, a certified Clean Facilitator and an accredited coach. She is director of Change Perspectives and a business trainer with PPD Learning Ltd.

# Author's Acknowledgements

I, like so many others, owe a huge debt of gratitude to the originators of NLP, Richard Bandler and John Grinder and the many other NLP developers who have contributed so much to the field – Judith DeLozier, Lesley Cameron Bandler, Robert Dilts to name only a few. As a result of their work people, businesses and communities are achieving so much more – this book is just one example of these achievements.

*Business NLP For Dummies* is based very much on my own experience of taking NLP into organisations to improve individual and business performance. That would never have been possible without learning from, and being supported by, some of the most outstanding trainers in the field. Particular mention must go to Judith Lowe, James Lawley and Penny Tompkins. Special thanks too to my dear friend and colleague, Mariette Castellino, from whom I have learned so much, and all those clients who had faith in the difference that working with us could make.

Thanks to the team at Wiley, including Simon, Sally and Nicole, for guiding and supporting me through the writing of this book, and to Chris for his diligent and knowledgeable contributions. Particular thanks to Brian Kramer, whose insights and incisive questions added so much to the end result.

Many thanks to friends and family for their forbearance. They've been sorely neglected, but much loved, through the process of writing this book. And last but not least, thanks to Glen, Victoria and Chelsey, who have encouraged, supported and nurtured me with tea and cake in the long hours of writing.

## Publisher's Acknowledgments

We're proud of this book; please send us your comments through our Dummies online registration form located at www.dummies.com/register/.

Some of the people who helped bring this book to market include the following:

*Acquisitions, Editorial, and Media Development*

**Acquisitions Editor:** Nicole Hermitage

**Publishing Assistant:** Jennifer Prytherch

**Development Editor:** Simon Bell

**Content Editor:** Jo Theedom

**Copy Editor:** Sally Osborn

**Technical Editor:** Chris Howell

**Publisher:** Jason Dunne

**Executive Editor:** Samantha Spickernell

**Executive Project Editor:** Daniel Mersey

**Cover Photos:** © Tetra Images / Alamy

**Cartoons:** Rich Tennant
(www.the5thwave.com)

*Composition Services*

**Project Coordinator:** Linsey Stanford

**Layout and Graphics:** Reuben W. Davis, Sarah Philippart

**Proofreader:** Susan Moritz

**Indexer:** Claudia Bourbeau

**Publishing and Editorial for Consumer Dummies**

> **Diane Graves Steele,** Vice President and Publisher, Consumer Dummies

> **Joyce Pepple,** Acquisitions Director, Consumer Dummies

> **Kristin A. Cocks,** Product Development Director, Consumer Dummies

> **Michael Spring,** Vice President and Publisher, Travel

> **Kelly Regan,** Editorial Director, Travel

**Publishing for Technology Dummies**

> **Andy Cummings,** Vice President and Publisher, Dummies Technology/General User

**Composition Services**

> **Gerry Fahey,** Vice President of Production Services

> **Debbie Stailey,** Director of Composition Services

# Contents at a Glance

# Table of Contents

# Introduction

*T*oday's workplaces can be stressful places to be – at least for some. Businesses are continually working to adapt to fast-changing environments, to stay ahead and make profits. Not-for-profit organisations are repeatedly challenged by the demands of achieving more with less. Individuals work harder under the constant pressure to perform better and achieve more. And many people are dissatisfied with their situation and want change – a more fulfilling job, career, or income, or an improved balance between their personal and working lives. I've written this book because this is the kind of feedback I get on a day-to-day basis when working with people at work – and because my experience has taught me that Neuro-linguistic Programming (NLP) is a valuable approach to making the improvements and transformations that these people seek.

NLP transformed my own life, in particular my working life. I used NLP to get in touch with what I really wanted, and to develop the flexibility and skills to achieve it. At the start of my journey I would never have imagined that I would change my career and use NLP full time, doing work I love – coaching and facilitating others to make positive change at work.

NLP enables you to understand what makes you tick; how you think, how you feel, how you make sense of everyday life in the world around you and how to take charge of your life. Whether you wish to put in place a few subtle changes to your performance, influence or achievements at work, or to turn your whole working life upside down, you'll find some fantastic tools in NLP to help you. I wish you well on your own personal voyage of discovery.

## About This Book

This book takes you through the practical applications of NLP within the working environment, and guides you through exercises and techniques to refocus and streamline your thought processes. Whether you're interested in improving your communication skills or polishing your leadership techniques, this hands-on guide gives you the tools you need to take control and achieve your goals within the workplace.

If you are new to NLP you can discover a whole variety of techniques in this book to learn and use to achieve your elusive goals and make improvements to your working life. If you already have knowledge of NLP, I trust that you'll find some of my ideas and approaches to using NLP in the workplace new and interesting.

I have selected the aspects of NLP that I have found most useful in supporting people to identify new possibilities, take action and achieve more, in my work with organisations. I have structured the book so that you can dip into any chapter to discover some practical ways of using NLP to handle the specific challenges you face at work, including:

- ✔ Improving your influence to achieve more
- ✔ Leading and motivating others
- ✔ Developing a vision – for yourself or the business
- ✔ Coaching others to perform well
- ✔ Accomplishing goals
- ✔ Handling tricky relationships
- ✔ Making effective change

You'll probably find some new stuff in this book – things which require you to think and act a little differently to your normal way of operating. Take the opportunity to use the techniques and exercises I've given you to build your understanding and skill. In my experience, the best way to learn NLP is to experience it. Test it out for yourself, and notice any disbelief slip away as you find yourself getting results.

## Conventions Used in This Book

To help you navigate through this book, I've set up a few conventions:

- ✔ *Italic* is used for emphasis and to highlight new words or terms that are defined.
- ✔ **Boldfaced** text is used to indicate the action part of numbered steps.
- ✔ `Monofont` is used for Web addresses.

# What You're Not to Read

I've written this book so that you can easily understand what you find out about NLP in a business context. Although after all this work I'd like to believe that you want to scour my every word, I've made it easy for you to identify material that you don't absolutely have to read. This is interesting stuff, and you'll benefit from it, but it's not essential reading:

- ✔ **Text in sidebars:** The sidebars are the grey shaded boxes that appear here and there. They share personal stories and observations, and flesh out the bare bones, but you can skip them if you wish.

- ✔ **The stuff on the copyright page:** Well, of course, read it if you will, but if you're like me, you'll not get excited about the legal stuff and reprint information.

# Foolish Assumptions

In writing this book, I made a few assumptions about you. I assumed that you work – maybe you have your own business or are employed by a large organisation. I've also assumed that you are attracted to this book because you've heard something about NLP (you may even already know and work with NLP concepts), you're curious to learn more, and you're interested in personal or business improvement. Learning more about how to use NLP effectively at work will be indispensable if any of the following apply to you:

- ✔ You want to improve your own performance at work

- ✔ You have a vision – a dream career, job, or income – that you just can't seem to reach

- ✔ You want to improve business performance.

- ✔ You find other people are often the biggest barriers to your success.

- ✔ You want to take back control of your working life.

# How This Book Is Organised

I've divided this book into five parts, with each part broken into chapters. The parts structure helps to keep related material together. The table of contents gives you more detail on each chapter, so you can dive in wherever you want to.

# Part I: The Difference That Makes the Difference

This part is where you get the basics on understanding and using NLP in a business environment. I introduce you to the NLP thinking behind engaging with and influencing others, increasing your flexibility to get the results you want, setting and achieving goals, and applying the principles of NLP to overcome barriers to success in the workplace.

# Part II: Building Working Relationships That Work

An important NLP concept is creating advantage through excellent relationships and effective influence. Part II gets up close and personal with the business of communicating in business, from understanding how other people's thought and speech patterns work through to building rapport and maximising influence in the workplace. I also delve into how to manage emotional states and motivating others – and yourself!

# Part III: Leading People to Perform

Wouldn't your working life be a whole load easier if others would just do what you wanted them to? This part gives you the tools you need to help your work colleagues perform to the max. I explain the importance of emotional intelligence in driving people's responses, how to inspire and enthuse others, and how to effect change in difficult relationships. I also cover the value of well-constructed feedback and positive coaching in supporting and developing employees to perform at their best.

# Part IV: Achieving Business Excellence

This part focuses on how to use NLP to effect real change in a business environment. Starting from the creation of a vision colleagues will want to buy into, and how to generate fast and sustainable change, I go on to explain the value of generating the sort of well-formed outcomes to which they will want to aspire. I also let you in on the secrets of modelling the strategies of those who have already met with success.

## Part V: The Part of Tens

If it's a *For Dummies* book, it has a Part of Tens, and this one is no exception. Here you'll find ten business benefits to using NLP, tips for using the principles in everyday situations, and run-downs of the best in NLP resources and books. The works, in other words, on the works.

# Icons Used in This Book

The icons in this book help you find particular kinds of information that may be of use to you:

This icon highlights practical advice to put NLP to work for you in work situations.

This icon is a friendly reminder of important points to take note of.

You'll find this icon beside stories relating real-life experience of NLP in action in business. Some are real; others have their names changed; while others are composite characters.

You'll find this icon highlighting things that you may like to experiment with to start to translate the theory into action for yourself, and to build your NLP skills.

# Where to Go From Here

You don't have to read this book from cover to cover, but you will benefit greatly if you capture it all at the pace and in the order that's right for you. Use the table of contents to see what you are attracted to first. For example, if you're keen to improve your business relationships , try Chapter 6 first. Or if you'd like to hone your coaching skills, turn to Chapter 12 first. One of the common themes of this book is flexibility, so feel free to approach the book in whichever order works for you.

# Part I
# The Difference That Makes the Difference

The 5th Wave — By Rich Tennant

"Henceforth, we shall try a new direction in management called neuro linguistic programming."

# In this part . . .

Welcome. The chapters in this part deliver the basics on understanding and using NLP in business. I introduce you to the NLP skills you need to engage with and influence others and increase your flexibility to get the results you want. I also show you how to set and achieve goals and apply the principles of NLP to overcome barriers to success at work.

# Chapter 1

# Achieving Business Excellence with NLP

*B*uilding a career, getting an interesting job, and finding opportunities to progress are important to most people. After all, you spend a huge amount of time at work. You hope that your career brings personal development, fulfilment, and, of course, the means you need to live a comfortable life. Yet sometimes your working life falls short of your expectations and hopes.

Making a success of your working life and achieving your professional goals and dreams depends on more than your qualifications, experience, and job-related skills. These days, getting on at work relies on exceptional communication skills and the ability to flex and change continually. Understanding the principles and tools of *neuro-linguistic programming,* or *NLP*, can help you become an excellent influencer, as well as acquire the self-awareness and techniques to adapt and change to achieve your aspirations.

If you're ready to take charge of your life at work – and to stop allowing your fortunes to be dictated by bosses, colleagues, employers, customers, or anyone else – then this book is a good place to start. Find out more about the value of NLP in business in this chapter, before moving on to discover dozens of ways to put its principles to use in the rest of the book.

# *Reprogramming the Mind for Success*

Making change happen at work often seems difficult. Have you ever found that, no matter how much you try, you're still frustrated in your efforts to make things better?

Maybe you've been so determined in the past that you worked harder and harder, yet still didn't get what you wanted. This experience isn't so surprising, certainly if you subscribe to a core NLP premise, explored more in Chapter 3, that:

If you always do what you've always done, you'll always get what you've always got.

So in order to get a different result, you probably have to make some changes and find alternatives to your tried-and-tested actions and responses to people, situations, and challenges. At the heart of NLP is the idea that if you about continually seek new choices and try different things, you achieve what you want.

The fact that you're reading this book suggests that you may well be ready to make some changes. Throughout the book I show you how to use NLP to discover the drivers of your thinking and behaviour. You can discover how to detect the patterns and habits that you hold unconsciously – and realise when these patterns and habits are very useful to you, as well as when they aren't.

Think of your brain as a bespoke computer, programmed to run you. As with any software program, you only notice the bit that comes up on the screen. The detailed and sophisticated program is running behind the scenes, out of your awareness. You may not realise that some of this software can be deleted, installed, or upgraded to get far more effective results. The same can be said of your unconscious mind. After you start paying some attention and observing how your mind is working, you have the choice to delete, upgrade, or install whichever bit of 'thinking software' you desire.

NLP offers you the keys to unlocking your own potential. Reprogramming your mind for success is in your hands. Removing previous limitations is inevitable. Your dreams become your goals, and they're goals you can achieve.

You can't change other people. All you *can* change is yourself and how you respond to other people. When people around you are ready to change, you can use many of the tools and approaches you discover in this book to coach and help them. Turn to Chapter 12 for more on coaching others.

# Defining NLP

One of the first challenges to face when discovering NLP is the name itself. *Neuro-linguistic programming* sure is a mouthful.

When you break the name down into its component parts, however, the relevance of each part becomes clearer:

- ✔ *Neuro* relates to your neurological system: how you use your five senses both to experience the outside world and to create your internal world by remembering and imagining. Your conscious and unconscious thought processes activate your nervous system, which influences your physiology (breathing, posture, movements and so on), how you feel, and what you do and say.

- ✔ *Linguistic* refers to the way people use language to make sense of their experiences, to talk to themselves, and to communicate with others. Everyone has distinct patterns in how they use language, and these patterns provide tremendous insights into people's thinking.

- ✔ *Programming* is just like computer programming, only relating to the human brain. A *program* – for a computer or in your brain – is a succession of steps designed to achieve a particular result. Your personal programs lead to the results you get and the impact you have on yourself and others.

Since its introduction in the 1970's, NLP has been defined in many different ways. The following sections delve into what exactly NLP is – and isn't.

## Studying and observing

Leaders in the field of NLP most commonly describe NLP as the study of the structure of subjective experience, which is a very obscure way of saying studying how individuals think and behave. Studying and observing very precisely what human beings think, say, and do is the cornerstone of NLP, giving insights into the internal workings of people's minds. Understanding how someone does what they do well allows you to create a model of that capability so you can replicate their excellence. You can also detect how you, or someone else, is managing to create the results you *don't* want – and then make changes to achieve your aspirations and goals.

NLP gives you skills and tools to find out how others achieve great results. You can build models of others' capabilities and try them out for yourself. In addition, NLP originators Richard Bandler and John Grinder (see the nearby sidebar 'The origins of NLP'), as well as many others in the field, have developed and created a wealth of models and techniques for creating change and influencing effectively.

## *Even more definitions*

The scope of NLP extends beyond business-specific skills and techniques and has led practitioners to develop many other ways of describing NLP's essence.

Some definitions focus on NLP's strength in the area of communications and define NLP as:

- ✔ The art and science of communication.
- ✔ A communication model based on working with patterns of thinking, language, and behaviour.
- ✔ The key to successful communication.
- ✔ A set of powerful influencing strategies.

Other definitions are concerned with excellence and define NLP as:

- ✔ A behavioural model of outstanding talent.
- ✔ A methodology for replicating behaviour that generates exceptional results.
- ✔ A user's manual for the brain.

Still other definitions focus on achieving goals, considering NLP as:

- ✔ A process by which you can achieve what you want in life.
- ✔ An attitude of mind.
- ✔ Skills and techniques for designing and creating your future.
- ✔ The difference that makes the difference.

As you can see, NLP can be many different things to many different people – from a science to an attitude.

In my experience, people who learn about NLP take what they want from the wealth of available insights and techniques. How you define NLP after you begin your journey of discovery is entirely up to you. What's important is that you explore, experiment, and have fun while finding out what NLP can do to support you to improve your business life.

# The origins of NLP

The seeds of NLP were planted in the early 1970s at the University of California, Santa Cruz. Richard Bandler, a mathematics student, and John Grinder, a professor of linguistics, started the collaboration that led to NLP. The duo studied three leading psychotherapists:

- ✔ Fritz Perls, the creator of the school of therapy known as Gestalt.

- ✔ Virginia Satir, an exceptional family therapist.

- ✔ Milton Erickson, one of the most influential hypnotherapists and psychiatrists of our time.

The success of these therapists intrigued Bandler and Grinder. Their styles and personalities seemed quite different, yet they were each achieving amazing change with clients with very significant problems.

Bandler and Grinder identified that some similar, fundamental patterns underlay all three therapists' work. In the mid-1970s they published their discoveries in *The Structure of Magic, Volumes 1* and *2*, and two volumes of *Patterns of the Hypnotic Technique of Milton H. Erickson, M.D.*

Many other leaders in the fields of communications, systems theory, (the study of complex systems in science, nature, and society), and psychotherapy informed the development of NLP. In particular, Gregory Bateson, an anthropologist with an interest in linguistics, systems theory, communications theory, and psychotherapy, provided a strong influence.

NLP was born out of the originators' development of specific models of excellence, aided by a number of colleagues and students, who themselves have made significant contributions to the field. These include Judith DeLozier, Lesley Cameron-Bandler, Robert Dilts, David Gordon, Stephen Gilligan, and many others. Over the last 30 years, others have developed and contributed new models (using the NLP modelling capabilities evolving in the field)and extended thinking in NLP. The quest to study human excellence continues.

In its very early days NLP was used primarily in personal development and therapy, Before long it began to be used in a much broader range of situations, including business.

## *Evaluating NLP for yourself*

In the many years I've been using NLP I've come across a few people who are resistant to NLP. They have preconceived ideas from things that they have heard – or indeed they may have just had a bad experience of working with an unskilled or badly trained practitioner.

Those few people I've met who have negative perceptions of NLP have described it as brainwashing or manipulation, pop psychology, even new age mumbo jumbo! Well, everyone is entitled to have their own map of the world (I talk more about maps of the world in Chapter 3).

My experience in working with NLP in business is that, used wisely and ethically, NLP opens up the opportunity to develop a better life and career for anyone – if that's what they want. Try it out for yourself and then draw your own conclusions. Everyone is entitled to their own map of the world – including you!

# Using NLP in Business

Over the years, the use of NLP tools and techniques has exploded around the world, in every conceivable walk of life. NLP is now applied in counselling, education, parenting, health, personal development, coaching, voluntary service, sport, and, not least, in business. New discoveries, new models, and new ways of thinking are continually emerging from the many people whose talents NLP has unleashed.

Business people now widely use NLP. Forward-thinking organisations embrace NLP because they benefit from its positive effects on individuals, teams, and overall business performance.

As you read this book you discover many ways to apply NLP to business, whether you wish to:

✔ Get better results for yourself

✔ Support others to achieve better results

✔ Drive change in your business

As well as the tools, NLP is also an attitude of mind that incorporates:

✔ **An awareness of self:** Noticing and understanding how you habitually think and behave.

✔ **A high sensitivity to others:** Paying close attention to others and using what you observe and hear to step into their worlds.

✔ **A future outcome focus:** Aspiring to make changes and achieve all that you desire.

Your journey through NLP is a voyage of discovery. With this book – and perhaps other books, workshops, and online resources – you can sail through the wide variety of valuable tools, techniques, and models on offer.

In this book, I introduce many aspects of NLP thinking and approaches that are employed successfully in business. Use as much or as little of this information as you please. I suggest you prioritise and use those parts of NLP that appeal to you most. Then build your skills and add more NLP gems to your tool kit as you're ready.

This is a book about NLP in relation to your work, career, and business. The book does not deal with NLP as therapy. But if you're suffering from serious personal issues, NLP can help. It has been an effective tool for curing phobias, overcoming post-traumatic stress disorder, and responding to anxiety and other major issues that affect health and happiness. I suggest you contact the Neuro Linguistic Psychotherapy & Counselling Association (www.nlptca.com) to locate an NLP specialist to help you with your specific issue.

The following sections address key benefits of including NLP tools and techniques in your business life: communicating, leading, and achieving the best results.

## Enhancing interpersonal effectiveness

Modern-day business success demands not only good interpersonal skills but also exceptional powers to influence and persuade. The need for communication pervades all business activities:

- ✔ **Within the business.** People need to work together, cooperate, negotiate, influence, inspire, and motivate others to get the job done.

- ✔ **With customers.** Good customer service is critical to keeping competitive advantage. Paying close attention to customers' wishes and communicating in ways that have meaning to customers are essential.

- ✔ **With the market at large.** Getting your message across effectively to prospective buyers and managing communication through broadcast and online media are constant challenges.

- ✔ **With others**. Communicating with and influencing stakeholders, including shareholders, financiers, community groups, and others, is extremely important. Good supplier relationships are also critical for success.

In their early analysis of highly effective therapists (see the sidebar, 'The origins of NLP'), Richard Bandler and John Grinder identified a range of key underlying patterns of communication that are critical to success. From this initial research, they developed *models* – representations of what excellent influencers were doing – that generate both personal change and highly influential communications. The models for greater interpersonal influence appear largely in Parts II and III of this book and cover the key themes of:

- ✔ Developing awareness of yourself and others
- ✔ Building rapport
- ✔ Influencing language
- ✔ Handling emotions

The following sections address the communication-based benefits of NLP.

### Understanding differences between you and others

The journey to becoming an exceptional communicator starts with discovering and understanding your own patterns of thinking. These patterns drive the way you feel, act, and react. Everything you've experienced in your life – and the way your brain has filtered this information – determines what you think, believe, value, and feel. To find out more about the unconscious mind and its filtering process, head to Chapter 4.

Right now you may not be aware of many of your habitual ways of thinking, evaluating, and making decisions. But your unconscious mind is steering you. Find out how to identify your patterns from the language you use and the things you do in Chapters 5 and 7.

Guess what? Other people aren't like you! While some people may resemble you, others don't at all. As you can read in Chapter 3, NLP adopts the principle that all people have different maps of the world. Even when two people share an experience, they notice different things, have different responses, and store different memories.

### Targeting your language

After you know how to detect patterns, you're likely to start seeing and hearing the patterns of others – and notice those that are different to your own. You can then adapt the way you talk to people so that you make perfect sense in their maps of the world!

Becoming more flexible in how you communicate is the key to developing exceptional influencing skills. Knowing others' patterns gives you the information you need to target your words to them, as if you're speaking their language rather than your own.

Turn to Chapters 4, 5, and 7 to find out how to use words and phrases so that someone whose patterns are dissimilar to yours can understand and respond. You may be amazed by what you can achieve with some subtle shifts in your language.

### Using rapport

*Rapport* is that natural connection between people when all conversation seems to be effortless. Discussions flow easily and everyone has a sense of respect and underlying trust.

You no doubt have some colleagues with whom you simply seem to get along well, and business conversations are just plain easy. These people are probably most like you in terms of their patterns, and rapport happens naturally. With others at work, this kind of rapport is much harder to find.

Persuading a colleague and getting him on your side is so much easier when you're in rapport with him. Thanks to the modelling work of NLP pioneers, you can create good rapport in situations where it previously seemed difficult, and influence more effectively. Find out all about rapport in Chapter 6, including how to use body language and words to attain it.

### Managing your emotions

Humans are highly emotional beings. Powerful feelings are wonderful when they work for you. In business, many emotional states can be useful: excitement, interest, calm, and confidence, to name but a few.

In contrast, strong negative feelings don't often help you work to the best advantage. Anger, anxiety, frustration, demotivation, and stress are some of the states I come across in business people, none of which supports best performance.

You may well have worked hard to control your emotions at times. Trying to manage or suppress a strong feeling is often a battle. Yet having the capacity to choose how you feel, rather than have your feelings control your reactions and behaviour, is essential for success in:

- ✔ Leading
- ✔ Influencing
- ✔ Achieving
- ✔ Negotiating

NLP tools and techniques help you find ways to choose your feelings. When you opt to modify your emotional response to a difficult situation, you can alter how you act and react and get a far more positive outcome. Chapters 8 and 9 hold an array of approaches to changing your emotional responses to get the results you want. You can also use these techniques to coach others to change their emotional states when doing so is beneficial to them.

## *Leading peak performance*

For business excellence, you need to get yourself and others working most effectively. This is a leadership job. Regardless of whether you have the job title of leader, you still lead people when you're:

- ✔ Guiding
- ✔ Directing
- ✔ Managing
- ✔ Controlling
- ✔ Influencing

Good performance comes from you, your team, your colleagues, or others on whom you rely, such as suppliers. As you communicate more effectively with yourself and others, you can influence and lead excellence to achieve business success.

### *Leading yourself*

Creating the life you want, including the kind of work and career that you desire, starts with self-leadership. Leading yourself is about taking charge of your working life to get where you want to go. When you lead yourself well, you:

- ✔ Establish your personal goals or outcomes
- ✔ Choose your emotions and state
- ✔ Become aware of your own unconscious patterns
- ✔ Build your behavioural flexibility
- ✔ Reprogram your unconscious for success

Discover all the wonderful ways in which you can make this happen as you read through this book.

### *Inspiring and motivating*

Getting people to listen to you, agree with you, or be inspired by you affects your success, whether you're the CEO or the new kid on the team. Businesses depend on people. People need to be persuaded, motivated, and enthused to back new ideas and put their best into their jobs.

NLP models and approaches for communication in this book are particularly useful if you want to:

- ✔ Gain agreement, approval, or consensus
- ✔ Call others to action
- ✔ Persuade people to join you in your opinions or judgements
- ✔ Encourage and motivate others
- ✔ Pass on information that you believe is important
- ✔ Generate passion or excitement

If inspiring others is what inspires you, I recommend you jump straight to Chapter 10. There you can find out how to choose your words to engage others' emotions positively.

### Coaching others

Coaching others to improve performance is considered increasingly important in business these days. The days of managers telling staff what to do, rather than coaching them to develop skills, may well be limited.

Many business leaders believe that NLP offers the most powerful coaching tool kit available today. Throughout this book you can discover insights and techniques for improved communication, as well as tools for personal change. All of these, including the specialist coaching models I present in Chapter 12, provide a wide array of approaches to incorporate in your coaching.

### Giving feedback

If performance improvement is important to you, then giving and receiving quality feedback is essential. In many organisations, feedback is still sparse and too infrequent. Feedback is all too often used only when bad news needs to be delivered, while praise and encouragement for a job well done are often overlooked.

Chapter 11 outlines how to use NLP thinking to direct meaningful and actionable feedback, so that others truly understand what they're doing well, where they need to improve, and what those improvements may look and sound like in order to increase their personal effectiveness.

### Handling difficult relationships

Most people find certain situations or individuals at work challenging to handle and seriously detrimental to progress. To get the best business performance, people need to be able to work well together and overcome difficulties and differences.

Getting past the problems caused by relationships that just don't seem to work or situations that seem complex and stuck becomes easier with NLP. The NLP models of master communicators identify what those with exceptional influencing skills do to change such relationships positively, and you can use their techniques to influence others.

Explore how to gain new insights into difficult relationships and build your flexibility to get the results you want in Chapter 13.

## Improving business results

Although the early NLP models were based on the study of individual excellence, they apply equally well to achieving great results across a business. If you want to maximise business performance, this book offers many NLP tools that can serve you well.

### Creating vision, values, and goals

All businesses have goals. Some have a vision. All have values, although they may not be the ones they say they have! I spend a lot of time in organisations of all sizes, and I rarely find an employee who's bang up to date with the company vision and values, and often not even the goals. After all, the vision is so often just a bunch of words that aren't easy to remember. Much the same can be said for the values. And the goals are a bunch of numbers that aren't really going to change the way anyone does his job.

Applying NLP to the process of crafting vision, values, and goals brings a whole new perspective.

- ✔ NLP focuses on sensory experience – what you see, hear, and feel. When a sensory description brings vision, values, and goals to life, people start to understand, anticipate, and align with them. To find out how to develop a compelling vision, meaningful values, and inspiring goals, look up Chapter 14.

- ✔ The NLP model for goal setting is known as a *well-formed outcome*, which you can find out more about in Chapter 16. This kind of goal is far more motivating to people within a business than is a brief description of financial targets.

### Effecting change

If one constant exists in business, it's the need to make changes, small or large, in order to be competitive, generate the desired results, and adapt to the rapidly changing environment in which the business operates. Business leaders frequently find major change difficult. Changes to structure, processes and systems are often complex and slow, and many don't achieve the hoped-for outcome.

Much of NLP has been modelled from successful personal transformation. These models, when used to support organisational change – which of course depends largely on individual change – are equally powerful. Using NLP to create change within a business involves:

- ✔ Influencing and motivating people to make changes more effectively.
- ✔ Setting well-formed outcomes and meaningful action plans that people buy into.
- ✔ Developing more flexible individuals as a result of greater awareness of self and others.
- ✔ Making changes at the right level of thinking.

The NLP *logical levels* model (more on this in Chapter 15) determines the kind of changes individuals should make in order to achieve their goal. Changing the right things is the difference that makes the difference.

### Modelling best performance

Modelling is the essence of NLP. Understanding how you or someone else intuitively does something exceptionally well is a valuable skill in business.

You can model exceptional performers in any discipline to determine precisely what they do that gets great results. You can then transfer this model to other people and other areas.

Modelling is a very different approach to attempting to improve performance through standard skills training. Very often good performers aren't aware of what they do to get results that's different to what others do. Modelling identifies subtle thinking and behavioural processes that separate average and exceptional performances.

Think of all the things you'd like to do well if you only could. If you want to raise standards and do even more things well, find out how in Chapter 17.

# Chapter 2

# Overcoming the Barriers to Success

. . . . . . . . . . . . . . . . . . . . . . . . . . . . . . . . . . . . . . . . . . . . . . . . . . . .

### In This Chapter

▶ Shifting your focus from problems to goals

▶ Using your senses to good effect

▶ Thinking and acting more flexibly

▶ Understanding and working with differences

▶ Taking control of your work life and your future

. . . . . . . . . . . . . . . . . . . . . . . . . . . . . . . . . . . . . . . . . . . . . . . . . . . .

**D**o you believe that barriers exist that prevent you from being successful at work? Or does this way of thinking about whether you get what you want make little sense to you?

Herein lies some of the essence of NLP: Noticing how you think about things. Being aware of how you use language to express your thoughts. Paying attention to how others think. And making changes as a result to reach your goals.

Take a moment to consider the title of this chapter: *Overcoming the barriers to success.* It's just the kind of phrase business leaders – maybe you use liberally. Except the phrase in the world of NLP is more than just a throwaway. It gives lot of clues about how the person who said it is thinking.

Consider what you can assume, or *presuppose,* from this title. You can assume that success is possible. Barriers exist. The barriers are probably metaphorical rather than literal. You can overcome them. Getting success involves overcoming barriers, which suggests that barriers are a problem.

Other unconscious thought processes may be wrapped up in this statement as well, although you may not be able quite to pinpoint them. For example, you may be curious to know: Success at what? How big are the barriers? How many barriers exist?

Paying attention to language and thought processes, being curious, and asking questions are all fundamental aspects of using NLP. In this chapter, you find out more about NLP tools and how to use them to help you overcome barriers to success in your work place.

# Working with NLP at Work

Choosing to use NLP to support you in getting the success you want in your working life may be the best decision you ever made. You really can overcome barriers, achieve exciting things, and realise your potential. NLP gives you a heap of wonderful tools and techniques. How well they work is up to you!

NLP does require you to do some things that you may not be doing currently. These are summarised in the *four pillars of NPL,*which, are:

- **Setting your goals.** I emphasise the importance of goals, or *outcomes* many times in this book. Establishing an outcome, is all about knowing exactly what you want, in any situation. After you establish outcomes you stop thinking about the problems you no longer want (or need to overcome) and focus on the future. See the section 'Achieving Elusive Goals', later in this chapter, and Chapter 16 for more on goal setting with NLP.

- **Using your senses.** Paying close attention to the world around you with all your senses – sight, touch, hearing, as well as taste and smell – is a critical part of using NLP well. As you develop your sensory awareness, you find out much more about how you and others act and react, and have the opportunity to make productive change. The section 'Noticing What You're not Noticing', later in this chapter, and Chapter 5 offer more on the power of your senses.

- **Behaving flexibly.** You want different results to what you're currently experiencing – otherwise why are you considering NLP? Everything you discover in this book gives you more options in how you think, what you say, and what you do. Keep on changing what you do until you get what you want, and remember: the path that leads to realising your goals isn't always a straight one. Check out 'Building Flexibility to Achieve More', later in this chapter, and find out many different ways in which to be more flexible throughout this book.

- **Building relationships.** You can't always achieve what you want in life in isolation from others. You may well need other people's co-operation or support. For that you need quality relationships built on trust, mutual respect, and responsiveness – all of which indicate great *rapport*, the connection between two people that enables good communication. As you find ways to create and deepen rapport with others, you can discover even more success. 'Building Positive Relationships', later in this chapter, and Chapter 6 explore ways to build great work relationships.

As you try out different aspects of NLP at work, you may find certain things confusing or awkward – or maybe things just don't go as you hope. Don't give up! What you're doing with NLP is trying things that are new and different. Sure, they may not feel natural or 'right' at first. But new approaches and skills rarely do. Stick with the strategies and techniques I outline in this book, even when you feel that you're venturing outside your comfort zone. That's where you're likely to learn the most.

# Achieving Elusive Goals

So much of this book is about achieving things that you may think I'm presuming you haven't accomplished all that much in your life to date! Just to set the record straight, my belief is that you're already a successful human being. Of course, *you* may or may not recognise how successful you are, but that's another matter.

NLP can support you to reach for your elusive goals – things you want but somehow never achieve. Whether your elusive goal is clearing your in-box, getting an unhappy person to smile, feeling full of energy on Monday morning, or completely transforming your business, NLP techniques and strategies can help, particularly if you haven't yet managed to reach your goal.

NLP concentrates on achieving goals by making adjustments to how you're thinking – specifically shifting away from solving problems and towards a focus on outcomes.

## Addressing the problem with problem thinking

When things aren't going right, people naturally focus on the problem – often on the problem *only*. Many organisations consider problem solving an important competence.

The only problem with problem solving is that you tend to think long and hard about the problem, and therefore use the same thinking that created the problem in the first place.

What do I mean by this? Well, a problem's only a problem if you find it so. Think of a scenario where two people get made redundant. Each has a different response:

> **Response 1:** I've lost my job. I hate having nothing to do. I need to get work before the money runs out.

**Response 2:** It's great. I'm getting a paid break from work so I can do some of the other things I've always wanted to do. Now I can concentrate on finding the much better job I've been wanting.

Both of these people have been made redundant, but which one of them experiences redundancy as a problem?

Turn to Chapter 9 to consider *reframing*, a way of thinking about a situation which helps you to explore alternative meanings, so that you've more choice about how you think – and feel – about something you experience.

## *Focusing on desired outcomes*

An *outcome* is the NLP word for a goal or something you want. To achieve an elusive goal, you need to think about the outcome – what you want – rather than what you currently have and don't want (the problem).

Figure 2-1 illustrates the way to separate a problem from an outcome. By moving away from where you are now, your present state, you can move towards where you want to be, your desired state.

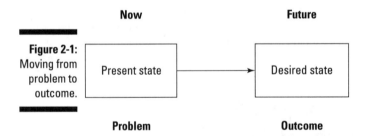

**Figure 2-1:**
Moving from
problem to
outcome.

You find out all about how to define your outcomes to ensure success in Chapter 16.

John, a regional manager for a retail pharmacy chain, regularly hired temporary pharmacists. He needed to ensure that on each branch pharmacist's weekly day off, a replacement pharmacist was in the shop. Temporary pharmacists were in short supply and some John booked just didn't turn up. John spent much of his time solving this problem from week-to-week. and month-to-month. When John stopped grappling with the problem and set an outcome – a reliable group of pharmacists to provide weekly cover, which were easy to organise – his thinking, and behaviour, changed. John employed two additional permanent pharmacists and staggered the branch pharmacists' days off. He then had guaranteed, reliable cover for his ten pharmacies at the same financial cost, and gained over eight hours back a week for himself to do his job more effectively.

# Noticing What You're not Noticing

Think about a regular journey you make, maybe your trip to work every day. What do you see? What do you hear? What do you smell? What do you pay attention to?

And even more importantly: What do you *not* see and hear?

NLP offers several techniques to expand your awareness of the physical world you inhabit and your inner world.

## Celebrating your senses

You have five senses:

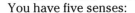

- ✔ Seeing
- ✔ Hearing
- ✔ Feeling
- ✔ Smell
- ✔ Taste

You can easily take your senses for granted, but when you tune into them they allow you to experience the world in wonderfully rich and vivid ways. With a little effort, you can use your senses to collect more helpful information for your conscious mind. Discover how to get more from your senses in Chapter 5.

And your senses aren't just valuable in your experience of the outside world. You also use your senses when you create or recreate things in your mind. So your memories and your thoughts are all formed with your senses. You may hear an inner voice talking to you, see pictures in your mind, and have feelings about situations long after, or even before, they've happened.

As you read about NLP, you realise the importance of having your senses on full alert and developing high sensory awareness of yourself and others. You start noticing things you haven't been seeing, hearing, or feeling.

How much more can you discover the next time you do that regular journey? Test yourself and discover at least ten things you didn't pay attention to before.

## Improving self-awareness

Paying close attention to yourself is something that's alien to many people. After all, many believe that you are who you are, and that's it.

Except self-awareness isn't about who you are. It's about noticing your patterns - your default ways of thinking and behaving. You may be surprised that others can predict what you think, say, and do! But you too can use your awareness of your patterns to achieve success. Simply being aware of your patterns helps you to spot those times when habitual thinking and responses are actually less than helpful and become a barrier to your success.

NLP requires you to take notice of yourself and pay attention to:

- ✔ What motivates you
- ✔ How you use your senses
- ✔ Where you put your attention
- ✔ How you put up barriers to your success
- ✔ How you do certain things well
- ✔ How you think about your goals

This self-awareness is the key to unlocking your potential, making changes, and achieving your dreams.

Getting to understanding your own thinking is a common theme in this book. Start with Chapters 5 and 7 to identify some of your patterns.

## Understanding how others tick

To be truly successful in business, you have to work well with others. Even if you're self-employed you still have to communicate with prospective customers, suppliers, accountants, and a whole range of other people. Understanding what makes other people tick can make all the difference.

Curiosity is crucial. When you start to be curious about other people and what leads them to speak and act as they do, you can be far more understanding and flexible when working with them. When you observe and listen to others carefully, you can detect what's behind some of those things they do or say – things you may find strange, irritating, or downright outrageous!

When you know yourself better (turn to the section 'Improving self-awareness', earlier in this chapter), you can make better sense of what you're seeing and hearing in others too. Using NLP tools you can get much greater insights into people's habitual ways of thinking and behaving – the things that you just don't know that you do – than ever before. You can appreciate another person's map of the world (more on this in Chapter 4), and learn to work with that more effectively to mutual benefit.

# Recognising choices

A while ago I received a call from my friend Alison. She wanted to cancel our planned evening out. This was the third time she'd cancelled me in four weeks. She sounded exasperated on the phone, telling me 'I have to work every evening this week again. I've worked every evening and weekend this month – I'm *so* fed up!!'

I was pretty fed up too – I had been looking forward to seeing her and was disappointed to be let down yet again. I asked Alison 'What leads you to choose to work all these hours?' Alison's response was indignant. 'That's how it is with this job. If you don't get the work done you lose your job. If I lose my job I can't pay the mortgage and I'll be homeless. I've no alternative – it's *not* a choice.'

At this point I realised *I* had some choices. For instance, I could sympathise with Alison and forget about my own needs for a good night out (again). I could express my pique and tell Alison not to bother to book any more dates with me until she was sure she'd make it. Another alternative was to question Alison further (gently) about her belief that she had no choices. This was the choice I opted for. After 20 minutes on the phone, we'd identified that Alison had over a dozen choices – including finding a new job. Alison's top six were:

- Delegating more tasks to her team
- Saying 'no' to new projects
- Reviewing her workload with her boss
- Prioritising projects differently
- Finding more efficient ways of working
- Requesting an additional team member

I left a more positive and relaxed Alison to decide on what to do next. A week later I heard from her. Alison was very excited. She'd implemented *all* of her top six choices and was already working far more sensible hours. We agreed to meet the next evening – and we did!

# Increasing Flexibility to Accomplish More

Having more choices sounds great – perhaps easy. After all, you're a capable individual. I'm sure you've made lots of choices in your life, important ones too: What work you do, where you live, who you love, and who you live with.

So how come you seem to have no choice about a whole range of small things? Think about the everyday situations where you may think you have no or little choice:

- ✔ Feeling frustrated when you're stuck in a traffic jam, late for work or an appointment.
- ✔ Getting irritated with someone at work who seems to get in the way of you doing your job well, time and time again.
- ✔ Experiencing despondency when your favourite sports team loses a vital cup match.
- ✔ Believing you must work late some days to get the job done.

Maybe you don't feel like you have a choice about what you do, how you react, or how you feel. (Well, not yet anyway!) NLP tools can help you build more flexibility into the way you go through life.

Right now, your unconscious mind is running its habitual patterns: something happens (the stimulus) and you respond, as Figure 2-2 illustrates. Your response is almost instant, as if your mind is programmed to respond in a particular way to a certain stimulus.

With NLP you develop the skill to change your habitual response. You extend the time between the stimulus and the response long enough to consider and evaluate more options. Of course, your brain is such an amazingly fast data processor, you don't notice a delay! Instead, the process becomes more like Figure 2-3 shows.

**Figure 2-2:**
Prog-
rammed
stimulus–
response.

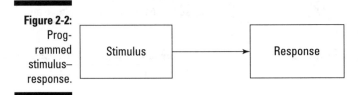

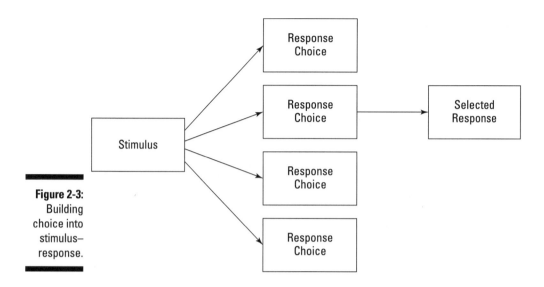

**Figure 2-3:**
Building
choice into
stimulus–
response.

With more choices you have flexibility. You can try something new. And indeed, if that doesn't get you what you want, you can try something else. Discover many ways in which to think and act more flexibly throughout this book.

# Building Positive Relationships

After reading the title of this section, you may be asking yourself, 'Why would I ever want to have a relationship with many of the people I work with?' By *relationship,* I'm not talking about dating, getting married, and starting a family. I'm talking about the ability to work well with another person, to have mutual respect, and to be able to communicate effectively. In short, a good work relationship is having rapport. (For much more on rapport, see Chapter 6.)

Other people are often some of the barriers to your success. Not usually because they deliberately want to get in your way – although you may come across someone who appears directly obstructive from time to time. It's more often the differences that exist between people that create the stumbling blocks. Other people unwittingly stop you achieving your goals for reasons including:

> ✔ **Goals**. Other people can have goals that conflict with yours. For example, you want extra budget to hire an additional person, but your boss wants to under spend budget to show his management capabilities and get promoted.

✔ **Beliefs and values**. Other people can believe in, or value, things differently to you (more on beliefs and values in Chapter 4), For example,
you need cooperation from a colleague to sell into a new market. You
believe it's a great profit opportunity. He believes it's a waste of time
and money.

✔ **Patterns of thinking.** You think in different ways and therefore talk
and act very differently, so you never seem to get agreement (turn to
Chapter 4 to explore this further). For example, you want to make some
improvements and discuss all the benefits of change with colleagues.
These colleagues don't like change, turn off to listening to the benefits,
and set themselves firmly against your initiative.

By being able to work well with people and get them on your side, your path
to success becomes much smoother. In Parts II and III of this book I show you
how NLP tools and techniques can transform how you and others perform at
work through more effective communications.

# Benefiting from NLP in the Work Place

NLP is full of useful, easy to grasp approaches and tools with which you can
make changes, influence more effectively and achieve much more. It's no
surprise then that so many business people are now utilising NLP in the constant quest for performance improvement.

As you develop new insights and skills through NLP, you work more effectively, generate better results for yourself and your business, and you're even
likely to enjoy your work more. With your newfound understanding of yourself and others, you can also help your colleagues to raise their game too.

## Appreciating other perspectives

Much of NLP concentrates on examining the structure of your own internal world, as well as comparing how yours differs from others'. Gaining
additional perspectives on your and others' ways of thinking and operating
opens up new possibilities. Having more understanding of what's behind any
behaviour, yours or someone else's, allows you to interpret things better and
respond differently – and hopefully, more effectively.

For example, do you know someone who's guaranteed to turn up late for
any scheduled appointment? I certainly do. I also know people who are so
punctual you have to plan for them to be early whenever they're due to meet
you. The difference between these people, as the process of *NLP modelling*
discovers (see Chapter 17), is that people experience time in different ways,
or *patterns*.

✔ Some people spend much of their time living in the present, fully experiencing what's happening for them right now. In NLP, this is known as *in-time*.

✔ Others view time from a distance, thinking ahead to the future or looking back into the past. These people are said to be *through-time*.

Each pattern of experiencing time affects not only people's behaviours but also where they think about things spatially. As Figure 2-4 shows, a person with an in-time pattern tends to see her future straight ahead and her past directly behind her. A person with a through-time pattern views her past and present as a continuum in front of her.

In-time and through-time are just patterns. Neither is right or wrong, better or worse. But both patterns can profoundly affect how someone appears to manage her day-to-day schedule. With the new perspective of in-time and through-time patterns, your reaction to someone delaying you or abruptly leaving you can be very different.

Start to tune your sensory awareness by noticing people operating in-time and through-time patterns.

✔ When being in-time, someone's less likely to think ahead to where she's scheduled to be next because she's so fully engaged in the current moment.

✔ Someone running the through-time pattern may suddenly break rapport to dash from an interesting conversation with you to ensure she gets to her next meeting on time.

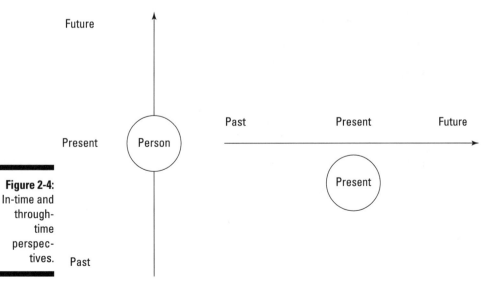

**Figure 2-4:**
In-time and through-time perspectives.

See Chapter 7 to explore other patterns that come into play in the work place.

## Transforming performance

Getting the best out of people – including yourself – in an organisation has many benefits, not just better-quality work and results. When people believe they're giving their best, they're receiving support to do so, and the organisation is rewarding and recognising them, the positive outcomes include:

- ✔ Good performance
- ✔ Energised and dedicated employees
- ✔ Personal satisfaction and fulfilment
- ✔ Talented people staying in the business

This all creates a much longer-term capability for good business performance.

Getting the best out of yourself at work and transforming your own performance can help you overcome many of your personal barriers to success. These transformations can be in the smallest things yet still have really useful results. Whether you just want to manage your e-mails better or achieve a major promotion, using the NLP tools in this book you can change the way you work until you get the outcomes you desire.

## Taking charge

NLP is all about taking charge of your thinking – finding out about your own thinking patterns and noticing when they become barriers to your success. When you know how you're blocking your own success, you can use your new insights to start to make changes.

Taking charge isn't just about taking charge of your thinking; NLP gives you the chance to take charge of your life. This notion is a revelation to many people when they think about work. The days of employers providing 'jobs for life' are long gone. People increasingly experience not simply job changes but career changes throughout their working lives, some by choice, others not. With the decline of certain industries and geographical shifts of manufacturing bases with increasing globalisation, employees these days must have greater flexibility. Yet still people are often quite passive about their career.

Are you one of those people who works hard and then assumes that others notice what a good job you've done? Maybe you believe:

- ✔ They should notice what you do.

- ✔ They need to understand your commitment to your job or the organisation.

- ✔ They must realise that not everyone puts in the sort of hours or effort that you do.

Unfortunately, these beliefs aren't very useful in the modern work place – and I question whether they were ever all that useful in the past. Other people's sensory awareness is often not as good as you expect it to be. Your boss or other key people at work may not be paying quite as much attention to your contribution as you want them to. Funnily enough, they aren't as committed to your job satisfaction or career progression as you are and need to be!

The preceding beliefs also contain some particularly problematic words – *they*, *should*, *need to*, and *must*. I examine these words and others in Chapter 12 and introduce you to ways in which you can challenge these beliefs.

Are you taking charge of your own working life and achievements, or are you giving away that power to others? Ask yourself the following questions:

- ✔ Do you expect others to notice and recognise what you do when you're quietly being industrious?

- ✔ Do you think that others can mind-read your desires and ambitions?

- ✔ Do you feel trapped in a job you don't like because you're telling yourself you need the salary, the pension, the status, or something else?

- ✔ Do you work for a corporate organisation and believe you have no power to make anything happen?

Answering yes to any (or all!) of the preceding bullets gives you a clear sign that you've created a barrier to your success. Realising that you're putting up obstacles for yourself may take some time to notice. But as soon as you're aware of how you're thinking, you're on the road to change. Now's the time to take charge of your working life and destiny. NLP gives you all the help you need.

## *Maintaining integrity*

NLP includes many tools and techniques to help you boost your communications skills. After all, if you can influence, persuade or inspire people more effectively you are far more likely to get what you want. People new to NLP sometimes raise questions about the integrity of this approach. They wonder whether NLP enables people to manipulate others or gain personal advantage at the expense of others.

## Unblocking the route to job satisfaction

Greg, an international marketing director for a consumer goods company, asked me to coach him. He disliked his job. He was away from home far more than he wanted, was challenged by attempting to meet the needs of nine different business leaders in many different countries, and had little job satisfaction. He hoped I could help him enjoy this job more.

I coached Greg to find out what he really wanted instead of a job he disliked. Deep down Greg really desired work that meant more to him, He wanted to work for a charity, and make a contribution to the community. The kind of work he could feel proud of. However, Greg had a family and a mortgage and lived well. He decided long ago that he'd have to stay in this job, or one just like it, to maintain the family's lifestyle. He just needed to find a way to get through each working days.

Using NLP tools to help Greg get more insights and understandings, and to increase his choices, I coached Greg through some key changes in his thinking. As a result he worked with his wife to identify how they could reduce their financial outgoings. He discovered that she was keen to return to work and earn an income again. And he found out that there were several charities looking for skills just like his in salaried positions. Eight months later Greg had made the move, he worked in a job he loved, had modified a somewhat extravagant lifestyle, and never looked back!

Well, the honest response to this concern is that anything's possible. If you have the intention to get ahead by acting without integrity towards others, then you probably do that whether you use NLP or not. And if you operate in that way, you're likely to have to take the consequences (some of which may be extremely painful or even disastrous). In my experience this self-serving approach doesn't benefit people in the long term. It's not a great way to win friends, for sure.

If, however, you use NLP with a positive intention for both yourself and others, in ways in which everyone wins, then manipulation isn't really an issue and success is much more assured.

# Chapter 3

# Utilising NLP Principles at Work

*T*en core principles underlie the thinking and approach of NLP. Getting the full benefit from living with these principles requires you to assume, or *presuppose,* that each principle is true. That's why in the world of NLP, these principles are known as the *NLP presuppositions.*

Flexibility is important when you try the NLP principles on for size. (See the later section 'Building Flexibility to Make Changes' for more.) At first, you might think that some of the principles don't fit with you. Indeed, you may well be able to come up with arguments to prove that various principles aren't true. However, what *is* true is that these NLP principles have been really useful to many people, in and outside of the workplace.

In this chapter, I share ten NLP principles that I've found help people make changes in how they think and act in the world of work – changes that have led to improvements in performance, effectiveness, and ultimately, the enjoyment of their jobs.

## Perceiving the World Your Own Way

No doubt you've been to many meetings in your time. You discuss issues, analyse problems, set objectives, and agree the next steps. Some time later, you have another meeting. One person hasn't done what you expected and now says the task is someone else's responsibility. Additionally, someone else has done something quite different to what you agreed. A debate ensues about what you agreed, who's responsible, and what needs to happen next. The meeting ends, but in a subsequent meeting the cycle continues, with people not following through or doing something different to what you agreed. Sound familiar?

The originators of NLP, Richard Bandler and John Grinder, (more on the origins of NLP can be found in Chapter 1), used this premise of mathematician, philosopher, and scientist Alfred Korzybski as a core principle of NLP thinking:

The map is not the territory.

In this expression, the word *territory* represents reality, what exists and what actually takes place. The *map* is just a representation, such as a picture or a model, of that reality. This principle explains that what exists – and how you experience it – are two different things. For example:

- ✔ The pain in your knee from banging it on your desk is *not* your knee.
- ✔ Your opinion of a colleague, whether good or bad, is *not* that person.

Every person has a different perception of reality, their map. Your reality is just that – *your* reality. As no two minds are identical, no one else shares that reality exactly. What you notice, and what you don't, form your impression of what's happening on any occasion.

Given the enormous amount of information bombarding your senses at any one moment, your brain has devised clever ways of filtering out most of this stuff before your system goes into overload and meltdown. (See Chapter 4 for more on filters.) So your perception and your colleagues' perceptions are different. Everyone has their own unique set of filters, resulting in unique maps. That's part of the reason those great agreements that you and your colleagues work so hard to achieve in meetings often suffer from the *different map factor* (everyone in the group is working from a different map), which holds back progress.

## Responding according to your map

You know that other people are different to you – some more so than others! Some seem to act in ways you just can't fathom. Others say what *you* think is the wrong thing at the wrong time. Their maps of the world drive their actions.

Performance appraisals are an interesting example of these different maps. Say you give three people the same piece of feedback: 'You need to concentrate more on the accuracy of your data input; your past work led to nine complaints.' You can get an infinite variety of responses to this statement, such as:

- ✔ Employee 1: 'You're right. I'm finding where I sit distracting and I want to make some changes if that's OK with you.'

> ✔ Employee 2: 'Well, Dan had 13 complaints, so I'm not that bad. I'm working as hard as I can, you know. I don't know what else you can expect me to do.'
>
> ✔ Employee 3 bursts into tears.

These three different responses reflect three different maps. They also illustrate another NLP principle:

> People respond according to their maps.

Everyone responds according to their individual map of the world. Keeping this top of mind helps you understand more about people who act in ways that you find unhelpful or unacceptable. When you remember this principle, you can move out of judging mode and become able to deal with what's happening more effectively.

A colleague and I attended a training seminar. The seminar's trainer reminded me of an eccentric old aunt – full of fun, loud, and lively. She had us doing lots of different exercises to familiarise ourselves with the material. I met some interesting people and discovered a lot of new, useful information.

At the end of the day I asked my colleague how the seminar had been for him (with bundles of enthusiasm at my good experience). His summary was that the trainer was overbearing, completely mad, and didn't seem to know her stuff. He found the exercises excruciatingly embarrassing and her visual aids incomprehensible. For him the entire day was a waste of time.

Hard to believe we attended the same event!

## Acting for good reason

Even when you take account of other people's maps of the world, comprehending their behaviour can still be challenging. People do all sorts of things that just don't make sense. You may wonder or not understand:

> ✔ Why someone risks their job by getting drunk at an important event.
>
> ✔ Why an employee is really aggressive towards others.
>
> ✔ Why a person takes sick leave for an in-growing toenail.

But rather than trying to figure out why (which is usually fruitless), you can instead start to think differently about the things that others do. This shift is part of another NLP principle:

> Every behaviour has a positive intention.

## Satisfying the need to feel confident and secure

I ran a team event for a management group of a financial services organisation. The brief was to get the team working more effectively together, and aligned with the team goals and strategy. Penny, a senior team member, made numerous witty but scathing comments about her peers. Mostly people laughed along, but they weren't all enjoying the joke. At lunch I took Penny aside and shared some feedback. From my perspective her behaviour was at odds with what the group was gathered together to do.

I worked with Penny to explore the positive intention behind what she was doing. She was the newest member of the team, only recently promoted. She wasn't confident that she was good enough to be on the team. She was insecure about being 'found out' by her new team members. Putting up her jovial act allowed Penny to highlight other's weaknesses and helped her to cope with her anxious feelings.

I then coached Penny to identify other ways to deal with her concerns. She later put these into action. For example, Penny identified two areas where she herself felt under-skilled and requested training. She worked out who she wanted performance feedback from – her boss, some internal clients, and a couple of peers. When she received their feedback, she was surprised by its positive nature.

Ten weeks later I worked with this team again to develop their leadership skills., Penny's contribution was very different. The funny but critical comments regarding her team had disappeared. She gave very positive and public feedback on colleagues' developing skills and achievements during the workshop. Best of all she still had her sense of humour, and used it to help the whole group have an enjoyable experience of the training. As a result the managers in the team were all talking more openly and the team spirit was much greater.

Simply, everything you do, you do for a reason. Humans are continually wanting to achieve something. A behaviour may be good – or quite the opposite – but an underlying positive intention runs through every choice.

Often these positive intentions have an emotional element that may not be obvious. For example, you've probably encountered a child who misbehaves to get attention, even though the attention he gets is not positive or nurturing. However, on closer examination, this child has an intention that is driven from some unconscious emotional desire for love, care, and security (all positive concepts).

This principle most certainly doesn't require you to be blindly positive. You don't need to start accepting intolerable, unethical, or illegal behaviour. Instead, it gives you the option to think about the things that people say and do at work that seem destructive, and be curious as to what they hope to achieve by acting in that way.

Think about a kind of unreasonable behaviour you face at work. Notice how you currently think about this behaviour. You might be tempted to label the behaviour – or indeed on the individual. You might use words like critical, negative, lazy, aggressive. Labelling often gets really personal and includes identity-level descriptions, such as when you say (out loud or in your head): 'He is a . . .'. I've heard many words to finish this sentence, not all of them printable!

If you can find out, or guess, the positive intention driving someone's seemingly negative behaviour at work, you can start to think differently and act more flexibly towards the person. You'll find some questions for discovering positive intention in Chapter 4. From that position you may well be able to help him explore other ways of acting that could also achieve his positive intention. See the nearby sidebar 'Satisfying the need to feel confident and secure' for an example.

Likewise, if you find yourself acting in a way that you don't like, see if you can work out your positive intention. Identifying your positive intention then gives you the choice to look for other ways to meet this need. You may be amazed by the changes you can make!

# Embracing Feedback, Forgetting Failure

Thoughts of failure aren't helpful, but most humans have them. You may even have experienced them yourself today or in the last week.

You stop yourself doing certain things because of fear of failure. What fantastic job did you never apply for because you expected to *fail* to get the position?

Some people can experience several incidents that they consider 'failures' and start to expect to fail. Failure becomes a state of mind. For instance, you may believe you're never going to get a promotion because you haven't received one in the last few years. With thinking like that, guess what – you may well be right!

## Eliminating failure

A very different way of thinking, encompassed in NLP, can be much more liberating. This NLP principle states:

> There is no failure, only feedback.

## Succeed or fail, win or lose: The language of business

Organisations have a strong focus on success. Success is often judged through comparisons to previous years' results, or budgets, or a competitor's performance. Certainly success is assessed by criteria that important stakeholders, such as shareholders, set, or in the case of public bodies, the government of the day.

The same is also true of individuals working in organisations. Their performance is similarly measured and judged against budgets and earlier years, and often against the performance of others.

When success doesn't happen, many people think of failure. Indeed, lots of business talk centres around succeeding or failing, winning or losing. When you don't meet expectations, you often hear things like: 'We failed to hit budget for the third month in a row' or 'We lost market share this year'.

In the current climate of change, unless you have truly mystical powers you have little chance of setting and successfully achieving ten-year goals. Given the economic, technological, and global political changes of the last decade, who can predict what environment you may be operating in in the future? So any middle- or long-term plan has a high risk of 'failure'.

The section 'Eliminating failure' offers some NLP-developed alternatives to this definition of failure.

This principle is a very powerful concept. When you consider the results and outcomes of your efforts merely as feedback, you have much more choice about what to do next. Thank goodness Thomas Edison didn't take the results of his first, second, third, or numerous other attempts to create an electric light bulb as 'failures' – otherwise you'd be reading this book by candlelight.

Treating the results of your efforts as information, rather than judging them, gives you the chance to adapt and to achieve what you want. The idea of failure drains energy and motivation – feedback can do the opposite. The sidebar 'Moving from failure to feedback to achievement' details one salesperson's compelling shift away from the notion of 'failure'.

Next time you have a setback, rather than criticising yourself or labelling yourself or the situation as a failure, ask yourself some questions:

- ✔ What feedback do I have? From others? From myself? From other sources?
- ✔ How much have I achieved so far?
- ✔ Is it still important to me to achieve what I set out to do?
- ✔ Given the feedback, what do I now want to achieve?
- ✔ What can I do differently?
- ✔ When can I start?

# Taking responsibility for communicating well

Getting others to hear, understand, and react to what you say is a big challenge in business, where influence is key and misunderstandings are rife. You may have noticed that people don't always receive and understand your messages, written or verbal, exactly how you intend – despite careful crafting and precise words.

Adopting the following NLP principle helps you change how you think, what you do, and the results you get:

**The meaning of the communication is the response it gets.**

When you notice that the reaction you get to your message is not what you hoped for, it's easy to start justifying what you have said, or blaming the other person for misunderstanding your meaning.

ANECDOTE

## Moving from failure to feedback to achievement

Steve was a sales executive selling computer networking systems to businesses. Steve who hadn't hit his sales targets any month since starting the job 15 months previously. His manager asked me to spend some time with Steve, who had a good track record in another division, to find out what was happening. The other sales executives in the team were meeting or beating their sales targets most months, so in the manager's eyes, Steve was failing. He'd decided that unless things improved, Steve was soon going to be out on his ear.

Steve explained to me how he worked. He used his previous experience to hone his current sales approach, but his techniques didn't generate the same results in this division, where the customers were much larger organisations and had more people involved in the buying process. Early on, Steve started to feel he was failing. He worked harder, but he still wasn't meeting his targets. Eventually, Steve decided he *was* a failure. He was looking around for another job, but his self-belief was so low he wasn't having much luck.

By encouraging Steve to focus on his sales figures as merely feedback, I was able to help him separate himself from his sense of failure. He was able to analyse what he did differently in his better-performing months and implement more of these behaviours in his work day. He shadowed a colleague to find out how she worked. He started to make changes in his attitude, style, and approach. Within three months he was beating budgets and exceeding the previous year's sales by over 20 per cent.

Instead, when you think of the response to your message as just feedback or information, you are able to take responsibility for the communication. Blaming other people for their response is no longer viable. If you don't achieve what you want, *you* need to make some changes and find a new way to convey your message. After all, influencing other people is critical to your success at work. Part II of this book offers many ideas, tools, and techniques to help you find new and different ways to communicate when you just aren't getting the result you want.

If you don't get the desired reaction to your communication, that's not failure, only feedback. The feedback helps you to be more flexible and try something else until you get the response you desire.

## Influencing isn't optional

When a salesperson is chasing you and you don't return his calls, he certainly gets a message – at least that he isn't your top priority.

Similarly, when you present the new organisation chart to the team (for example) and get no response to your request for comments, you're still receiving feedback.

Another NLP principle says:

> You cannot not communicate.

The words humans use form a very small part of communication. Tone of voice and body language often say much mo re than the words people use. Even silence can be communication. (See Chapter 5 for more ideas on the numerous ways in which people communicate.)

Sarah, a coaching client, complained to me one day that her boss wasn't talking to her. He was avoiding her, not responding to messages, and answering emails only when absolutely necessary. By asking more questions and digging further, I heard that Sarah and her boss had had a big disagreement over strategy the previous week. Both took a particular position and didn't shift. By *not* talking to Sarah, the boss was communicating very clearly – if not very professionally – his dislike of conflict and his frustration at the situation.

## Realising You've Got What You Need

Humans are incredibly useful beings. We have many capabilities and the potential to do phenomenal things. In the last 50 years humans put man on the moon, combined gramophones and cameras into handkerchief-sized mobile phones, and created truly global businesses.

Think about your own desires, goals, and dreams for a moment. Can you think of something you want to do? Maybe you want to:

- ✔ Get rich
- ✔ Become board director
- ✔ Give up work and sail around the world
- ✔ Run your own business
- ✔ Make a greater contribution to the community

What are you doing to achieve your goal? Do you believe you can do it? Well, others have done all these things, so why not you?

Another powerful principle behind NLP says:

People have all the resources they need.

Think about this principle within the context of your job. Maybe you don't have all the internal resources you need – *yet*. However, you do have the resources to discover and develop new resources. And you have the resources to find good external resources. So someone running his own small business, for example, may not easily acquire the skills of financial management, but he can still find and use a good accountant.

When I went on my first skiing holiday at the age of 35, I thought it would also be my last. Neither cold nor exercise was my thing, and potential limb-breaking activity was a real no-no. Despite all that, I ended up on a snowy mountain like an over-dressed, over-mature Bambi – and I had the time of my life. Don't get me wrong. I didn't became an overnight qualifier for the Winter Olympics. However, to my astonishment, I *did* have the resources to overcome my fears (just enough), to pay for some expert tuition in ski school, and to put my body into positions never before imagined.

# Building Flexibility to Make Changes

You may know the story of the English speaker on an overseas trip. Unable to speak the local language, he continues to repeat the same English phrase – loudly – in the hope of being understood. (I thought it was a parody until I started travelling and witnessed it for myself!) The reaction of the locals? They just keep on looking bemused and shrugging their shoulders. After all, as the saying goes, 'If you always do what you've always done, you'll always get what you've always got.'

Being flexible is not about compromise or giving in to others. Rather, flexibility comes from having a number of alternatives to how you approach an activity or conversation, in order to make sure you get the best possible outcome.

Some years ago there was a dreadful storm in the south of England, causing unprecedented damage and uprooting millions of trees. A colleague and I both lived in the same part of town and both wanted to attend an important meeting that day. My colleague found trees blocking her route to work and turned around and drove home. I encountered the same obstacles, turned around and drove to a train station on the one route that had remained in operation and headed towards the location of our office. After a train ride and 20-minute walk I arrived for the meeting and achieved all I wanted to do. And just in case you are wondering why I didn't share my options with my colleague, this was the days before mobile phones and the land lines had been put out of action by the storm!

## Doing something different

Dawn is a learning and development manager who's moved companies during the six years I've known her. Her previous job was, she said, a 'nightmare'. Dawn takes on *everything* people ask of her. She inevitably ends up with too much to do. So she does what she always does: she just works harder and harder until she stops being effective. Dawn has recently started telling me that her current job is also a 'nightmare'.

Repetitive, unproductive behaviour occurs in workplaces all over. The behaviour can be an individual pattern, like Dawn's, but inflexible behaviour is also commonplace across businesses. In fact, many of these unwavering actions are part of an organisation's culture. For example, I work frequently with companies where structured weekly or monthly meetings are the norm – yet for many they serve no useful purpose. When I challenge this assumption, clients tell me that these meetings are 'just the way we do it here'.

What these organisations – perhaps you – need comes from another NLP principle:

> If what you're doing isn't working, do something different.

This notion seems so simple, so obvious – yet this is so often not what people do.

The key is flexibility. When you're flexible, you think about what you can do differently to help the situation change. When you're inflexible, you focus on how others in the system can change.

# Flexing for advantage

Having more flexibility gives you more opportunities to accomplish your goal. When others are involved, as they inevitably are in business, being more flexible than the other people gives you the best possible chance of getting what you want. This is summarised in the NLP principle that says:

> In any system, the person with the most flexibility controls the system.

OK, 'control' may be a bit of an exaggeration – and for some people this word has negative associations. This principle does not intend to suggest that you control others, and there are no guarantees that you can control what happens. Rather, having a range of choices in how you try to achieve your outcome sure gives you a good prospect of doing so. And what about that word 'system'? It may sound technical, describing some complex computing or engineering work. Actually, a system is just something that only exists as a result of the interaction of various things. For instance, the natural environment is a system. So is your body, your business and your family. Each is made up of various parts that interconnect and work tog ether in some way.

You can think of your working relationships as systems. When you want to persuade or motivate someone to do something that they're reluctant to do, the more flexible your approach, the more likely you are to get the result you're seeking.

You have many ways to behave more flexibly in order to get the result you want through negotiation with a colleague. (In Part II of this book, I explore a whole range of new ideas.) Some initial ways to act with great flexibility include:

- **Making your point using language that is not your normal style.** For example, instead of asking "What do you think about my suggestion?" try appealing to someone's senses. For example: "How does my suggestion sound to you? Can you see a way to make it work?"

- **Asking questions about another's objections to your ideas or proposals objections.** For example: "How could we improve the design so that you do feel it will work?"

- **Adopting a different tone of voice.** For instance, if this is something that you are very excited about, slow down, breathe deeply and speak more calmly and assertively than you naturally would.

✔ **Using a different presentation style.** Try out new styles such as formal, informal, humorous, and so on

✔ **Changing location.** For example, rather than trying to influence someone in the usual meeting room or office, find a more relaxed location such as a coffee shop

✔ **Drawing pictures or diagrams.** Illustrate and emphasise your point of view rather than just using words

## Choosing to have choices

Choice is a critical aspect of flexibility and this NLP principle sums it up:

Choice is better than no choice.

Business people tell me quite frequently that they have to stay in their current job or career, for reasons such as:

'I need to carry on to get the pension benefits.'

'I've got the school fees to pay.'

'Retraining and working my way up again takes too long.'

'No other company is going take me on at my age.'

TIP

---

### The NLP principles in brief

Remembering the NLP principles when you've only just discovered them can be hard, especially in difficult situations. Well, recalling them was for someone with a memory like mine!

When I was new to NLP, I typed myself a summary and put it where I saw it often. Your desk, wallet, bathroom mirror, or car dashboard are all good places to post this list.

In fact, feel free to use this sidebar as your personal copy of the principles.

✔ The map is not the territory

✔ People respond according to their maps

✔ Every behaviour has a positive intention

✔ There is no failure, only feedback

✔ The meaning of the communication is the response it gets

✔ You cannot not communicate

✔ People have all the resources they need

✔ If what you're doing isn't working, do something different

✔ In any system the person with the most flexibility controls the system

✔ Choice is better than no choice

These comments aren't from happy, fulfilled people. They think they have only one choice – and one choice is no choice at all. When they start to think more broadly, they may find that they have many more choices than they originally imagined:

- ✔ Starting their own business and making much more money
- ✔ Moving the children into state-funded schooling
- ✔ Cutting back on unnecessary outgoings so retraining and a lower salary is feasible
- ✔ Looking for an employer who appreciates experience and maturity

Many of the principles of NLP – as well as the thinking, tools, and techniques you uncover in this book – are based on the idea that the more choices you have, the more you can manage your own destiny.

# *Making NLP Principles Work for You*

As I say at the start of this chapter, you choose whether you accept the NLP principles – or not.

Some principles don't work for you? Relax. Most people can buy in to some more than others. For example, trying to fathom the positive intention of the guy who snatches your bag on the way to work challenges the best of us. The choice is yours. All I say is don't dismiss a principle until you try it.

Of course, the principles are generalisations (a topic I address in Chapter 4) and they maybe don't match with your current beliefs. However, one of the pillars of NLP is *behavioural flexibility*, and therein lies the challenge. If you want to make changes in your working life (and I'm going to make another generalisation I believe that's why you're reading this book), then flexibility is key.

So, test the NLP principles in this chapter for yourself. You may need to consciously remind yourself of the NLP principles for a while before thinking this way becomes second nature. Start with those that appeal to you the most. After all, there is no hierarchy of importance in them. Which you work with first, or most, is up to you. For example, if the idea that everyone has a different map of the world, or perception of reality, is a new and interesting way of thinking for you, keep that top of mind. Next time you notice someone responding to a situation in a very different way to how you would, remember that person has a different way of thinking to you, an alternative map. How does it change how you think and feel about that person and their behaviour?

# Part II
# Building Working Relationships That Work

The 5th Wave · By Rich Tennant

"As a manager, I think you're beginning to rely a bit too much on non-verbal communication."

## In this part . . .

An important NLP concept is creating advantage through excellent relationships and effective influence. This part gets up close and personal with the business of communicating in business, from understanding how other people's thought and speech patterns work through to building rapport and maximising your influence in the workplace. I also delve into how to manage emotional states and motivate others – and yourself!

# Chapter 4

# Understanding More, Achieving More through Communication

## In This Chapter

▶ Discovering the traits of a master communicator

▶ Taking charge of communications

▶ Finding out how people form their maps of the world

▶ Paying attention to others' responses

▶ Adapting to others' maps

*M*aximising your personal success – at work or elsewhere – depends on your ability to communicate well. Being good at what you do almost always includes being able to relate to other people well, irrespective of your other abilities and skills.

Good leaders use strong communication skills to persuade, inform, inspire, motivate, give feedback to, and engage others. Effective team members are those who can negotiate, collaborate, and get along with others to progress towards team goals.

NLP founders John Grinder and Richard Bandler discovered that great communicators all had a number of things in common:

✔ They know what they want to achieve.

✔ They are good at noticing others' responses to their communication.

✔ They are skilled at adapting what they say to match others' language.

✔ They act flexibly to alter what they say and continue adjusting their communication until they achieve what they want.

As a result, NLP integrates these traits so that you too can become a master communicator. This chapter looks at how communications work – and don't work. I investigate how you can take responsibility for the communications you're involved with and explore how you can start your journey to becoming an exceptional communicator.

# Winning People Over

*Communication* involves a minimum of two people interacting with each other. People interact through a variety of *channels* and in many different ways – face to face, on the phone, through dancing, e-mails, letters, touch, and more.

To become a more effective influencer – a person who can win over people much more of the time – you must develop the skill of paying very close, conscious attention to the person or people you're trying to connect with. As I described in Chapter 2, there are many things which you may not currently be noticing. You'll discover a whole range of things to notice in others in Chapter 5, including:

- ✔ Language
- ✔ Eye movements
- ✔ Physiology

## Communicating with more than words

In the modern business world, communication takes place though an increasing variety of channels. Letters, face-to-face meetings, telephone calls, and faxes all still happen. Yet so many more channels bombard workers today as new communications continue to be introduced, including SMS messaging, mobile phones, video-conferencing, and so on. Even if you sit behind a computer most of the day, you probably spend a huge amount of time using this piece of hardware to communicate with others.

Research that Professor Albert Mehrabian of the University of California (UCLA) has undertaken into how communication between people actually works is enlightening. Mehrabian's experiments identify what people notice and react to during face-to-face communication. Surprisingly, only 7 per cent of what people respond to comes from spoken words. Figure 4-1 shows that the most important aspect of communication in Mehrabian's research is body language (55 per cent), followed significantly by voice tone (38 per cent).

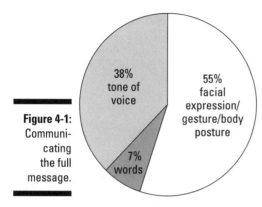

**Figure 4-1:** Communicating the full message.

When you're with people and talking to them, even your most positive and encouraging words will only be believed if your body language (physiology) and voice tone support your words. (Chapter 5 explores the roles of body language and tone further.)

When your communication is *not* face to face, it's harder to communicate the whole message. A humorously intended comment in an e-mail, written with a smile on your face, may not be received with humour by your reader. Face to face, the recipient can see your smile and (hopefully) understands your joke.

## *Focusing on people power*

As the western world continues to shift industry emphasis away from manufacturing towards service-, retail- and leisure-based businesses, polished communication skills become increasingly important. The focus of business is less and less on making things and more and more on interacting with a customer, supplier, business partner or the community.

Of similar importance is communicating within and across an organisation, whether a company, a public body or a not-for-profit organisation. The *Oxford English Dictionary* includes people in its definitions of these two modern workplaces:

  ✔ **Organisation:** An organised body of people with a particular purpose, for example, a business.

  ✔ **Company:** A number of people gathered together.

In my experience, the biggest barriers to success in organisations are misunderstandings, difficult relationships, and blaming. All these are people-centred issues.

When I work with groups that have open communication, that give people the chance to contribute and influence, and that motivate and support one another, good things happen. The employees are engaged, energised, creative, and willing. And funnily enough, these groups typically achieve their goals and more.

## Responding to others' responses

Communication takes place in an ongoing *system*, known as the *response–behaviour cycle*. For example, when you communicate with someone else:

✔ The other person has an *internal response* and then reacts (their *external behaviour*), creating a *feedback loop*.

✔ You perceive the other person's reaction, which in turn triggers *your* thoughts and feelings (your *internal response*).

✔ Your thoughts and feelings drive what you do and say next (your *external behaviour*), and the cycle continues, as Figure 4-2 shows.

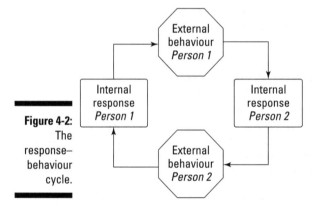

**Figure 4-2:** The response–behaviour cycle.

To envision the response–behaviour cycle in action, imagine your boss congratulates you on a recent job well done. You feel good as a result of the praise (your *internal response*). You smile, thank her, and add that you only did it with her good leadership and support (your *external behaviour*). In turn, your boss's *internal response* to your thanks and praise is embarrassment. She flushes pink, stammers slightly, and changes the subject (her *external behaviour*).

In this example, the response of the boss – embarrassment – was not what you were intending to create when you thanked her. Lots of people would have been delighted to receive such feedback. However, we are all different, and can have quite different reactions to the same experience. Read more about this in the later section: *Working with Different Maps of the World.*

# Taking charge of communications

Taking responsibility for all the communications you're involved with is the first step to becoming a great communicator. This involves:

✔ Believing that you can achieve what you want through influence

✔ Trusting that you can communicate effectively with just about anyone

✔ Knowing that if you don't get the response you want, then it's down to you to try something different

This attitude towards communication may not seem true or even possible right now, but after you read more of this book and build your skills, you may well be amazed at the improved outcomes you get.

A number of the core NLP principles that I discuss in Chapter 3 are worth considering. Think about how the process of communicating with others connects to the following five principles:

✔ **You cannot not communicate.** Even if you sit through a meeting without saying a word, your body language will be speaking for you!

✔ **The meaning of the communication is the response it gets.** If someone is offended by a remark you made, it becomes offensive even when your intention had only been to make them laugh.

✔ **There is no failure only feedback.** When you take responsibility for the effectiveness of your communications, should you not persuade someone to do what you had hoped, that is useful information. It tells you that the way in which you have communicated so far hasn't worked.

✔ **If what you're doing isn't working, do something different**. Adapting your approach, like the master communicators, is the key to getting different results.

✔ **In any system the person with the most flexibility controls the system.** When you are flexible and ready to try different things, you are more likely to convince or prompt others to follow your ideas.

# Working with Different Maps of the World

Your thoughts influence everything you say and do. Your thoughts give signals to others – what you think, believe, value, and want.

Your *map of the world* guides your thoughts. Your life experiences and what you've noticed about them build this map. Given that everyone receives and processes information differently, understanding how someone else sees things differently to you can be extremely helpful.

Differences in people's maps of the world result from the fact that stimuli coming into the brain via the senses continually bombard everyone. Some researchers contend that people face up to 2 billion bits of information every second. I don't know if this statistic's true, but I'm certain that information in just double figures is likely to overwhelm me!

In fact, over 50 years ago Professor George Miller, an American psychologist, claimed that the conscious human mind can deal with a finite number of pieces of information at once. The number? The clue was in the title of his paper: *Seven Plus or Minus Two*.

According to Miller's research, whether you handle nine or five pieces of information (or anywhere in between) depends on how you're feeling and how much interest and excitement you have in what's coming in.

So, your brain selects what it consciously and unconsciously takes in – what you see, hear, feel, smell, and taste at any point. How does it do this? Through very sophisticated filtering systems that develop into patterns over time. Your filters are unique, leading to your exclusive map of the world. I discuss filters in the section 'Filtering: Creating individual maps', later in this chapter.

## Judging from your own maps

You usually interpret someone else's actions and reactions by comparing them to your own patterns. Figure 4-3 illustrates what happens when you have an experience of someone else's behaviour.

As you pay attention to what you see, hear, or feel, you compare experiences with your own patterns of behaviour. When you find a match, you generally attach meaning to the other person's behaviour – the meaning that behaviour would have if it was something *you* had said or done. In many instances, your meaning may be very different indeed from the other person's.

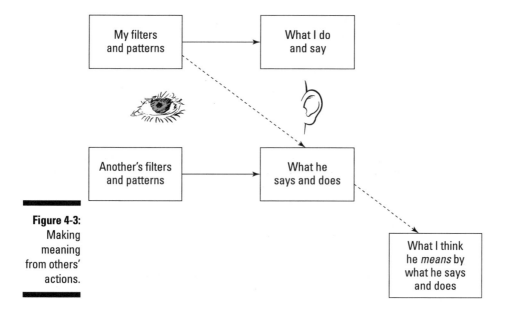

**Figure 4-3:**
Making
meaning
from others'
actions.

For instance, if your boss continually checks your work, you are likely to notice this checking and give it meaning. In your map of the world, the checking may mean that she doesn't trust you to do a good job. As a result, you may feel irritated or demotivated. For your boss, this checking behaviour may mean that she wants your work to be presented at its best to others so she can help get you a promotion.

If you only allow for interpreting someone else's actions meaning one thing – what those actions would mean if *you* did them – you can only react to that other person in one way. When you stop and remember that someone else has a different map of the world to you, you have more choices in how you react. In the example of the boss checking your work, if you find out more about her map of the world, or just decide for yourself that there could be a number of reasons for her behaviour, some of which would be to your benefit, you may well start to feel quite differently about the situation.

Simon, a leader I was coaching, complained of a lack of cooperation from Tom, a member of his team. When Simon asked him to do something, Tom often replied with a brief e-mail saying who he had delegated the task to. Simon interpreted Tom's behaviour as lazy and uncooperative. However, Tom was delegating so he could keep focused on his own schedule and thought his boss would value his use of initiative to ensure the jobs were completed quickly.

# Filtering: Creating individual maps

People put a wealth of different kinds of filtering systems to work, unconsciously, to form the maps from which they develop their individual patterns. I introduce these filters in the following section, and you can delve more deeply into some of these in Chapters 5 and 7.

### Deletion

Given the bombardment of stimuli that you receive at any one time, you quickly develop the ability to delete much of the information in your surroundings. You pay attention to certain things that happen around you but just don't notice others. This is a natural process that starts very early on in life.

As you read this book, are you aware of the feeling of the book in your hands? Are any background sounds happening – birdsong, the noise of a train or traffic, electrical buzzing, or conversations – that you haven't been paying attention to? Until I direct your attention, these very real experiences may well have been some of the information that your system was filtering out and deleting, without you ever knowing.

Everyone deletes information to make sense of the world differently. So when communicating, you may well delete the data or information that doesn't appear on your radar without knowing you're doing it.

A coaching client, Andy, reported that many of his colleagues told him they didn't understand him. Further investigation showed that his thinking process was often so fast that he didn't notice he was missing out bits of information that they needed to respond to him. He'd say something like' I found a good fix for that glitch that was causing all the problems. You might want to do the same for your machines.' Andy's colleagues were left wondering: 'What glitch? What problems? Who had the problems? When? What machines might I need to fix, and why? What is he talking about? Andy developed the ability to slow down and pay attention to what he wasn't communicating. His work relationships improved substantially.

### Distortion

You distort information that your senses take in. You're not consciously manipulating your experience; rather, you're misinterpreting information.

When communicating, people distort what they hear and see by filling in extra bits from their own experiences. The process is quite normal – everyone does it to make sense of what other people are communicating. However, filling in someone else's message is a type of mind reading and is therefore quite often wrong!

For instance, you may find yourself distorting the meaning of other people's word or actions. You may also distort what someone says or does to believe you know what she's feeling.

Maybe you accuse someone of being grumpy when you want him to buy into your enthusiasm – just because something else is distracting him. Or you believe someone's feeling good because she's joking around – when actually she's very concerned she's about to be made redundant.

You can never know *exactly* how someone else is feeling because you truly cannot get inside another person's mind and body. Yet how many times have you heard or said the immortal line: 'Oh, I know just how you feel'?

Mark was explaining to me how nervous he became when he made a presentation to a client. He got flustered, his face turned pink, and he stumbled over his words. We explored what triggered his nerves and discovered that the expression on the face of one of the clients was particularly potent. 'She had a look on her face. I knew she didn't like what I was saying as soon as I started,' Andy told me. Of course Andy's interpretation was a distortion – he didn't know instantly how his client felt. When I suggested that the client may have just had bad wind, Andy started to see the funny side of the situation and began to plan a whole different approach for his next client presentation.

## Generalisation

You generalise from your experiences to form your opinions and beliefs. When you burn yourself on a hot stove, you generalise pretty quickly that stoves are hot and not safe to touch.

Although people can generalise after just one or two examples of something happening, sometimes they need a whole lot more evidence to formulate a sound generalisation. For example, people at work may need to let you down a number of times before you make the generalisation that you can't trust your colleagues.

Maintaining your belief system depends on generalisations. Let's assume you are employed by an organisation that pays you monthly, on the promised day of the month, and you have worked there for three months or more. You *generalise* from your experience and *believe* that your employer will meet that commitment. This ensures that you work hard, and rest easy, in the comfortable belief that you will be paid on the said date. If you didn't generalise from your experience, you may be reluctant to accept monthly payments, or anxious from day to day as to whether you'd see a pay cheque at the end of the month.

Sometimes you distort or delete (see the preceding sections) to make sure that what you're currently experiencing fits in with your generalisations. You may hear a friend wax lyrical about a talented child, set to be an international concert pianist. When you're finally subjected to the performance of a shy and miserable teenager plonking out a none too tuneful piece, you realise that the mother has generalised from early feedback about the child's talents – and distorted and deleted other evidence.

### Sensory-specific thinking

You use your senses to experience the world, form memories, and create new ideas within your mind. Over time, people start to use one of the senses of sight, hearing, or feeling somewhat more than the other two. This preference in turn becomes a filter on your experiences, meaning that two people do not have an identical experience of the same occasion or incident.

For example, maybe you've had a conversation like this:

> **Jack:** 'Do you remember the conference we went to last year?'
>
> **Susan:** 'Do you mean the one where they played a big fanfare for the speakers?'
>
> **Jack:** 'Yes, that's the one. Where the keynote speaker wore that purple suit and showed a lot of slides with graphs on.'
>
> **Susan:** 'Well, I remember that suit, but not the slides. He was the guy who talked about the economic forecast and told us how grim things were going to be this year.'
>
> **Jack:** 'Did he? I was just thinking about how good that stage set-up was and whether we can copy it for our next event.'
>
> **Susan:** 'Was there anything special about the stage? I recall the sound system was a bit crackly. We surely don't want anything like that.'

Notice the differences between the two people's memories of a shared experience. Although Susan remembers the purple suit, which she sees in her mind's eye, she mainly remembers things she heard. By contrast, Jack remembers hearing the fanfare but remembers far more of the things he saw.

Chapter 5 offers much more about sensory thinking, including how to spot what sense someone's using and how to use this preference to have more influence.

### Metaprograms

*Metaprograms* have been identified by early NLP developers as some of the habitual patterns of thinking that control how you like to work and what motivates you. They're probably the most unconscious filters you have, so you may not be aware of them.

When you and a colleague are running very different metaprogram patterns, you're guaranteed to have difficulty understanding each other, at least some of the time.

Consider possible metaprograms related to problem solving and achieving goals. (I discuss six other important workplace metaprograms in Chapter 7.) Which of the following is most like you:

✔ **Task oriented:** You like people, of course, but when you've a goal to achieve, you prefer to put your head down and get things done. Tools and processes are important, and you see little room for emotion at work.

✔ **Relationship oriented:** You're focused on people and relationships. Your and others' feelings are of the highest importance, and your attention is often on keeping people (including yourself) engaged with projects, working together and motivated.

When you're task oriented and determined to hit a target and you're working closely with someone who's relationship oriented and centred on how people are feeling, friction may, unsurprisingly, occur.

When my colleague Mariette and I run training workshops together, we often get some way through the day and find we are behind schedule. This is invariably due to me. When I run discussion sessions I'm keen to encourage everyone to participate and to feel heard and understood, so often allow more time than planned. By lunchtime, Mariette can be beside herself with frustration, 'We are behind and we have so much still *to do*.' Guess which one of us has a strong relationship pattern and which one is very task oriented!

The good news is that language actually flags up the metaprograms people are using – if you have a well-trained ear, of course. To identify a preference towards one or the other end of the task/relationship-oriented metaprogram pattern, listen to what people are saying. Table 4-1 highlights the different kinds of language that let you know whether someone is more task oriented or relationship oriented in the workplace.

| Table 4-1: | Task or Relationship Orientation Signs | |
|---|---|---|
| *Orientation* | *Talks about* | *Sentence structure* |
| Relationship | People, feelings, emotions, individuals by name | People are the object of sentences. (For example, 'The sales team all seemed to enjoy my presentation. My boss was delighted.') |
| Task | Systems, processes, things, tools, goals, tasks | People become 'objects' and are referred to as 'they', 'you'. (For example, "My presentation went well. They all seemed to get something from it so we should see increased sales.' |

Ann orientation towards achieving *tasks* is neither superior nor inferior to an orientation towards *developing* relationships. Like all metaprograms, these orientations are just different. In fact, the most successful teams often have people representing both extremes – as well as some people in between – to ensure the job gets done but in a cooperative and collaborative way.

You may be tempted to stereotype a metaprogram pattern based on gender. Indeed, many women are relationship oriented, while many men are task oriented. However, beware! Never assume someone's metaprograms based on gender. Always test out your observations by carefully watching and listening.

Chapter 7 has lots more on six common metaprograms that have a strong influence on how people operate at work. I tell you how to spot various metaprograms in yourself and others – and how to make changes in order to work better with other metaprogram patterns.

### Beliefs

Beliefs are very powerful. If you believe you *can't* run a marathon, write a book, or build a house, you're most probably right. And if you believe you *can* be a CEO, fly a plane, or become a millionaire, again, you're most probably right. Beliefs are an important influential filter on your experience.

You start to acquire and form your beliefs from birth and continue adding to and refining them throughout your life. Many of your beliefs come from what and how you generalise. One person may believe that they won't be wealthy as they have never been wealthy, nor has anyone in their family. Another person may believe that as they want to be wealthy they will be, because they generally get what they want when they put all their energy and drive into a goal. Additionally:

✔ Some beliefs may change when new evidence contradicts what you believe. For instance, you may believe someone at work is not committed as they frequently take sick leave. You subsequently learn they are suffering from a serious condition and actually are working more time than their doctor advises. You now believe this person is incredibly committed to the company.

✔ Some beliefs stick with you, and you may not always realise they're there. Maybe you believe that you should always help others at work ahead of working on your own projects. This belief will direct how you spend your day, and what results you achieve and yet you aren't even aware that's how you are thinking.

Beliefs come from various sources, including:

✔ The attitudes and beliefs of your family

✔ The people you associate with throughout your life – school, social groups, voluntary organisations, work, and so on

✔ Your education

✔ Your culture, including your religion and the beliefs of your community

✔ Repeat experiences that you have (losing jobs, getting pay rises, broken relationships, sporting successes etc.)

✔ Significant life experiences (redundancies, traumatic events, illnesses, relationship breakdowns etc.)

✔ All forms of media

Your beliefs are mostly formed from generalisations of your experiences. For example, if a colleague snaps at you several times, you may generalise that experience and develop the belief that she's always aggressive. If IT support people fix your PC quickly twice, you may generalise this experience and believe that IT supplies good service.

What then happens when you speak to other colleagues who have different experiences and believe differently? Sometimes the collective experiences, beliefs, and opinions of others colour and change your beliefs. For example, you discover that the colleague who snapped at you is generally regarded as a very amenable, helpful and pleasant person to work with, until she was recently under threat of redundancy. You now believe her anxiety led to her aggressive behaviour and that she is actually a nice person. You may also find out that colleagues have been left waiting two weeks for critical IT updates and repairs and that this delay is seriously damaging their ability to do their jobs. You now believe that IT service is variable and not to be relied upon.

Given the difference in life experiences from individual to individual, people unsurprisingly develop different, sometimes contradictory, beliefs.

Your beliefs play a key part in filtering what's happening around you, which then affects what you think, say, and do. Knowing that others' beliefs drive them to different thoughts, opinions, and actions to yours is the first step to communicating more effectively with others by understanding more about their maps of the world.

I explore more about the role of beliefs in the world of work in Chapter 14.

### Values

Values, like beliefs, differ from person to person and serve as significant filters on the world. Whereas beliefs are what you perceive as the facts of life, your values tell you what's important to you and direct how you act as a result. You don't tend to attach emotion to your beliefs. – they're just things you believe, such as the belief that the train will get you to work. Values on the other hand are more like beliefs about what is right and wrong, good or bad. When the train is severely delayed you start to feel distressed because it's really important to you to get to work on time.

Values are powerful motivators, or *drivers,* of behaviour, both constructive and destructive. You also use your values to evaluate yourself and others.

For instance, if you value honesty, you're more likely to be open and candid with others, including your co-workers. If service is important to you, you do your utmost to do your best for customers. If you value loyalty and honesty and notice a colleague taking some stationery home, you may well find yourself in conflict – whether to be loyal to your workmate or inform someone about the potential theft of company property.

Business often develop formal values that they ask employees to subscribe and work to. Many organisations also have a *sub-culture of values.* Some companies – certain financial institutions, for example – quietly value people working long hours, but you don't read that up on the wall on the list of company values.

Julia, a friend of mine working in an investment bank, admitted that she just used to hang around at night until she thought it was an acceptable time to leave the office according to her manager, (usually at least 13 hours after arriving). Julia valued her home life and family, and eventually found the conflict between the implicit corporate values and her own values caused her too much upset. She eventually left the bank.

Conflicting values are a continual source of challenge to effective communication and cooperation in business. A few examples of things that people hold quite opposing values around include:

✔ **Timekeeping:** Does it matter whether things are late as long as you do them well, or do you think being on time is important?

✔ **Effort:** Is working harder more important than working smarter? Do you put value on the amount of hours you spend on the job, or do you value work–life balance?

✔ **Image:** Do you value being dressed formally or professionally for work, or do you value choice, comfort, and informality in appearance?

✔ **Organisation hierarchy:** Do you value being able to speak to anyone, or do you think following hierarchical protocol is important?

Forming a greater understanding of the difference in values that are acting as filters on someone else's viewpoint can help you bridge a communications gap. You can find out more about values in Chapter 14.

# Mastering Communication

Your various patterns of thinking and behaving are well programmed into your system. Your unique set of filters on the world defines your attitudes, opinions, and thoughts. You can be quite proud of these patterns. They have certainly got you to where you are today. However, you maybe haven't been fully aware of them.

## Constructing connection

The next time you want to communicate something at work, take some time – even a few seconds – to plan before you speak.

✔ **Work out your goal beforehand.** What do you want to have happen as a result of this interaction? Be specific with yourself. For example, 'I want to get agreement to spend a particular sum of money on advertising.'

✔ **Try to be curious about the other person.** What filters – deletions, distortions, generalisations, sensory-specific thinking,

metaprograms, beliefs, or values – may she be using that are affecting how she hears you?

✔ **Pay attention to all feedback.** What responses are you receiving? Are you getting the types of response that you want?

✔ **Keep experimenting.** If what you're doing isn't working, try something different. How else can you communicate something that may connect with the other person?

Now's the time to become conscious of your patterns, so that you can have more choices in how you think, speak, and behave. If you discover these patterns in yourself, you can then find ways to effectively influence others, through speaking so that people can hear, understand, and respond positively.

# Chapter 5

# Making Sense of Other People for Better Influence

---

---

**A**s I discuss in Chapter 2, one of the four pillars of NLP is *sensory awareness* – using your senses to experience the world and form your own reality.

You only have to watch babies on their voyages of discovery as they explore their surroundings through looking, listening, touching, tasting, and smelling to know how important the senses are. As you grow, your senses continue to play a critical role in shaping your understanding of the world.

In this chapter, I explore the senses in depth: how you use them, how to exploit them in new ways to notice how others think, and finally, how to build flexibility in using your senses to become a more powerful influencer.

## Celebrating the Senses

Humans use their highly sophisticated senses – sight, hearing, touch, taste, and smell – to discover new things and develop throughout life. As you grow and mature, you also use your senses to engage with other people and things, and to create the basis of your emotional connections and experiences.

Similarly, you use your five senses to create your *internal version* of the world. When you remember an incident or imagine something that may happen, your mental processes use your senses.

Take a moment to remember an occasion at work when you were very successful. Simply recall a time when you did a good job and got a great result.

When you think back to that time, *how* do you remember? I often hear people declare what they think and commenting on what others think. They so often put attention on the *what*. In contrast, this chapter's all about the benefits of noticing and reacting to *how* people think. ? (Indeed, *how* can be even more important and revealing than *what*.)

When you think back, maybe you can see a picture in your mind – possibly even a kind of moving film of what happened. You may see an object, people's smiles, or just a bigger pay cheque!

Spend some time thinking about the sounds of the event:

✔ How did the voices of other people sound?

✔ Was there applause or cheering?

✔ How did the voice inside your head sound?

Think about your other senses during the event. Can you remember how you felt at that time? Maybe you can even experience some of those good feelings right now as you think about it. You may even recall a smell or a taste – perhaps a celebratory glass of something? – as you think back.

None of the experience you're having when you think back on the event is happening right now. You're having memories of a past occasion. Yet through your senses you recreate the experience in your mind.

Now, imagine that you're giving an important presentation next week. How can you know what to say and what to do before you start? Unless you're very spontaneous, you're likely to prepare. Perhaps you may:

✔ Think in advance and plan what you want to say.

✔ Prepare some visual aids or props.

✔ Plan some answers to possible questions.

To do any of this you have to use at least some of your senses. For example, you may make pictures, hear words, and experience feelings about the presentation – but everything happens internally.

# Making Sense of the Senses

The developers of NLP (you'll read more about them in Chapter 1) explored *how* humans use their senses to represent their experience to themselves. Funnily enough, the developers of NLP then named the senses *representational systems*. Over time, the senses have become informally known among people versed in NLP as *rep systems* for short.

To keep things easy in this chapter – and throughout the book – I use the short form for various rep systems. VAKOG is the acronym used to describe the five senses:

- ✔ V –visual
- ✔ A– auditory
- ✔ K – kinaesthetic
- ✔ O – olfactory
- ✔ G – gustatory

The first three, which I call VAK, are the ones I concentrate on in this book, as these are the three that everyone uses for the majority of their thinking.

You use your senses (VAKOG) to interact with what's outside yourself and to make sense of that within yourself.

So what's the big deal about that? Well, it's this: Everyone uses their senses differently. Further, knowing more about how you use *your* senses – and discovering how others use *theirs* – helps you find a key secret to becoming a master influencer.

## Doing it my way

In the words of Ol' Blue Eyes, when it comes to using my senses, I do it my way. And by extension, you do it your way, and everyone else does it their way.

The point here is that however you do it, it's never exactly the same as me. Why not? Well, how people use their minds to remember and create things is something they develop, usually unconsciously. Over time you develop preferred senses to filter your experience. (Check out Chapter 4 for more on filters.)

## The how of writing this book

I seem to do most of my thinking kinaesthetically, although I do see lots of pictures as well. This doesn't mean that I can't use my auditory sense – thank goodness, or this book would never have been written! Although my preferred sense is feeling, I do use all three senses – and so will you.

As I sit at my desk writing this book, I hear words in my head before I type. Then, after they're on the screen in front of me, I read the words back to hear how they sound – again, in my head. As I hear them, I sometimes get a feeling inside that

what I've written doesn't seem quite right, so I make changes. I read them back to myself and check out if it 'feels right' now.

I see my typing errors by looking at the words and noticing I've spelt some words incorrectly. How do I know that I need to change a word? Well, I compare what I see on screen to my memories of how particular words should look. These memories are stored as pictures in my mind. I'm using all three main senses while writing, not just my preferred sense.

Each person tends to develop a preferred rep system – one sense that you use more than the others. This doesn't mean that you don't use all your senses some of the time, but one of your senses is your lead sense most of the time – even if you don't know which sense it is. (See the later section, 'Detecting Visual, Auditory, and Kinaesthetic Thinking', for several ways to figure out your lead sense.)

Because thinking drives behaviour, what you do and say shows and tells someone else how you're thinking. Due to people's differences in thinking, they act and talk in different ways – a recipe for misunderstanding and confusion. Bottom line: If you're not thinking the same way, you aren't talking the same language.

Consider this example: When discussing a training programme I designed with my colleague Mariette, I asked, "How do you feel this may work?" She struggled to answer. I quickly understood that Mariette doesn't make judgements through her feelings. Instead, I now ask her, "Does this look like it may work?" Mariette uses her own approach, which is to run a series of pictures in her mind and then give me feedback. And interestingly, her feedback is typically about what the aspects that need changing may *look like*. Having changed just one question I use with Mariette, our collaboration on training design is now smooth, easy and effective. I do like an easier life!

## Identifying your VAK patterns

If you think you already know which rep system you use the most, then the rest of this chapter can help you test out your belief. If you aren't sure, try the following.

Remember something good that you recently did. Do you get a picture, sound, or feeling first? Try some other memories too. Think back to your last holiday, what you did last weekend, your best day at school. Test out what you discover by exploring lots of memories. Good, bad or neutral memories all count, but why not spend time enjoying some good times again?! If the sense you use first is always the same, you can be pretty sure that you've discovered your lead rep system.

Following are some other clues to figuring out your VAK thinking. As you study these characteristics, does any rep system seem more familiar to you?

- ✔ **Visual.** You may enjoy art, images, symbols, or graphic design. You may be good at seeing how things may look, keeping an eye on things, or getting things into perspective.

- ✔ **Auditory.** You may enjoy reading, drama, writing, speaking, poetry, or music. Ideas may resonate with you. You may seek harmony with people and like to talk things through.

- ✔ **Kinaesthetic.** You may enjoy dance, sports, yoga, or other physical activity. You may be comfortable with touch. You're often able to get a handle on things or grasp a situation. You like to make an impact.

You can continue to identify your lead rep system as you read through this chapter and find out more about sensory thinking clues, particularly in the following section, 'Detecting Visual, Auditory, and Kinaesthetic Thinking.' After you know how you currently think, you can begin to exercise your thinking patterns and stretch your capability to utilise other rep systems. That way you have more choices to work with and influence others who use different rep systems to you.

# Detecting Visual, Auditory, and Kinaesthetic Thinking

Discovering other people's preferred rep systems can be fun. You can get many clues by watching and listening closely to three telltale signs:

- ✔ Eye movements: The direction in which people's eyes move during thinking.

- ✔ Language: The kinds of words and phrases people use.

- ✔ Physiology: People's posture, breathing, and gestures.

After you develop the ability to spot the rep system that someone's using most, you can then work out ways to be so much more successful in influencing them. (See 'Using VAK Awareness to Influence', later in this chapter, for more information.)

## Following the eyes

Next time you ask someone a question, pay close attention to his eyes. Do they travel upwards, downwards, or to one side?

You need to watch what happens *immediately* after you ask the question and before he answers. The eyes move as the other person thinks about his answer. Look hard – it can all happen very quickly!

The early developers of NLP observed that people's eye movements are not random, but actually correlate with which rep system they're using. Extensive research found distinct patterns of movement in six directions. Each movement clearly shows how a person is thinking.

Only a small percentage of people don't follow these patterns, and a number of these people are left-handed. Being from a different culture or race has little bearing on the results. The movements, and what they mean, remain the same.

The following sections describe the eye movements for individuals with various rep systems. You'll learn what kind of thinking each eye movement represents and find out how to practise paying attention to eyes in action.

### Eye movements for visual thinking

When someone's eyes travel upwards, you can be sure that their owner's seeing pictures internally. Visual thinking is quite noticeable, but the eye movements can be fast. If you watch carefully you can see movements like those Figure 5-1 depicts.

**Figure 5-1:** Eye movements for visual thinking.

Eyes up and to the right

Imagined or constructed images

Eyes up and to the left

Remembered images

As you can see in Figure 5-1, remembered pictures are accessed up on the right as you look at a person, and new, imagined pictures up on the left. If you notice someone looking into the middle distance with his eyes defocused, he's also likely to be thinking in images.

Find out for yourself how the eye movements for visual thinking work by asking a friend or colleague to experiment with you. Ask the other person a few questions and notice where his eyes go. Ask several questions – that way you can observe multiple eye movements and check that the movement patterns match the majority. The kind of questions to try include:

✔ What can you see from your workstation?

✔ What colour is your front door?

✔ What was the first thing you saw on your journey to work this morning?

✔ How would your work environment appear if painted fluorescent pink?

✔ Can you imagine people's faces when they see you arrive at work on a camel?

✔ How would your colleagues look if dressed up in cowboy costumes?

### Eye movements for auditory thinking

Remembering where the eyes travel to indicate that someone's thinking in an auditory way is easy. The eyes move from side to side, as if looking to the ears. Figure 5-2 illustrates this in action.

**Figure 5-2:** Eye movements for auditory thinking.

Eyes to the right side

Imagined or constructed sounds

Eyes to the left side

Remembered sounds

Like eye movements for visual thinking, memories are accessed on the right as you look at someone, whereas new sounds are created on the left.

Test out the eye movement patterns for auditory thinking with your friend or colleague by giving instructions or asking questions such as:

✔ Hear your mobile phone ringing.

✔ Remember your favourite song.

✔ What does the fire alarm at work sound like?

✔ How would your boss sound speaking in the voice of Arnold Schwarzenegger?

✔ Hear your chair as a talking weight machine, announcing your weight loudly to your colleagues each morning.

✔ How does your name sound with Lord or Lady front of it?

### Eye movements for self-talk

Another eye movement is associated with auditory thinking – looking down and to the right as you look at someone, as Figure 5-3 shows. This movement is a distinctly different kind of hearing activity. It tells you a person's talking to himself. Don't worry – *internal dialogue*, or *self-talk*, is perfectly normal and not a sign of madness. Everyone does it!

**Figure 5-3:**
Eye move-
ments
indicating
self-talk.

Eyes down and to the right

Feelings and emotions

To spot self-talk in action, ask your willing co-experimenter a few questions such as:

✔ What kinds of things do you say to yourself when you're having a bad day?

✔ What can you say to open the next performance feedback session you run?

✔ Ask yourself what your ambitions are.

### Eye movement for kinaesthetic thinking

The eye signal that someone is thinking with his feelings is a look down and to the left as you face him, as in Figure 5-4. When you see this it will indicate that the other person is doing one of the following:

✔ Using his emotions, for example feeling pleased

✔ Having an internal sensation in his body, like the *gut feeling* some people describe

✔ Thinking about a tactile experience, such as remembering a friendly embrace

ANECDOTE

# The eyes tell the story

A former colleague and his wife invited me for dinner. I hadn't seen them for a while and didn't know their relationship had hit a difficult patch.

They sat opposite each other at the two ends of a rectangular table, while I sat between them. As dinner progressed, their desire to talk to me about their marital issues grew. Like a tennis fan I turned my head from side to side to hear their respective complaints.

When Angela spoke, she looked up high. When Peter spoke, he seemed to be examining the table, looking down and slightly right. After a number of exchanges, Angela turned to me and said: "And I'm so fed up that he can't even *look* at me when he's speaking to me."

Angela was right, Peter wasn't looking at her, but not for the reasons she imagined. Peter's internal world is kinaesthetic. He was working hard to make sense of the complaints and accusations Angela was making – all delivered with much more speed than he was able to handle. He was stuck deep down in his feelings as he tried to work through it all, and therefore he was eyes down at the table. Angela meanwhile, kept looking up high, seeing her thinking in pictures, with her preference for visual thinking.

**Figure 5-4:**
Eye move-
ment
showing
kinaesthetic
thinking.

Eyes down and to
the left

Self talk
(internal dialogue)

TRY THIS

To see kinaesthetic thinking in action, persuade a friend or colleague to have just a bit more fun playing with this stuff. Give him instructions like:

✔ Remember the feeling of hot sand under your feet.

✔ Feel cotton wool.

✔ Feel any points of tension or soreness in your body.

✔ Feel enthusiastic.

You may need to be patient with the person you're observing here. Feelings can take a little longer to access than other senses.

## Listening for language clues

Language is a real giveaway to which VAK system a person's using. Actually, realising how much of yourself you flag up with just a few unconsciously selected words and phrases is quite scary!

Start to listen carefully to others, and you're likely to hear a lot of words and phrases that tell you what rep system they're mainly using.

Table 5-1 lists some sensory-specific words and phrases you may hear people use – or indeed you may use yourself. Of course, many more language-based clues than those in the table exist, so listen well.

| Table 5-1 | Words and Phrases that Indicate Specific Representational Systems | |
|---|---|---|
| **Visual** | **Auditory** | **Kinaesthetic** |
| I see | Tell me | Feels like |
| Focus on | I hear that | Real impact |
| Big picture | Sounds like | Get a handle on |
| Clarifying matters | Listen | Support |
| Illustrative | Let's talk | Drive |
| Viewpoint | Out of earshot | Tied up |
| Show me | So you say | Touch |
| The outlook | Don't ask me | Warm |
| New perspective | Dialogue | Solid |
| The vision | Harmony | Tight grip |
| With hindsight | Tone | Flow |
| Graphic | Rings a bell | Hard |
| Perceive | That resonates | High pressure |
| Colourful | Same wavelength | Soft |
| Enlightening | Strikes a chord | Heated |
| Paint a picture | Spell out | Stretching |
| Look out | Discuss | Driving forward |
| Insight | The question is | Pushing ahead |
| Appears to me | Clear as a bell | Rough |

As you begin paying greater attention to people's use of language, you also hear olfactory and gustatory (smell and taste) words from time to time. Because people don't tend to have smell or taste as their primary rep systems, you don't hear these words as frequently as VAK words. A few examples include the following: I smell a rat, bitter sweet, clear the air, fresh, palatable, juicy, bland, cheesy, savour the moment, whiff, stale, spicy.

At work you can listen to language for a while to detect whether someone's main language is visual, auditory, or kinaesthetic. However, two factors may trip you up:

> ✓ **A lot of business-speak misses out altogether on sensory-specific words.** Some of what you hear is logical and conceptual. Think about legal documents – they rarely include sensory words.
>
> Also, language used in a typical organisation has many 'neutral' words that give no clue whatsoever as to the rep system of the speaker. Look through the e-mails you receive this week and notice how many or how few sensory-specific words they contain.
>
> Examples of words that are not sensory-specific include organisation, analyse, introduce, goal, experience, strategy, understand, utilise, analysis, appraise, decision, buy, sell, success, communicate, and learn.
>
> ✓ **Businesses develop their own jargon.** People within an organisation start to repeat stock phrases, which often feature in the company's mission, vision, and values statements. This jargon becomes the *lingua franca,* or common language, of people within the company.
>
> And some of this jargon may seem to suggest a particular rep system. Phrases like client focus, the vision, in discussion, a hearing, moving forward, and beating the competition sound like they have sensory connections. Everyone in the company may use these phrases – but not necessarily because they have meaning to everyone's rep system.

One of my colleagues says something regularly that always leaves us laughing. It's quite a common expression in fact: 'I see what you're saying.' Taking her words literally, I can be forgiven for thinking that she actually reads my words, as if they've physically flowed out of my mouth and are now hanging in the air. She can't do that, of course. But she *does* see what I'm saying because she immediately makes pictures in her mind so she can understand and make meaning of my words. Guess which is her primary representation system?!

## *Looking for signs*

People's *physiology* – how they hold and use their bodies – gives away further evidence as to which rep system they are using. The speed at which you talk and the associated breathing characteristics are very good indicators of a dominant rep system. Your posture and where you point with your hands give additional signs. Table 5-2 gives you an overview of what to look and listen for.

| Table 5-2 | Physiological Clues to Specific Representational Systems | | |
| --- | --- | --- | --- |
| *Clue* | *Visual* | *Auditory* | *Kinaesthetic* |
| Breathing | High and shallow | Through the diaphragm | Deep in the abdomen |
| Voice tempo | Fast | Fluctuating | Slow |
| Posture | Leaning back, head up | Leaning forward, head cocked | Head and shoulders down |
| Gestures | Gestures above eye level | Pointing towards ears | Touching chest and stomach |

Some say that discovering how to pay attention to eye movements, voice, breathing, posture, *and* language all at once is impossible, a bit like steering, signalling, looking in the rear-view mirror, and changing gear. Don't expect to do it all perfectly when you start. Keep practising!

ANECDOTE

## Slowing down the pictures

Julia, a marketing manager, reported to Martin. Julia used to dread their weekly meetings. Martin listened to her review of recent progress and then discussed next steps. Full of ideas, questions, and suggestions, he typically leaned back, looked up, and talked (in Julia's words) "at what feels like the speed of a rocket". Often, Julia just couldn't make sense of what Martin was saying. She swung between feeling completely intimidated by his sharp mind and wondering if he was a bit mad as he sometimes talked nonsense.

Julia looked downwards as she steadily explained this situation to me. She admitted she felt uncomfortable talking about her boss in this way, but she was feeling very stressed about these interactions with Martin.

After Julia indentified and understood the different rep systems that she and Martin were using (kinaesthetic and visual, respectively), she started to feel better. The next week she explained to Martin: 'You're much better at seeing in pictures than me. You see things so quickly in your mind's eye that when you explain them to me, you skip a few things. So when I try to picture what you're saying, I can't run a full video for myself. I need to slow down the pictures a bit so I can get a gut feeling for your idea.'

Martin was intrigued and wanted to see if this new insight helped them work together better. Martin started to slow down his explanations and give a bit more information. Julia felt comfortable in asking for clarification when she needed it. They laughed at times about their different styles whilst becoming a very successful team.

# Using VAK Awareness to Influence

After you know how someone uses their senses – and which sense they rely on first and most – you can begin using this new-found understanding. ('Detecting Visual, Auditory, and Kinaesthetic Thinking', earlier in this chapter, provides several tools for spotting the different ways in which people think – and therefore behave.)

By adapting to others' rep systems, you can increase rapport, which I explore in more detail in Chapter 6. After establishing greater rapport, you can create stronger working relationships, be better understood, and get the responses you want more often.

The following sections consider some of the areas where you can use your VAK flexibility.

## Communicating one to one

Do you just seem to connect with some people? Do you see where they're coming from? Can you easily get on the same wavelength?

If you spend some time to work out what these individuals' main rep system is, you may well find it matches yours. (If it doesn't, then you may find you have other things in common in your thinking process, which you can read more about in Chapter 7.)

No doubt some other people are a bit more tricky to get along with or to communicate well with. Humans just don't seem always to understand each other's ideas or opinions. In particular, difficulties can arise between someone with a high visual preference and a person with strong kinaesthetic thinking, leading to confusion and conflict.

So, when you need to influence people who aren't like you, VAK skills can come into their own to help you get the results you want.

### Getting face-to-face

One-on-one meetings give you the perfect opportunity to study someone for clues about which rep system he's using – and to experiment with matching his system to find out what different results you get.

When you're face-to-face you can watch eye movements very closely, and notice posture, body movements and breathing, as well as listening to someone's words. When you get your clues from several sources you're even more likely to work out a preferred rep system accurately.

I sometimes find that the clues I am getting lead to me to narrowing down someone's lead rep system to two, but I can't decide which as I am getting evidence for both. If this happens to you why not start to use a lot of words indicating one of the senses, and notice if you seem to be influencing effectively? If that doesn't work, switch to the language of the other rep system!

You can try out various sensory words (see Table 5-1) in all sorts of face-to-face situations including performance appraisals, negotiations, planning meetings, feedback sessions, selling opportunities, and motivating discussions.

Words aren't the only tools you have. Consider the following scenario:

> Brenda, a facilities manager, is trying to persuade John, a department head, to agree to change the working environment of his team by moving them to another part of the building.
>
> After some discussion John says: "Well, I just can't see how this can work."
>
> In response, Brenda gives lots of reassurance that it *can* work, but she doesn't convince John.
>
> If Brenda listens to John's words, she now knows that John needs to *see* how something can work.

So a sensory-specific response to visual-thinking John may be to *show* him some things, inviting him to *look* at an office layout, *view* some flowcharts of work moving through the new location, and to take him to the other part of the building to *point out* where things can be situated.

### Talking on the phone

With the advent of the mobile phone, people seem to spend more time than ever in telephone conversations these days. Unless both you and the person you're speaking to are using the latest video technology, you can't see each other while you're chatting.

So determining which rep system another person's using is more difficult because you can't actually look at eyes, posture, or gestures. Of course, the other person's probably still displaying all of the signs – you only have to watch someone talking on a phone to know that it's a full-body experience. But unfortunately, you can't see any of this useful information.

When talking on the phone, your main clues about another person's rep system come from his language.

In addition, you can listen out for the speed at which he's talking (see Table 5-2 for more information). Take note, though, that occasionally fast talking on the phone is because the other person needs to finish the call to attend to something you can't see, rather than being a sign of visual thinking. Slow talking on the phone normally indicates a kinaesthetic rep system, but may also be a result of your caller being distracted – again by something you can't see!

With only the words to listen for, spotting a rep system can be challenging, especially if you don't have a well-developed auditory sense. To help, put a copy of the list of sensory-specific words and phrases in Table 5-1 by the phone on your desk. Listen out for any patterns, and after you guess the person's preferred rep system, test your choice out by using some appropriate sensory words. If your vocabulary for some senses needs more breadth, again, rely on the words in Table 5-1. Ways to develop your least preferred senses are outlined at the end of this chapter.

### Conversing electronically

With so much communication these days taking place through email, you often need to do some important influencing with no personal interaction at all. When compiling an email think in advance about the rep system of the recipient. If this is someone you meet face-to-face or on the phone, make sure you do all you can to detect her rep systems when speaking with her, as suggested in the *Getting face-to-face* and *Talking on the phone* sections above). You can use this knowledge to target the words in your email to her lead rep system.

If you never get to speak with this person directly – and these days that's not so uncommon – then pay attention to her emails to you. Do her words give you any clues? Is she using sensory-specific words, and if so are they predominantly visual, auditory or kinaesthetic? Use what you detect is her preference and tailor your email language accordingly.

It's possible that you'll not find any strong clues in another person's email as to their most used rep system. If you don't get a chance to talk with them either then you may never be certain which language to use. In such a case, use a good mixture of VAK language in your email. For more ideas on how to do this read the following section, *Influencing a group.*

## Influencing a group

Speaking to a group is more challenging than a one-on-one meeting – unless you know everyone in the group really well and they're all using the same rep system (which can happen if the group's very small, but it's rare).

In general, assume you're interacting with a mix of sensory thinking in your audience. Plan to make the biggest impression on them by using visual, auditory, *and* kinaesthetic words throughout your talk. The following sections offer some specific examples.

If you have a really important message you need to get across, take the time to prepare key words and phrases in advance. Otherwise, you have a tendency to fall back on what comes naturally – the language of your own rep system – and you end up leaving some people out.

### Making a presentation

When you're presenting information to a group with a mix of sensory thinking, imagine that your audience is made up of people who literally speak three different languages. So every time you say something important, you must say it three times in each language.

The following quote shows how you can display your viewpoint from just one rep system. (This example's quite graphic. Can you see what the dominant rep system is? How many clues did I put in that sentence?!):

> I envisage that by investing in this customer relationship management system we can:
>
> • See customer satisfaction scores rising.
>
> • Watch the level of complaints falling.
>
> • Focus on looking for new business referrals.

Notice how different the same scenario sounds when using descriptions from all three senses.

> I envisage that by investing in this customer relationship management system we can:
>
> • Watch customer satisfaction scores rise because we talk more effectively to customers so they feel we care.
>
> • Observe complaints figures falling because customers have less to tell us they're unhappy about.
>
> • See sales growth because customers feel more valued and tell their friends about us.

Of course, influencing a group of people isn't just about what you say. After all, the auditory people are still the ones most likely to notice your words. Words form only a small part of communication, as I explain in more depth in Chapter 4. Voice tone and body language also play an important part.

When presenting to a group, you can enhance your message through your voice and physiology.

- ✔ Ask yourself what impression visual people are getting of you. Specifically, what you're wearing and how you're presenting yourself can be really important.

- ✔ Pay attention to how much or little you move. Kinaesthetic people may notice and be swayed by your stillness or movement.

- ✔ Mismatching your voice tone and physiology with your words doesn't persuade. For example. words like *energy, excitement,* or *passion,* delivered in a monotone, just don't cut the mustard!

- ✔ Use additional media to help influence others:

    - • Visual aids can deepen the understanding of visual people. (Just avoid those dull death-by-PowerPoint presentations, please!) Share relevant, clear posters, illustrations, diagrams, and pictures on screens, walls, and handouts to help sell your message.

    - • Video clips appeal to both the visual and auditory senses.

    - • Audio clips, quotes, music, and poems all appeal to auditory thinkers.

    - • Items to touch, examine, and try out help to engage kinaesthetic thinkers.

### Training

You can train, coach, and teach people in all kinds of settings. Whether in a formal or informal setting, one on one or with a group, distance learning or online programmes, you must appeal to people's senses to get your message across. You bring your subject matter to life when you engage people's rep systems. You strengthen their ability to learn and retain new knowledge and skills.

Introduce as much VAK vocabulary (turn to Table 5-1) as possible into training materials such as manuals and online training packages, as well as training presentations. Then pay attention to how you design the learning experience to suit individuals with different rep systems.

## The museum business comes to its senses

When I was young – okay, that was some time ago – a trip to the museum involved looking at things and not much else. You saw artefacts, stuffed animals, model aeroplanes, real trains, rocks, dinosaur skeletons, and so on, but you only touched something at your peril!

Nowadays, museums appeal to *all* visitors' senses. Good museums have something for everyone: portable audio devices, films, activities, interactive exhibits, computers, simulators, and more add further dimensions to the museum experience. You sometimes even get the chance to taste and smell something to recreate times gone by, which isn't always a pleasant experience!

At a training event, your trainees gather information through all their senses. Don't restrict yourself to your preferred rep system. Instead, have:

- ✔ Visual people look at illustrations, view diagrams and charts, examine models, or watch demonstrations and video clips.

- ✔ Auditory people read around the subject, listen to presentations or audio clips, take part in discussions, and complete written assignments.

- ✔ Kinaesthetic people do activities, make things, move around, try out skills, and engage their emotions.

## *Writing with VAK*

Before you write an e-mail, letter, or even instructions to an individual, determine whether you already know or can guess his rep system. If you can, go ahead and use the words and phrases that appeal to his preferred sense. If you don't know the other person's rep system, bring a variety of sensory words into your letters and e-mails. When writing for a bigger audience, you probably already know what you need to do. Newsletters, reports, proposals, advertisements, and so on all need to use a range of VAK vocabulary to appeal to all readers.

The presentation of a document can be very important to a visual thinker, while you may need to choose the words well to influence the auditory thinker. A kinaesthetic thinker may pay attention to the weight and texture of the paper. Whenever possible and appropriate, pictures, images, and graphics enhance the persuasiveness of the document by engaging the visual sense.

The written language you use can attract or put off good potential candidates when hiring people. Be sure to include a variety of sensory words in all your recruitment advertisements and job descriptions.

# Chapter 6

# Building Rapport: The Heart of Successful Relationships

*U*nderlying all good communication is *rapport*. But what is rapport exactly? You certainly know it when you have it.

Rapport happens when people are relating to each other well – when they trust, respect, and understand each other, even unconsciously. Rapport is the ideal good foundation for discussion, negotiation, and decision making.

People make business decisions more often as a result of good rapport than on the merits of an idea or proposal.

You build strong rapport over time, through ongoing relationship building. For this reason, you may notice that leaders who join your organisation often bring some of their relationships with them and use these to:

✔ Recruit previous employees

✔ Engage suppliers they've worked with before

✔ Bring clients with them

Forward-thinking organisations are now realising that getting people working well together is critical to business success. Rapport is an essential ingredient of good relationships, enabling mutual respect and trust.

In this chapter you find out how to notice when you are – and when you're not – in rapport. You discover some NLP techniques to help you build rapport when you need to improve relationships, have more productive meetings, and influence others more effectively.

# Appreciating Rapport

When two people are in rapport, they connect in some way. They're on each other's wavelength and they see each other's point of view. Rapport is like being in step with one another, like dance partners.

The Encarta English dictionary defines rapport as

> *an emotional bond or friendly relationship between people based on mutual liking, trust, and a sense that they understand and share each other's concerns.*

Rapport generally happens when two people have an interest in each other, when they can understand, accept, and respect one another's opinions, even when they're different. Trust runs through the entire encounter.

## Creating success through rapport

In business, getting the job done is usually the top priority. Historically many organisations have been managed through:

- ✔ Exerting power and authority by controlling behaviour.

- ✔ Dominating through fear – with implicit or explicit threats to make things happen.

- ✔ Rewarding people for certain aspects of performance, while not valuing other actions.

The preceding are all *carrot-and-stick methods*, which either buy people's co-operation through rewards (the carrot to motivate the donkey) or coerce it through fear (the stick to drive the donkey). These methods constitute influence without rapport. Only people in positions of power – and usually with inadequate relationship skills – can use these methods to get much of anything done.

Business leaders are becoming increasingly aware that managing via rewards and fears doesn't bring out the best in people. The key to getting the job done well lies in the quality of the relationship. Good relationships are fundamental to just about all aspects of business. Following are a few types of work where building relationships and rapport make a significant impact on success:

- ✔ Selling
- ✔ Negotiating
- ✔ Gaining buy-in to ideas
- ✔ Appraising
- ✔ Resolving conflict
- ✔ Coaching
- ✔ Communicating change
- ✔ Serving customers
- ✔ Team working
- ✔ Motivating

The increased awareness of the importance of how you work with and talk to others in business has led to much more prevalence of skills-based training in influencing, coaching, selling, and negotiating. Leadership development programmes also emphasise relationship and influence in leading effectively. The more leading-edge training programmes include the development of rapport skills.

## Noticing rapport

Given that rapport is essential for good relationships and effective communication, humans curiously don't often realise when they have it. Rapport is such an unconscious, instinctive state that many people just don't think about it. A bit like breathing, really. In fact, you're probably more likely to notice when you're *not* in rapport than when you are.

### Yourself in rapport

You may have noticed that you find some people very easy to be with, while with others you just don't feel so good.

When you find yourself in rapport with another person, you may attribute this feeling to:

- ✔ A similar sense of humour
- ✔ Interests in common
- ✔ Stimulating conversation
- ✔ A shared enthusiasm for something

When you feel easy with people you're in rapport with them, and when rapport exists you probably notice how much smoother and more straightforward discussing, agreeing to, and acting on things are.

### Others in rapport

Spotting when other people are in rapport may be easier for you initially. Whether in a meeting, at the lunch table, or even walking along, pay attention some of the tell-tale signs of rapport:

- ✔ Matching body posture and movements
- ✔ Similar facial expressions
- ✔ Eye contact
- ✔ Similar voice pitch, tone, volume, and speed
- ✔ Identical words and phrases

# Building Rapport, One to One

When rapport happens naturally at work, progress happens – and smoothly. You share ideas with someone else, discuss your concerns, reach conclusions, and move on to other things. But what about situations where rapport doesn't just happen?

You can still create good rapport with people at work with whom you don't have anything obvious in common – even people who seem very different to you. The early developers of NLP identified what people do when they're in rapport. You can consciously choose to do the same stuff that you normally do unconsciously – even when you don't relate so well to certain people. See the section 'Matching others', later in this chapter, for more.

# *Identifying rapport experiences*

Before exploring how to build rapport, take some time to think about your current work relationships that may benefit from having more rapport. These may include your relationship with:

- ✔ Your boss
- ✔ A particular colleague or team member
- ✔ Somebody much higher up in the organisation
- ✔ An internal or external business partner
- ✔ Anyone who can help you get your job done effectively

Try the following technique to figure out what you already know about rapport.

1. **Identify someone at work with whom you want to have better rapport.**

   Consider the preceding list for ideas or come up with someone from your own experience. Think about how you currently relate to this person. What do you do and say? How do you feel while interacting with this person?

2. **Think about someone at work with whom you have *good* rapport.**

   Select a relationship where spending time together is hassle free. What do you do and say? How do you feel while interacting with this person?

3. **Compare the relationships with these two people.**

   What are the differences you notice?

Fortunately, you can bridge the differences between your rapport-rich relationship and your more challenging one. You create and build rapport in four main ways:

- ✔ **Listening and watching:** Paying close attention to the what the other person says, his speed and tone of voice and what he does, particularly, his body language.
- ✔ **Matching and mirroring:** Finding commonalities and matching aspects of the other person.
- ✔ **Pacing:** Continuing to match, acknowledge, and respect the other person.
- ✔ **Leading:** Encouraging that person to think or act differently.

The following sections cover each of the techniques in greater detail.

## Listening and watching

Paying full attention to what another person is saying – giving someone else's thoughts and opinions due consideration – is an important part of creating rapport. Yet, you may notice in business meetings that sometimes your mind drifts or you're busy thinking of what to say next to counter, or even agree with, another person's point of view.

In my experience with organisations, people are driven by their need to have their opinions heard. In a meeting about a contentious matter, I hear voices becoming louder and words tumbling out more quickly, as the people concerned compete to express what they have to say.

Getting your own point across doesn't necessarily help achieve agreement, which is usually what you really want. Instead, listen intently and consider what another person has to say. In so doing, you begin to build respect and trust into your relationship – a good starting point for establishing rapport, which can lead to compromise and agreement.

It's also really useful when you want to build rapport to watch carefully what someone else is doing. His posture, gestures, movements and more give you clues as to how they're thinking (more on this in Chapter 5), and are things that you can actively use to build rapport, as you can discover in the 'Matching others' section that follows.

Practise taking a few minutes in meetings to become an 'observer'. You may want to do this initially in meetings with more that just one other person, so that you can perform this observation while others are in animated conversation and won't think you've drifted off because you can't answer the question they've just asked you!. Concentrate on one person. Notice everything you can about how she is sitting or standing, moving and gesturing. Is she speaking quickly or slowly? Are there phrases or words that she repeats regularly? Do this as often as you can – you can even do it by watching conversations on TV – to build your skills at listening to, and watching, others.

## Matching others

People watching is something that many like to do. You may have noticed that you can tell quite a lot about the relationships between people by observing them, even when you can't hear their conversation.

If you've ever looked around a bar, restaurant, or coffee shop and noticed two people sitting across a table from each other, you know immediately when they're in tune with each other. You probably notice that they're *matching* each other – in their movements, facial expressions, gestures, and posture. Even if you can't hear them, the conversation seems to flow while the silences are easy and comfortable. You're witnessing people in rapport.

When you can actually hear people talking, as well as observe them, you may also discover some additional clues as to how much rapport they have. When you hear comparable tone, volume, and speed of voice, as well as similar words, you can be sure those people are in rapport.

Of course, you can equally notice when people *aren't* in rapport. Next time you spot an interaction not going well, take note of the differences between the individuals. Can you see or hear any matching?

You have many aspects of communication you can choose to match. The following sections cover those most people find useful.

### Matching and mirroring the body

Even from a distance, you can spot whether two people are in rapport just from their bodies. Good rapport includes similarities in body posture, angle, movements, and so on.

---

## Beware putting meanings to body language

Theories of the meaning of body language are plentiful. Perhaps you've heard or read that:

✔ Eyes cast down can be interpreted as the person being nervous.

✔ Arms crossed mean she's not open to what she's hearing.

✔ Lack of eye contact means someone isn't listening.

In some cases these interpretations may be true – but not always. Making generalisations about body language can lead to inaccurate assumptions.

Many years ago I had a boss who gave me the feedback that I didn't seem to be open to new ideas. After considering this feedback for quite a while, I realised that his comment was because I often crossed my arms in his office as the air conditioning was up high and I was cold!

Rather than drawing conclusions from what you see in another person's body language, match the posture, gestures, and movements yourself. Then you're able to think and feel a little more like her. You understand more about her, have more empathy, and be in deeper rapport.

When two people are in rapport, they start to match each other with their bodies, either directly or, when opposite each other, by *mirroring* the other's posture. For example, you may notice someone crossing her left leg over her right. The person opposite may well then cross her legs too, but with the right over the left, which mirrors the first person's movement.

Body matching and mirroring are natural processes in rapport. Mostly you're not even aware that you're doing them. The originators of NLP discovered, however, that by *consciously* matching another person's posture and movement, you can create and build rapport in a situation where previously it didn't exist.

Next time you want to get into rapport with someone, pay attention to what she's doing with her body. Experiment with matching or mirroring what you see. Pay attention to the following aspects:

- ✔ **Head:** The angle, whether the person is looking up or down.
- ✔ **Arms and hands:** Arms crossed, arms open, hands behind head, hands playing with something, rubbing hands.
- ✔ **Gestures:** Waving or pointing with arms or hands, nodding head in a particular direction.
- ✔ **Legs:** Crossed at knees or ankles, open, outstretched, tucked under.
- ✔ **Breathing:** Shallow, deep, fast, slow.
- ✔ **Face:** Relaxed, smiling, serious, furrowed brow.
- ✔ **Movements:** Head nodding, finger tapping, foot swinging.
- ✔ **Body:** Overall position, general posture.

When you practise matching and mirroring another person, you're doing something that happens naturally but just isn't happening for you at a given moment. Matching and mirroring may feel strange at first, like any new skills, but keep practising and you get used to them.

When matching body movements, be subtle. Make *similar but smaller* movements compared to the other person, rather than outright mimicry. If you keep your movements small, others don't notice and rapport starts to build.

### Matching voice

Using your voice to match another person can be a great aid to getting into rapport.

- ✔ **Speed.** If you tend to speak quickly and you want to influence someone who speaks far more slowly, you can create better rapport by slowing down.

✔ **Volume.** If you want to influence someone who has a fairly quiet voice, quietening down your own voice to a similar level can help.

✔ **Other aspects:** Matching the pitch, rhythm, and musicality of another's voice can assist you to build better rapport.

Make sure your matching efforts are subtle so you don't come across as imitating the other person. And be careful not to copy someone's accent, as this is noticeable and she may well interpret it as mimicry.

### Matching words

You can improve rapport if you match another person's language. Listen out carefully for:

✔ Words

✔ Phrases

✔ Metaphors

Pick out some specific key words to match. You can choose those that the other person seems to emphasise or repeat, or maybe just those that seem unusual. For example, if you hear 'Let's keep *focused*' you can use the word *focused* or another variation, such as 'Well, *focusing* on the matter in hand . . .'

Phrases can be particularly powerful when you use someone's exact words rather than paraphrasing them. So when the other person tells you she wants to '*get this signed off today*', your response should *not* be: 'What needs to happen for us to put this to bed today?' Instead, to increase rapport, you ask: 'What needs to happen for us to *get this signed off today?*'

Everyone uses metaphor, whether they realise it or not. Your metaphors describe how you're perceiving and thinking about a situation. You can substantially improve rapport by working with another person's metaphor. For example, if you hear 'We're going to *fight this one all the way*', you're respecting the metaphor and can build rapport by talking about things like *front-line troops*, *ammunition*, and *winning the fight*, as well as reiterating the original statement.

### Matching patterns

Over time people develop particular styles and patterns of thinking, and that does make everyone different. (Thank goodness – or else the world would be a very boring place!)

## Traffic light sport

A fun way to practise your rapport-spotting skills is to watch two people in the front seats of a car. Whether you're crossing the road or in a nearby car, take a second (when it's safe and the lights are red!) to notice how people can be in rapport when sitting alongside each other.

They may have no eye contact, yet you often see a range of similarities in their positions, head angles and movements, and facial expressions. You may also be able to observe the rhythm of their speech as they talk and make subtle head and body movements. And you can certainly notice when they laugh together!

By noticing other people's patterns and matching them, you can increase rapport and improve your influence. You can also train yourself to be aware of the most revealing behaviours associated with common patterns.

One useful set of patterns to notice is how people use their senses when they think and express themselves. You see, hear, and feel things in your mind that you remember or imagine. The chances are that you use one of these three senses far more than the others. I explain this in more detail in Chapter 5 – plus I give you clues about the language, body, breathing, and eye movement patterns associated with each sense.

So if you want to increase rapport with someone who's thinking visually, for instance, match their words, body, and breathing – but you can also use *other* visual words, and maybe present an idea to her as a picture or diagram.

Other important patterns are *metaprograms*, which are patterns of motivation (more on this in Chapter 7). Like sense-preference patterns, you can detect metaprogram patters from what people say and do. So after you identify a pattern that the other person has, you can make good use of this information and match the pattern. For instance, if you like to communicate a lot of detail and depth to support an argument but you notice that your colleague seems to do the opposite, you can choose to match her pattern and give top-line information only.

### Acknowledging values and beliefs

No matter what else you match, building rapport is tough if your values and beliefs contradict the other person's.

You can't change at will what you believe and what's important to you, and pretending you have is superficial and doesn't help to build a long-lasting relationship. However, you create far better rapport by listening to, considering, and respecting what others believe and value – and affirming their rights to have those beliefs and values.

Spend time acknowledging what drives another person's thinking. Find out what's important to them through attentive listening and watching. You'll hear people emphasise certain things, and see their passion and conviction about something in their face and body language. If possible, ask them questions: 'What's important to you about this?' and '*Why* is that important?' will tell you what's important to other people and how and why they care deeply for something. Even if you disagree passionately, remember that you're creating rapport.

When negotiating with someone on an important matter, drawing out her beliefs and values – as well as knowing and respectfully sharing your own – is a good starting point. When both sides know and respect one another's values in the negotiation, you can build rapport and more easily work towards a mutually acceptable outcome.

I once met with an account manager of a design agency who wanted to win some business from me (when I was a marketing director years ago). He asked me about some key values in selecting a supplier. 'What's important to you in a design agency? What qualities do you need?'. I explained that I wanted a supplier I could *trust* – people who would do what they said they'd do – and that *responded quickly* and effectively when I needed something. The account manager then told me his values – at the same time, carefully weaving in and matching mine. He told me: 'What I value in a customer is openness and honesty. I need to *trust* that if anything is going wrong, I'm told straight away so I can *respond* and fix things *quickly*.' You guessed it, he got the business!

### Matching culture

Another way to improve rapport with others is to match elements of their culture, where doing so seems appropriate. With the increasing globalisation of business, people are working across cultures, races, and religions. The more you match aspects of another culture, the better rapport you can achieve.

Cultural characteristics to consider matching include:

- ✔ **Styles of communication.** For example, the Japanese are very polite and deferential, which is quite different to most western cultures. So changing some of the way you speak and act in a meeting with Japanese people can help you to build rapport.

- ✔ **Food and drink.** For example, avoid alcohol when dining with a Muslim businessperson; consider joining a Dutch colleague in drinking milk at lunch (a fairly traditional drink for Dutch lunch table). Match food and drink choices where you can.

- ✔ **Social rituals.** British business people tend to shake hands in welcome, but many other Europeans kiss or embrace. Becoming more flexible and matching the greeting style of the other culture will get you off to a good start in building rapport.

Even when operating in your own country, thinking about organisational culture can be useful. By organisational culture, I really mean 'the way we do things around here'. Every business has its own subtle yet pervasive styles, language choices, rituals, and habits. If you pay attention to what happens in your own organisation, or in others that you deal with, you're sure to find many things you can match.

For example, if you work with clients or suppliers who dress formally in suits and ties, you build better rapport by adopting this style of dress, even if your own style of work wear (or your organisation's dress code) is more casual. If being on time for meetings is the 'done thing' in your business, matching other employees' promptness can start the process of being in rapport with the people you meet.

Matching people when you don't have good rapport with them takes practice. Why not try practising one of the types of matching that I outline in this section each day for the next 10 working days? You can choose to match posture, gestures, breathing, movements, facial expressions, voice speed, voice volume, word choice, patterns, or beliefs and values.

## Pacing and leading

Once you're matching someone well – whether with physiology, voice, language, patterns or more – keep on doing it! In this way, you *pace* the other person and continue to increase the rapport between you. If you've ever watched middle distance runners in a race, you may have noticed that the front runner sets the pace for the race. Other runners follow that pace until it's time to strive to take the lead. You're doing much the same here, although it's a whole lot more subtle!

You need to continue to pay full attention to another person and match and pace some key aspects of their thinking, language and behaviour before you then start to take over the *lead*. Having matched someone, then paced that matching (see the section 'Matching others', earlier in this chapter), you're in a much stronger position to influence by leading them to hear and understand your opinions.

For example, let's say you have a meeting with a customer who you wish to persuade to buy something from you. You notice that this person speaks incredibly quickly, and uses a lot of phrases that indicate he's seeing things in his mind, such as 'I can't see that we'll get a good financial return from buying this.' You're concerned that at the pace things are going this meeting will be over and no sale made within a few more minutes. Drastic action is needed! You introduce some words that match his pattern – things like 'I need to give you the full overview. Picture how it will be when . . .'. You then speed up your speech and start to talk at the same rate as your customer over the next few minutes. Then you gradually slow down the speech, until you reach a more comfortable pace in which you can explain all the advantages of investing in you product. You get the sale and the customer is satisfied.

In leading, you start to move the other person to a different way of thinking, feeling, or acting. You may wish to lead someone to:

- ✔ Consider a new idea or proposal
- ✔ Speed up a conversation
- ✔ Hear and accept bad news
- ✔ Slow down and think about something in more depth
- ✔ Change her emotional state (for example, to move from anxious to calm)
- ✔ Accept and respect you for saying 'no' or delivering bad news
- ✔ Change the other person's energy level

When you're ready to lead, start by testing out how much rapport you have by making a small lead and noticing whether your colleague follows. For instance, you may choose to change position by sitting right back into your chair (see the section 'Matching others', earlier in this chapter). If the other person makes a similar change to her sitting position, you're ready to lead. From here you can start to make changes to your breathing or movements if you want to change the other person's emotional state, energy, or pace. If this is successful, introduce a more difficult thing that you want to talk about or point out some area where you and your colleague disagree. If the other person doesn't follow your lead when you test it out, keep on matching and pacing the other person, test again and keep on going until you're confident you have enough rapport to lead.

## Front-line anger management

A Health Trust asked one of my colleagues to train hospital staff to handle challenging patients. On occasion, people in discomfort who've been kept waiting for a consultation or treatment become frustrated and angry. These patients can become aggressive and even threatening to front-line staff such as receptionists.

Previously, administrative staff stayed sitting at their desks and spoke calmly and quietly to try to calm the distressed patients standing in front of them. With my colleague's advice, they were instead trained to stand and face angry patients and match the speed and volume of the patient's voice (although not matching the emotions). Doing this enabled the receptionists to better match and pace the patient. Gradually slowing and quietening their own voices, the receptionists were able to lead patients to do the same.

Patients' complaints dropped from an average 10 per month to one.

## Building credibility while disagreeing

Michael, a friend of mine, is a marketing consultant. One of his biggest clients had briefed him to undertake an urgent market research project that the organisation had decided to commission.

Michael values client service and has a history of not saying 'no' to his clients. On this occasion, however, he had two challenges:

✔ He believed that the client was having a knee-jerk reaction and that the data may not give the client what it needed. How may he change the client's mind about the nature and approach to the project?

✔ His time was already over-committed for the period in which the client wanted the job done.

Michael called a meeting with the client and put all his attention on building rapport. He matched the client's body, voice, and words, and eventually matched and paced the client's business concerns that had led to the request for the research.

Eventually, after ten or more minutes, Michael started to lead the client, explaining other ways in which the organisation may acquire the information needed quickly and cost effectively. He explained a different approach, recommended an alternative consultant, and made clear that he wasn't always able to be available at a moment's notice for an urgent project.

Michael did all this without damaging the relationship – or his credibility – with the client. In fact, the client was happy with his response and followed his advice regarding the different approach, and worked with the consultant recommended by Michael. The client continues to work with Michael to this day.

Don't match and pace anything that the other person isn't happy with, or doesn't like about herself. For example, if someone has a mannerism – a stutter, nervous tic, limp, or something of that nature – matching and pacing behaviours associated with the mannerism are likely to destroy rapport.

# Developing Rapport with Groups

Building rapport with a group is more complex than developing individual rapport (see the section 'Building Rapport, One to One', earlier in this chapter). Matching and mirroring everyone in the group is probably a step too far. You may blow a gasket and your colleagues may think you're having a breakdown!

However, you can still do things to create rapport within a group – and to pace and lead the group more effectively (see the section 'Pacing and leading', earlier in this chapter).

Developing group rapport is particularly useful in one of those long drawn-out meetings that just don't seem to be going anywhere. Following are a few tips that you can use whether you are running or facilitating the meeting or just one of a number of attendees but you want to have influence:

- ✔ Greet everyone in the group at the start, making sure to use her name (of course, if you don't know people's names, asking them and then using the names is a great place to start).

- ✔ Match and then pace any dominant style of the meeting in terms of its formality, any humour, level of detail, reports, and so on. This may be evident at the start of the meeting, or when you know the people concerned, or you may have to wait a short while to ascertain the style, which may be created by the meeting's leader. For more on pacing, see the section 'Pacing and leading', earlier in this chapter.

- ✔ Make eye contact with each member of the group at several points during the meeting – particularly when you're expressing your views.

- ✔ Match some aspects of the last person to speak each time you have something to say.

- ✔ Use key words, phrases, or metaphors that others express. See the section 'Matching words', earlier in this chapter.

- ✔ Match or mirror the body posture or movements of the person you need to influence most (for example a decision maker or an objector to your ideas).

When you're confident that you've matched and paced other people, test out whether you can lead the group or key people in the group, by making a simple change to your pace of speech or a body movement, and notice if others follow. More on this in the preceding section, 'Pacing and leading'.

Once there is enough rapport for you to lead, you can start to introduce a controversial idea, or to disagree with others' opinions or ideas, or even speed the meeting towards a conclusion.

Rapport is a natural phenomenon. Mostly people get into rapport without realising they've done so. So you may find yourself with groups where great rapport already exists across the group. You feel comfortable and notice that conversation flows well. If you look closely, you can see lots of matching and mirroring of body posture across the group. This is a group that will find it easy to agree on things, an atmosphere where disagreement may be heard and listened to respectfully – and where meetings might just go on an on as good rapport can be hard to break!

# *Talking with No Body: Rapport in the Digital Age*

The advent of the Internet, satellite technologies, improved travel, and more are causing a rapid transformation in how people work. Many businesses nowadays are truly international operations, with multicultural virtual teams operating around the globe, people working from home, and communications tools that connect people to their desks and each other 24 hours a day.

I work regularly with people in business who know that good interpersonal relationships are essential for success and want to find ways to improve their influence. Yet many of these people spend very little face-to-face time with those individuals they most want to influence. If they only saw them regularly, they may face far fewer influencing challenges with these colleagues or clients.

So the challenge if you work remotely from others is how to build rapport when you can't watch another person closely and then match, pace, and even lead key aspects of their physiology. In short, how do you build rapport when you have no body to watch? The following sections tackle this most modern – and challenging – of questions.

## *Matching the communication medium*

You may remember the excitement of using the earliest fax machines, or the scary business of personal assistants being replaced by computers and other digital equipment. Technological advances have only continued; today's business world is filled with extraordinary communications tools.

You have an incredible amount of options in what you can use to connect with another person these days – and with the rapid development of technology your choices are going to continue to expand.

In business currently, you probably use at least some of the following media to communicate:

- Face-to-face conversation
- Telephone
- E-mail
- Text messaging
- Internet telephone

✔ Video conferencing

✔ Internet messaging

✔ Fax

✔ Letter

The following sections offer tips and tricks to help you build rapport, even when you aren't face to face with someone.

## Fostering telephone rapport

Despite the extensive use of e-mail these days (see the section 'Creating e-mail rapport', later in this chapter), almost everyone in business depends on telephones – in fact, you probably carry one around with you wherever you go.

The extra flexibility of mobile phones means you can influence more people, more often when you're apart than ever before.

Many business decisions are made over the phone, either through one-on-one calls or teleconferencing. To be successful, you need to build rapport virtually.

To gain rapport on the telephone, concentrate on matching:

✔ Voice

✔ Breathing

✔ Words

✔ Values and beliefs

✔ Patterns

The section 'Matching others', earlier in this chapter, covers each of these aspects of rapport building.

To match a person at the other end of the phone, you need to listen very attentively. If the meeting isn't taking place in your first language, your complete attention is even more important, as you need to pick up the subtleties of the words being spoken. If you aren't confident that you can remember words (auditory thinking may not be strong for you – more about this in Chapter 5), write down key words and phrases that the other person uses. Then match these words later in the conversation. Having some of the other person's words in front of you may also help you to identify her sensory thinking patterns and metaprograms (see Chapters 5 and 7).

# Is your communication medium working for you?

To gauge whether you're getting the most from your communication options, consider a person with whom you have less influence than you want and ask yourself the following questions:

1. **What medium are you currently using to talk with this person? Is it her preferred medium – or yours?**

   For example, I have one colleague who uses text messaging a lot. I know that if I want to get a quick response from her, I need to text her rather than e-mail, even though texting isn't my preferred medium.

   If you're unsure of people's preferred communication medium, ask them. (Simple, huh?) Their answers may surprise you and definitely help focus your communications activities.

2. **Does the medium you're using allow you to build enough rapport for you to discuss and agree this issue?**

   For example, words can be misconstrued and emotions arise out of people's interpretation of language in an e-mail, whereas a

quick face-to-face discussion (which adds vocal qualities, body language, and other cues) often allows faster resolution.

If the medium you're using is getting in the way of you creating rapport, change it – but remember to use all you know about the person and the words they use to build rapport.

3. **Is this medium really suitable for getting the message across?**

   For example, long e-mail dialogues around a decision can be slow, convoluted, and unproductive, whereas a phone call can often sort matters out effectively.

   If you find yourself needing to move from an email discussion to telephone, remember to match, pace and lead. Reply with an email that matches and paces the other person's email style and language – and then lead with the suggestion that a telephone chat would help to resolve the issue and offer some specific times that you're available.

I work with Guy, a leader in a global organisation who's frequently involved in international teleconferences. Before he knew how to build rapport, Guy complained how boring and directionless these meetings were – and how little seemed to be achieved in them. He admitted to sometimes paying minimal attention to what was being said and doing other things while on the call (because there was no video or Webcam link and he couldn't be spotted typing e-mails or reading paperwork). After Guy applied his newly acquired rapport skills to these telephone meetings, he started to effect change. He listened carefully, matched, paced, and started to lead. Consequently the conversations moved along much faster, attendees became more energised, and decisions were made. Guy now reports fewer, shorter teleconferences – and that they are a worthwhile use of his time.

Teleconferences, with a number of people holding a telephone meeting, are much trickier to build rapport in than a one-to-one call. Not only can you not see the others but you've got time lags and the problem of people speaking at the same time – or not at all. If you know something about people's patterns in advance, keep a list of key influencing words by your phone in order to pace and lead key people in the meeting. In addition, remember (or write down) key phrases that people have used on the call. You may not get the chance to respond immediately to a point someone's made in a teleconference, so you need to return to a speaker who has made a point and repeat back some of the key things they've said, matching and pacing as much as possible about their speed, volume and tone, before attempting to lead.

## Creating e-mail rapport

Since the advent of the telephone, no other medium has revolutionised communications as much as e-mail. Love it or hate it, nearly everyone has to use it at work, and most people choose to use it at home. For many, e-mail is now the most-used means of talking to others. So how do you build rapport through a computer?

The principles of e-mail rapport are just the same as any other form of communication: match, pace, and lead. You build a better relationship via e-mail by matching the e-mail style of the person you're in dialogue with. In my experience, even those with excellent face-to-face rapport skills often fail to do this in e-mail.

Study the e-mails you receive from people you need to influence. Take note of the following aspects of how they write e-mails and then match them:

- **Length:** Note how many lines or screens their e-mails tend to cover.
- **Detail:** Pay attention to whether the e-mails tend to be full of detail or very top line.
- **Sentences:** Are they short and punchy – or long and complex?
- **Tone:** Determine whether the overall attitude is formal or informal.
- **Greeting:** How does the e-mail start – for instance *Hi, Hello, Dear,* or no greeting at all?
- **Sign off:** How does the e-mail conclude – *Regards, Best wishes,* just a name, or nothing?
- **Language.** Look for words, key phrases, metaphors, and words that seem to indicate patterns, values, or beliefs.

If you want to influence someone who you haven't found getting into rapport with easy, think carefully about the medium you're using. E-mail is an excellent tool, but when you're struggling to build rapport with someone, some face-to-face matching or vocal matching over the telephone may be a better first choice than e-mail. After you establish some rapport, shift to communication and further building rapport through e-mail, providing that you're sure the medium is right for your message and that you continue to match the other person's style of e-mail.

# Breaking Rapport: When the Chat Needs to Stop

If you're naturally good at developing rapport, you may be less skilled at *breaking* rapport. And if rapport's a good thing, why do you ever want to stop having it?

Have you ever been in a situation where you just can't get away? Maybe you've attended a networking event or a work social event where you've been chatting to one person for some time. You've exchanged all the information you need to and are both ready to move on to speak to someone else. Yet how do you politely and effectively break that fabulous rapport you've created?

The key to breaking rapport without damaging the relationship or appearing rude is to make some subtle changes. For example, a brief glance away, a small step backwards, or a change in your posture means that you're now doing some mismatching rather than matching. These behaviours are often enough to make the other person aware that the conversation's coming to an end, without you having to say anything.

Years ago I had a team member who regularly popped into my office to ask for help with a problem or issue she was facing. Being keen to support my team, I agreed to listen and give advice where I was able. Rapport was easy with this person and so a good conversation ensued. However, I was often very busy with tight deadlines, and the rapport meant that it was difficult to bring the impromptu meeting to a close. I didn't know about rapport then, but I discovered over time that the only way to get my colleague out of my office was to stand up and move out of the office myself. So strong was the rapport that I was able to lead her to follow me out of my office! From there I explained that I needed to get a drink or collect something. She went happily on her way and I got back to my desk and my deadlines.

You can break rapport quite easily – and often quite dramatically. For instance, you can turn your back on someone, stand up and walk out of a meeting, or raise your voice. These more extreme changes may be appropriate at times, but mostly you can be much more effective if you can pace and lead to break rapport gently and subtly.

Of course, if you're trying to bring a telephone conversation to a close, slight body changes aren't really an option. Here, rapport is all achieved through your voice (tempo, volume, and so on), breathing, and words. On the phone, you need to make a change in at least one of these to start to break telephone rapport. However, to achieve this some movement on your end helps, even though the other person doesn't see it. For example:

- ✔ If you're sitting down, stand up.
- ✔ If you're standing up, start walking around.
- ✔ If you're sitting and can't stand (maybe you're in a car or train), change body posture or breathing.
- ✔ Change the pace, volume, or tone of your voice.

Changing all the body movements in the preceding list has an impact on your physiology, which affects your breathing and your voice. The other person can pick up these small changes as cues, probably unconsciously, and rapport weakens sufficiently for you to move towards ending the conversation. Of course, although the other person will pick up the signs that you're ready to bring the conversation to an end, he might still have something important to say! If he resists your attempts to lead the discussion to a conclusion, then you just may have to break rapport. Remember, when you do this – for example by stating that you just have to do something else right now – do it respectfully. After all, you want to maintain the relationship so that rapport is easy to achieve next time you speak with this person.

# Chapter 7

# Using Words to Get Results

*In This Chapter*

▶ Recognising language and behaviour patterns – your own and others'

▶ Matching people and jobs successfully

▶ Using pattern-specific language to influence others

*W*hen leaders talk about embracing diversity and harnessing its benefits in their businesses, they're often restricting their thinking to differences of ethnic origin and faith.

However, the differences that exist within any group of people, which in organisations can quickly hamper performance, come from the diversity of people's habitual patterns of thinking and acting, no matter what their colour or creed. In NLP, these patterns are known as *metaprograms*.

In this chapter, I look at six metaprogram patterns that are particularly important in the workplace and I show you how to gain an understanding of these metaprograms and then use highly targeted language to achieve amazing results in business.

## *Pinpointing Patterns: Metaprograms*

*Metaprograms* are unconscious filters that people develop to allow themselves to handle and respond to the high level of information and stimuli that they receive every moment of every day. After all, human beings aren't computers, thankfully. You can't process every piece of information that comes at you. (Flip over to Chapter 4 for more on filters.)

Metaprograms are patterns of motivation and working. They drive where you put your attention, what you respond to and what motivates you. They shape how you interact with the people and environment around you. They are your preferred way of thinking and operating. These patterns run behind the scenes, just like computer software - so automatic that you most likely don't realise they are there.

## All about patterns

My colleague Mariette and I ran a team align-ment and leadership skills programme for a lead team. The client's project sponsor was Neil, a senior director, with whom we had carefully contracted what and how we planned to run the programme, as well as what the client expected to get out of it.

After the first of a number of planned work-shops, which delivered what we promised, Neil briefly outlined some things he wanted to be different. Mariette and I are good at flexibility, so we worked hard to put in place the changes he requested.

The second workshop went well and feedback from the participants was good. We heard from Neil, who wanted to make more changes. Again, we modelled supreme flexibility.

By the third workshop the team were really making great progress – improving their lead-ership skills and getting good results. But we heard from Neil again. Yes, you guessed it – he asked us to make some more changes!

Our training programme was tried and tested. In fact, many companies had benefited from the content and style of this course. The training was already making a difference to the leader-ship team. So what was wrong?

Nothing. Neil had some extreme metaprogram patterns. In fact, he was at the end of the spec-trum for four of the six metaprogram patterns I discuss in this chapter. These extreme posi-tions were driving his requests to us.

After Mariette and I worked out that Neil's pat-terns were motivating his demands, we adapted how we dealt with him, and the rest of the pro-gramme went like clockwork.

Later on in the programme, the team identified their metaprogram patterns, and Neil started to notice the impact that his patterns made on what he perceived he needed from us, and other people too!

You can develop the ability to detect metaprogram patterns in yourself and others because:

✔ Some metaprograms show up in the structure of people's language and the words they use.

✔ Other metaprograms are apparent in the way people behave.

## *Finding a place on the spectrum*

As you build your awareness of metaprograms, and how to listen and look for them, you'll spot some patterns in some people quite quickly - they'll be fairly obvious. You'll also discover that it's quite tricky to work out some pat-terns in other people, as they are not so extreme.

Think of the patterns that I outline in this chapter as appearing on a spectrum, as Figure 7-1 indicates. The descriptions at the two ends represent the two extremes of each spectrum. You may well find that people operate somewhere in the middle of that spectrum, with flexibility to do some of both behaviours - and they are often the people whose pattern is more difficult to detect.

**Figure 7-1:**
Meta-
program
patterns are
distributed
over a
spectrum

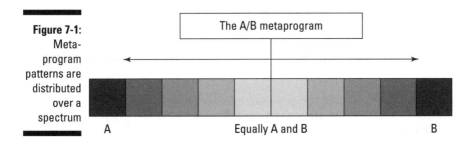

# Metaprograms, past and present

Noam Chomsky, renowned linguist, philosopher, political activist, and scholar, proposed in 1957 that people create their own model of the world by filtering their experiences in three different ways (which I cover in more detail in Chapter 4):

- ✔ **Deletion:** Selectively paying attention to certain information experienced through the senses yet excluding other information.

- ✔ **Distortion:** Altering information that you receive to fit in with your beliefs or preconceived ideas.

- ✔ **Generalisation:** Placing an experience in a category or group. For example, "I never win anything in the office Christmas raffle" after two Decembers working for a company.

So far so good, and pretty straightforward. However, Leslie Cameron-Bandler took Chomsky's work further in the 1970s to develop particular types of deletions, distortions, and generalisations, which appear in how a person behaves. She identified a few more different patterns. These became known as *metaprograms*. A few more? Okay, about 60!

But don't panic. Rodger Bailey, a student of Cameron-Bandler's, decided to test these concepts in the business context. He created the Language and Behaviour (LAB) Profile, reducing the number of patterns to 14. Phew.

Bailey further categorised these metaprograms into:

- ✔ Motivation traits, which are the patterns that drive people to act.

- ✔ Working traits, which are the preferences in internal mental processing that people use in particular situations.

Thanks, Rodger.

No right or wrong positions on these spectrums exist. Furthermore, no one pattern is better than another. As you become more familiar with metaprograms, however, you may notice that the people you have most difficulty communicating and working with are often individuals who have directly opposite preferences to you in at least one pattern.

## Meeting the metaprograms

Many identified metaprogram patterns direct how humans think, make decisions, act, and react. (See the sidebar 'Metaprograms, past and present' for more.)

In Chapter 4, I introduce the *task-* and *relationship-orientation* metaprograms and briefly explore how they show up in business, In this chapter I focus on another six.

In selecting metaprogram patterns to include in this chapter, I used my experience of working with organisations. Of all the patterns you can identify and use, the following six metaprograms make the most difference to my clients:

- ✔ General/Specific
- ✔ Proactive/Reactive
- ✔ Toward/Away-From
- ✔ Sameness/Difference
- ✔ Options/Procedures
- ✔ Internal/External

The following sections cover each of these six metaprograms in detail, including ways to identify specific patterns and recommended language to communicate more effectively with each pattern.

## Being heard and understood

You don't have to be a hypnotist to influence people. Besides, hypnotism is covered in a whole other book!

But identifying and knowing some key metaprograms that others may have gives you a great advantage in the workplace – and in life. When your metaprogram preferences differ from another person's and you speak in the way that reflects your pattern, the other person has to do some additional work to make sense of your words. However, if you use *the other person's* language, your audience hears you, understands you, and can be convinced much more easily.

When you adapt your communications to better suit others' metaprograms, you quickly gain *rapport.* Rapport is present when people connect and relate well. Conversation between people in rapport is smooth and easy. If you, for example, point out how a new project benefits a team member in a way he quickly understands, you'll improve rapport and he is much more likely to agree and commit. You can find out more about rapport in Chapter 6.

*Rapport* exists when the relationship between people has a certain, almost indefinable quality: a connection or alignment in the moment. You know rapport when it's happening – you can feel it.

In my work with organisations, I often hear that of all the influencing skills and tools that I help people to develop, the metaprogram patterns are the most effective. As people start to understand why they are frustrated or irritated by others who are 'not like them', they can work positively to improve working relationships.

All kinds of business communications benefit from an understanding of others' unconscious patterns. Selling, recruiting, negotiating, and giving feedback can be done more effectively when you notice and use other people's patterns.

## *Putting square pegs in square holes*

Competitive businesses need to develop high performance. Many organisations I work with invest well in their people – undertaking in-depth assessments for recruitment and promotion, designing targeted skills training, and creating sophisticated performance management systems. Yet these same companies continue to worry about the performance of individuals, teams, or functional areas.

In my experience, business performance only gets better when you understand and use metaprogram patterns. When people are able to work effectively with their patterns, they are more productive. When they can adapt to others' patterns, they influence more effectively.

In contrast, people struggle when a poor match exists between their job's patterns and their own patterns. The job holder in this situation often feels stressed by the way in which the job seemingly needs to be done, irrespective of the experience and qualifications that he holds. His effectiveness and outputs then suffer, putting further stress into the workplace. As his boss focuses more attention on performance management, his energy and motivation start to wane.

# Talking Generally or Specifically

The general/specific metaprogram pattern determines how people operate at their best based on what is, for them, the right amount of information. It defines what scope of information they work with effectively in terms of understanding and communicating – *general* or *specific*.

Someone running the *general* pattern is likely to work well with an overview of a situation. Someone with the *specific* pattern requires much more information and detail.

- ✔ **If you operate at the general end of the spectrum,** you probably think in concepts rather than lots of detail or itemised sequences. You want outlines of a situation and often turn off when you encounter too much information. Of course you can handle some detail, but not too much or you feel overwhelmed or just plain irritated by the sheer quantity of facts and figures in front of you.

- ✔ **If you operate at the specific end of the spectrum,** you handle small pieces of information well and like to work step by step. Your attention to detail is likely to be first-rate. You do your best job when you can break a project down into smaller components. When you only have the big picture you'll not be able to work effectively with it unless you can get more specific data.

Rodger Bailey's research into this pattern in the workplace identified the following spread of people across the general/specific spectrum:

| | |
|---|---|
| General | 60 per cent |
| Specific | 15 per cent |
| Equally general and specific | 25 per cent |

## Recruiting with general/specific

When recruiting, make sure you understand the level of specific, sequential detail a job-holder will be required to use. For instance:

- ✔ Bookkeepers usually need to have a high preference for specific information.

- ✔ Leaders mostly tend to operate more effectively towards the general end of the spectrum.

- ✔ A financial director can be effective only if he can flex between general and specific, in order to identify the important details but also provide an overview to others.

## Matching the proposal to the decision maker's pattern

My company was recently asked to provide a proposal for a leadership development programme for a senior HR team in an international organisation. The Head of Learning and Development requested some in-depth explanation of content and benefits. She was impressed by our subsequent seven-page proposal document, and I was invited to meet the HR Director.

Soon into the meeting I realised the Director hadn't read the proposal, but he was very interested in finding out about what we could do for his organisation. Listening to what he had to say, I noticed that he only wanted the big picture. I checked with him and he admitted that reading seven pages made him – in his words – 'lose the will to live'. Not wanting to drive a good client over the edge, I of course offered to rewrite the proposal.

The new document was two pages long with the key data presented in bullet points on the first page. That hit the spot – the client commissioned the job.

As my colleagues and I continued working with the organisation, I made sure that review meetings were never longer than an hour. And I rarely sent an e-mail to the Director that was more than a few sentences long.

The programme was successful. It met the client's outcomes and exceeded expectations. The final evidence was my evaluation of the impact of the programme – a one-page summary.

One organisation I work with has a CEO with a high specific pattern. His need for detail drives his executive team, who nearly all have a high general pattern, absolutely crazy.

## *Identifying general/specific patterns*

Identify where someone is on the spectrum between *general* and *specific* by asking him about a project he is working on. Listen carefully to his response.

✔ **A *specific* pattern emerges** in answers presented with lots of detail, in step-by-step sequences, and with lots of adverbs and adjectives. For example, a specific person may say:

"Well, at first it was difficult as there was so much to do, and we didn't really know if we had enough of all the right kind of resources. So the team has now met – quite an interesting bunch of people, and very keen – and we have created a more detailed and achievable action plan to gradually work towards completing the first stage of the project. I now feel more confident that we have thoroughly explored all the aspects of this stage and can now work through what we need to do."

- ✔ **A general pattern appears** in answers comprising overviews and summaries, often presented in a random order and using simple sentences. For example, a general person may say:

  "We're on track for completion of the first stage. The team's met and we've got a plan. Seems like a good team, and everyone's motivated."

Each person's patterns can vary from context to context. A CEO who typically just needs a strategic overview of this month's sales figures may want very detailed feedback on his son's school report!

## Influencing based on general/specific patterns

To influence people more effectively, use expressions that have meaning for their general/specific pattern. For example:

- ✔ **For general people:** in summary, the overview, essentially, the main concept, the important thing is, the big picture, in brief
- ✔ **For specific people:** exactly, in detail, specifically, precisely, step by step, on plan, first . . . second

Adapting your preference for amount and scope of information to another's has strong impact. Give less or more detail than you usually would if that's what someone else needs. In that way you experience more success in persuading, training, or instructing someone to do something. Give more information, in sequential order, to someone who works best in that way.

Identifying the general/specific pattern in the context of e-mail is usually easy and invaluable. To influence someone effectively by e-mail, notice how much detail goes into his own e-mails. You're sure to find extremes, from three words to three pages. So match the other person's style. If you want something approved and his e-mails are very short, keep yours short too and detail free – just offer a concept or outline. If someone sends a detailed e-mail to you requesting information, respond with lots of specifics.

# Discovering People's Level of Initiative: Proactive/Reactive

The proactive/reactive pattern plays out dramatically in the workplace every day.

✔ If you're more inclined to initiate things and get things started at work, you're operating at the *proactive* end of the spectrum.

✔ If you tend to let others take the lead while you wait and evaluate the best course of action, you're at the *reactive* end.

## Finding a place for everyone

When you're putting together a team to create and manage a change programme, you need people with a proactive pattern. Similarly, any job involving lots of initiative and self-starting needs a proactive bias. The following positions are often well suited to individuals with a proactive pattern:

✔ Sales people

✔ Business franchisees

✔ Senior leaders

When managing proactive people, you need to be continually channelling their energy. Someone with a proactive pattern is likely to get irritated by delays or interruptions, as she just wants to get the job done. So focussed is she on doing things that she might even upset others along the way! She'll certainly have little time for bureaucracy, interference or company politics.

If you are leading a reactive person, you'll find that he much prefers not to initiate projects or ideas. He works better if he can contemplate and analyse issues presented to him. He certainly has a role to play in slowing down a proactive person to make sure that all the options and implications of a solution or approach are taken into account.

The reactive metaprogram is useful in roles in:

✔ Customer service

✔ Research and analysis

✔ Jobs involving 'fire-fighting' and problem solving.

The majority of people (60-65 per cent according to Rodger Bailey) have a mix of the proactive and reactive pattern – pretty useful in most jobs where you need to be able to instigate certain things and to react to other people and situations. Despite pressure in some organisations for people to be more proactive, reactive people are invaluable in evaluating issues before they act, and bringing in an element of caution.

## *Identifying proactive/reactive patterns*

To spot people's *proactive* or *reactive* pattern, listen to the structure of their language *and* watch their body language.

If you notice a strong bias towards one list of sentence structures or body language characteristics that appear in Table 7-1, you know that the person is part of the cluster of people whom researchers identify as being very proactive or highly reactive (15 to 20 per cent of the working population for each category, according to Rodger Bailey's research. With the remainder being a mix of proactive and reactive).

| Table 7-1 | Proactive and Reactive Characteristics | |
|-----------|------------------|------------------|
| | *Sentence Structure* | *Body Language* |
| Proactive | Short sentences | Fast speaking |
| | Crisp sentences | Lots of movement |
| | Direct | Fidgeting |
| | Active verbs | |
| Reactive | Incomplete sentences | Stillness |
| | Passive verbs | Ability to sit for long periods |
| | Long, convoluted sentences | |
| | Conditional words, including would, could, should, might | |

## *Influencing based on proactive/reactive patterns*

To influence people based on their proactive/reactive pattern, use expressions that have meaning to them given their pattern. For example:

- ✔ **For proactive people:** go for it, let's do it, get the job done, now, don't wait, take control, make things happen

- ✔ **For reactive people:** why not think about it, consider, could, might, analyse, think about, take your time

# *Moving Towards Goals or Away From Problems*

The *toward/away-from metaprogram* pattern focuses on what causes people to do something. People act either because:

- ✔ **They want to move *toward* something:** A goal or target, perhaps.
- ✔ **They want to move *away from* something:** a problem or difficulty, for example.

In the workplace, if you determine people's motivation direction, you can achieve more and avoid potential problems.

People motivated by a *toward* pattern are fixated on what they want. They may work towards:

- ✔ Achieving a key business goal
- ✔ Getting a promotion
- ✔ Leaving the office on time that day

Targets and outcomes, large and small, energise these folks. As they concentrate on what they want to accomplish, they tend to set priorities well.

When operating at the extreme of this pattern, people can struggle to identify potential problems or recognise possible barriers to success. When also running a strongly proactive pattern, they can become dangerously gung-ho.

The towards metaprogram can be helpful in a variety of roles, where:

- ✔ Important targets, such as sales, need to be hit
- ✔ New businesses are to be built
- ✔ Leadership is required to achieve a major goal

Individuals with a strong away-from pattern tend to put their attention on what may go wrong in a particular plan, project, or situation. They are stimulated by:

- ✔ Solving problems
- ✔ Averting crises
- ✔ Looking for real and potential difficulties

Individuals whose motivations are truly away-from are likely to be easily distracted from objectives because they're compelled to deal with problems. Previously agreed priorities are forgotten as they troubleshoot the latest issue to emerge.

If someone with an away-from pattern is leading an organisation, the whole operation probably runs in crisis management mode.

The kind of roles that generally benefit from an away-from pattern include:

- ✔ Compliance officers
- ✔ Quality control managers
- ✔ Maintenance operators
- ✔ Proofreaders

People working together from different ends of the spectrum sometimes have great difficulty. Those with the toward pattern can judge the away-from people as negative or cynical. And the away-from people in turn perceive those with a strong toward preference as naïve and gullible for not noticing potential obstacles.

However, teams often benefit from having *both* patterns represented well among team members. This mix ensures a drive towards goals supported by thorough contingency planning.

## Identifying the toward/away-from pattern

Just a few questions about what a colleague considers important can help you discover his motivation direction – toward or away from – at work. For example:

Questioner: What's important to you in your work?

Respondent: To create new business opportunities.

Questioner: What about creating new business opportunities is important?

Respondent: Then I can do well and earn a good salary.

Questioner: What does that do for you?

Respondent: I can buy a bigger house and stop worrying about affording the kids' university fees.

# Negatively doing a good job

I coached Susan, an experienced project manager who'd just left a fast-growing young business. The energy, enthusiasm, and entrepreneurial spirit of the 120 staff had attracted her to the company. They were going places and that excited her.

Once established in her role, Susan found her director-level boss, Malcolm, to be very forward thinking and visionary. The broad-brush strategies he put forward, Susan and her colleagues needed to make happen. Susan wanted these plans to succeed – except she expressed this desire differently. She didn't want these plans to fail.

So Susan did what she did best: she identified all the areas where things could go wrong and pointed them out. Where possible, she offered alternative approaches. Susan worked hard and was committed and motivated.

Over time, Susan's contributions increasingly frustrated Malcolm. He struggled to conceal his feelings every time Susan told him how the latest plans may fail. When Malcolm eventually gave Susan an appraisal, he expressed concerns about her negativity. Susan was devastated. She didn't understand. She felt so positive and was as committed to achieving business success as anyone. She worked the longest hours in the department and was passionate about what she did.

Following her appraisal, Susan made an effort to avoid pointing out potential pitfalls in the department's plans. She watched as a key project floundered because the problems she spotted early on, and the contingency plans she recommended, were ignored.

Susan became increasingly disillusioned and her work suffered. Eventually she left the company by mutual agreement. Malcolm was confused about what had gone wrong. Susan's colleagues were demotivated over losing a valuable, experienced colleague. Susan's self-belief and confidence were damaged.

Fortunately, after I helped Susan to realise that she was motivated to succeed by moving *away from* problems, while Malcolm's entire focus was on moving *toward* his goal, her energy was restored. She then looked for a job where her away-from skills were useful *and* appreciated. Even better, in her next position she started to notice people with a motivation pattern that was more toward. She adjusted how she talked to them yet still got her message across.

In the preceding example, the first responses suggest a toward pattern. Yet more questioning leads to an answer that has both toward and away-from elements.

These patterns are opposite ends of a spectrum. A person's preference in any given situation can be somewhere between the two ends of the spectrum.

## Influencing based on toward/away-from patterns

Around 40 per cent of people at work are believed to have a toward pattern, and the same number have an away-from pattern, according to the research work of Rodger Bailey. For these groups to work together and communicate effectively, each group needs to be able to use the kind of language that the other speaks.

To motivate people with strong toward/away-from patterns, use words and expressions that have meaning to them. For example:

- **For toward people:** get, attain, achieve, accomplish, you get, the advantages, you can have, obtain what you want

- **For away-from:** fix it, prevent, avoid, steer clear of, find out what's wrong, there will be no . . . , solution, remove

# Selling Change: Focusing on Sameness or Difference

The sameness/difference metaprogram pattern is particularly relevant in today's increasingly fast-paced workplaces. Hang around the leaders in just about any organisation these days and you're sure to hear expressions like 'managing change', 'transforming performance', 'revolutionising products and services', and so on – probably as often as you hear their BlackBerries ring. The mantra 'we're operating in a fast-changing environment' and all the implications that this has for modern business are very exciting – for some.

How a person reacts to change is described in the sameness/difference metaprogram:

- **People with a sameness metaprogram** are most comfortable working in a highly stable and unchanging environment. They want consistency and to know where they stand, in terms of their location, role and management.

- **People with a difference metaprogram** thrive on change. They reinvent and reorganise their working environment repeatedly. Some thrive on continual and even dramatic change in their work environments. You may notice them changing jobs frequently – even moving organisations.

In between the preceding extremes fall another two patterns:

- **People with a *sameness with exception* metaprogram** like things to stay largely the same but with some minor changes or improvements. Rodger Bailey found that at work the majority of people – about 65 percent – fall into this category. (See Table 7–2.) For these people, change needs to be evolutionary, not revolutionary.

- **People with a *sameness with exception and difference* metaprogram** have a double pattern. You're happy with small and big changes at work, as long as the major changes are every so often. You'll make sure you have a significant change at work every three to four years.

All four change metaprograms have an important place in today's organisations and companies. When matching people and jobs, remember:

- Individuals with sameness patterns are well suited to administrative, manufacturing, or service roles where change is not a feature of the job.

- By extension, if the administrative, manufacturing, or service aspects of a department or group need improving through gradual changes, this motivates those with the sameness with exception pattern.

- People with the sameness with exception pattern will also like work involving gradual change, as long as they can move functions or locations every so often.

- Someone with a difference pattern needs a job with lots of different things to work on. He may also be motivated by situations where radical changes need to be introduced.

## *Considering customer sameness/difference patterns*

If you're in sales or marketing – or indeed have *any* contact with customers – make sure you're aware of the main sameness/difference pattern for your market.

If you have a well-established, loyal customer base, what drives that loyalty?

- Can your product or service be relied on because it's stayed largely the same (maybe with some improvements) for many years?

- Does continual innovation and change motivate your customers to continue to buy your product or service?

Be sure your advertising messages match your core market's most likely metaprogram – or you may soon be losing market share and firing the agency.

## *Identifying sameness/difference patterns*

One of the best ways to quickly find out which of the four patterns someone's using at work is asking the following question:

> What is the relationship between your job this year and last year?

Note the precise wording of this question. Odd though it may sound, its value is that it doesn't 'lead the witness'! It doesn't ask what's changed or stayed the same. Instead, the question invites a comparison – any comparison that people care to make.

After you ask this question, pay very close attention to the answer. Listen for clues that tell you the person falls into one of the patterns. Typical responses by pattern include:

- ✔ **Sameness:** The person tells you how things are the same or explains what hasn't changed.

    Example: 'I'm still running the same team.'

- ✔ **Sameness with exception:** The person describes how things are similar but with some change. He makes comparisons and uses words such as more, less, improved, better, fewer.

    Example: 'I still manage the same team, but we've taken over more of the responsibilities of the old southern region.'

- ✔ **Difference:** The person points out how things are new and different. He may even look at you as though you're mad because he doesn't understand the question.

    Example: 'Things are completely different now we've taken over customer management.'

- ✔ **Sameness with exception and difference:** The person uses responses from the preceding sameness-with-exception type and difference type.

    Example: 'Some major changes have happened as we took on customer management; the team have developed well and are working more efficiently.'

# All the same – apart from the differences

I worked with Ellen, the manager of a radiography department in a hospital, coaching her to lead her team through a major change that included moving to a new building, installing state-of-the-art equipment, and introducing different procedures alongside the new technology.

Top management in the Trust was very excited about the pending changes. This was the culmination of a major new build, some hard-fought investment in new capital equipment, and the opportunity to offer an improved service. However, the managers communicated their excitement with the language that motivated them. Words like new, different, changed, transformed, leading edge, next century, all tumbled out of their mouths and appeared in press releases.

The team members the changes primarily affected were almost exclusively long-serving specialists who'd worked in the same department in the same hospital for over seven years. They were people committed to giving a good service and doing what they do well. But funnily enough, they were having just the opposite reaction to the changes as senior management.

By contrast, the team members were resistant, unhappy, distracted, and demotivated. Guess which metaprogram they were operating from? Yes, some of the group were motivated by sameness, some by sameness with exception. (See the section 'Selling Change: Focusing on Sameness and Difference' for more on these metaprograms.)

The manager was having a pretty hard time. While monitoring the new facilities and their final installation, planning and preparing for the move, and maintaining an acceptable service to patients, she had to deal with the team's negative reactions to the upcoming change.

So Ellen and I identified all the things that were going to stay the same for the team. For example, the building was on the same site. Their journeys to work remained unchanged, as did their hours, uniform, lunch break, and terms of employment. Some of the existing equipment was moving with them. The new equipment did the same job as the old, and some new machines featured similar controls. And so the list continued.

This team's manager did a sterling job of communicating to the team – in their own language and being mindful of their sameness/difference patterns – from then on. Attitudes began to soften and the move went smoothly. The team settled in to their new environment quickly and easily. And yes, patient waiting times did go down and the quality of the team's output improved.

Rodger Bailey identified some predictability in the frequency of change within people's working lives, as Table 7-2 notes. So knowing a bit about someone's work history can give you another clue to his attitude to change.

| Table 7- 2 | Sameness and Difference Analyses | | |
|---|---|---|---|
| | **Type of Change** | **Frequency of Major Change** | **Distribution in the Work Context** |
| Sameness | None | 15–25 years | 5 per cent |
| Sameness with exception | Evolution | 5–7 years | 65 per cent |
| Difference | Revolution | 1–2 years | 20 per cent |
| Sameness with exception and difference | Revolution and evolution | 3–4 years | 10 per cent |

## Influencing based on sameness/difference patterns

To influence based on people's response to *sameness* and *difference*, use words and expressions that have meaning to them. For example:

- ✔ **For sameness people:** as you know, as usual, staying the same, as is, unchanged, identical

- ✔ **For sameness-with-exception people:** more, fewer, similar, better, the same except, upgraded, enhanced, improved

- ✔ **For difference people:** completely different, new, revolutionised, transform, unique, total change, doesn't compare

- ✔ **For sameness-with-exception-and-difference people:** use the preceding words recommended for sameness-with-exception and difference patterns

# Getting Work Done: Creating Choices or Defining Procedures

Another useful metaprogram pattern to keep top of mind at work is termed *options* or *procedures*. This pattern is all about how you tackle your work. Are you frequently looking for alternative ways to do things – or do you like to follow tried-and-tested procedures?

✔ **You're probably motivated by the options pattern** if you're motivated by choices, variety, and the chance to do something differently or better than previously. You may be very good at drawing up procedures for getting the job done, but you have no interest in following the procedure yourself. You initiate a new project with gusto but don't see any particular need to complete it.

✔ **You're probably motivated by procedures** if you believe a 'right' way to do things exists. You like your work to have a start point and an end point – basically you get things done. You can find having too many choices about how to handle things difficult.

Rodger Bailey identified that about 40 per cent of people at work have the options pattern, 40 per cent the procedure pattern, with just 20 per cent with a mix of the two.

Having a clear idea of which of these patterns you need when recruiting makes a big difference to the success of anyone you put into a job. If the job requires someone to set things up, design operations, and *create* procedures, you're looking for someone with an *options* pattern. Anything that involves maintaining things, using existing processes, or following scripts is ideal for an individual with a strong *procedures* pattern.

## *Identifying options/procedures patterns*

Someone's options or procedures preference is usually expressed in how he speaks.

✔ Someone with the options preference uses a lot of 'I can' and 'I could'.

✔ Someone motivated by the procedures preference uses a lot more of 'I must' and 'I should'.

If these word usages don't give you enough evidence to detect someone's pattern, ask the following question:

Why did you choose your current job?

Stick to the phrasing of the question outlined here as it's been designed very carefully to bring out the clues you are looking for, which are all in the *structure* of the answer, as well as the words - listen carefully! You'll find that:

✔ An options-motivated person is likely to tell you what choices and options he had and the criteria he used to decide.

✔ A procedures-motivated person is more likely to tell a story, detailing how he happened to end up in this particular job. You don't hear any criteria or suggestions of choice.

## Influencing based on options/procedures patterns

To influence based on someone's preference for options or procedures, use words and expressions that have meaning to them. For example:

✔ **For an options-motivated person:** possibilities, choice, 'play it by ear', alternatives, options, new, break the rules, variety

✔ **For a procedures-motivated person:** the right way, tried and tested, first . . . second . . . and then . . .

# Giving the Right Amount of Feedback: Internal/External

*Feedback* takes many forms. In business, people use numbers, scores, statistics, ratings – indeed a whole smorgasbord of measures – to gain evidence of what's been achieved – or not.

HR departments have managers give feedback to teams, and even on occasion to peers and bosses, within performance management systems. Plus of course, every day offers all sorts of *informal feedback* through what people say and do (as well as what they *don't* say and *don't* do).

✔ You're *internally* **referenced** if you believe you know whether you've done a good job, no matter what anyone else says. You have your own internal standards that you use to judge the quality of your work.

✔ You're *externally* **referenced** if receiving lots of feedback is important to you, in terms of telling you how well you're doing. This feedback pattern means that you need external information to assess your achievements.

If you're running the external pattern, then you're only motivated if you get the feedback you need. You want hard evidence and others' thoughts to assess how well things are going.

By contrast, if you're running the internal metaprogram pattern, you may have difficulty accepting the opinions of others when they're in conflict with your own. Instead, you're more likely to question or dismiss others' views and stick fair and square to your own conclusions.

## Managing based on internal/external patterns

Managing *internal* people can be challenging. They don't desire feedback and tend not to act on it. They often take direction and instructions as information – all very interesting but not necessary to act on. They need to make their own decisions, whether you as their manager have given them licence to or not.

To get the best from people running a strong *internal* pattern, give them as much space to do their own thing as possible. Allow them to make their own decisions. When this freedom isn't appropriate, negotiate standards in advance so they can make decisions against those standards.

Managing a person motivated by *external* information needs a very different approach. At the extreme, this pattern leads to people taking information and questions as instructions. An innocent enquiry such as 'Has the delivery arrived yet?' can lead to a flurry of unnecessary phone calls to chase suppliers and couriers, when the matter isn't urgent (well, not yet at least).

You must give people running strong external patterns a lot of feedback. They just aren't able to function well without it.

And if you personally run a strong *internal* pattern, motivating a strongly external person can be a struggle. Consider giving yourself written reminders to provide feedback, because doing so certainly doesn't come naturally to you.

I was once employed to introduce a whole new communications function into an industrial services organisation. Throughout the project, I felt constrained and frustrated that I wasn't able to do my best work. Yet my manager was continually patting me on the back for doing a good job. In his eyes I truly was doing good work, but I just ended up feeling even worse – because my internal standards seemed to be considerably higher than my manager's! He was baffled that all his positive words weren't motivating me. Every time he told me I was being success I felt compelled to disagree. The mismatch between my internal feedback pattern and his external pattern started to make our relationship quite difficult. If only I'd known then what I know now.

## Matching positions to internal/external patterns

When searching for the right person for a job, ask yourself the following questions:

- ✔ Does the job holder need to be self-motivated and make decisions and judgements about what to do?
- ✔ Does the job holder need to take heed of continual feedback and be prepared to flex to meet changing requirements?

Finding someone with an internal pattern with be very important to their success in a job calling for self-motivation, whereas a position where adapting to feedback is a requirement certainly needs an external pattern.

People with the internal pattern are often appropriate for leadership roles because leaders set standards and make decisions. Many artists and creative people run an internal pattern.

People running the external pattern are ideal for sales roles, positions in the travel, hotel, and leisure industries – in fact, any job where front-line staff work to meet customer needs. The external pattern is also useful to help meet internal customers' needs, such as human resources staff.

## Identifying internal/external patterns

To find out whether someone is motivated internally or externally, just ask the following question:

How do you know you've done a good job?

Listen carefully to the person's responses.

- ✔ An internally motivated person is likely to say something along the lines of 'I just know. In my experience this is how it is. I've decided.'
- ✔ An externally motivated person is likely to say something like 'Well, I find out from other people. If my boss doesn't let me know I go and ask. And of course the figures show an increase.'

## *Influencing based on internal/external patterns*

To motivate people based on their feedback pattern, use phrases and words that have meaning to them. For example:

- ✔ **For internally motivated people:** you know, you may wish to consider, you may want to think about, only you can decide, a suggestion for you, up to you, what do you think?

- ✔ **For externally motivated people:** the feedback is, results show that, [the person with authority] says, what I've noticed, the word on the street is, opinions are, statistics show

# *Becoming the Monsieur Poirot of Metaprograms*

If you're like most people, you're busy. Asking lots of questions to find out someone else's metaprograms can be time consuming and hard work. And of course, do too much of it and your colleagues may wonder what on earth you're up to.

So I suggest that, to start with at least, you keep your metaprogram analysis simple. The following sections cover a couple of relatively easy things to try.

## *Practising trial and error*

Sometimes you aren't able to do all the work required to detect another person's metaprogram patterns. After all, you can hardly pop into the office of the CEO to ask how he knows he's done a good job to identify his feedback pattern preferences!

So, in cases where you have limited contact with a person whose patterns you're trying to assess, try the following steps:

1. **Guess**

2. **Test**

Chances are, you may have some clues about a person's patterns based on something he said or did, but the jury's still out. When you just don't have enough evidence, make your best guess and then start using the words and expressions in the preceding section that you think are appropriate for the assumed pattern. Then pay very close attention to the response.

For example, you say something like 'You know best what to do in this situation' to a team member on a project you're leading. You get the response 'Well, actually I was hoping that you had an opinion and would advise me.' You know you need to change tack quickly!

If you start to talk about transformation and major changes and you get enthusiastic nods and agreements, keep talking about differences. You've tapped in to a difference metaprogram. If you get a stern-faced response or anxious questions, you may well have uncovered a sameness patter, so adapt what you say to emphasise the things that will be staying the same within the change ahead.

## Taking just one bite at a time

You may have heard the answer to the question 'How do you eat an elephant?'. That's right. The only realistic answer is 'One bite at a time.'

I don't recommend attempting to work out *all* of someone's metaprograms at once, as you can quickly tie yourself up in knots. Instead, I suggest that you approach your metaprogram detective work in the following way.

By the way, if you already know you have a strong preference for options (see the section 'Getting Work Done: Offering Choices or Defining Procedures' earlier in this chapter), you probably don't want to use the following technique – it's a procedure!

1. **Decide (or guess) your own patterns at work.**

   Ask yourself the various questions I offer in the preceding sections on each of the six metaprograms. Ask others – such as colleagues or your boss – for help if you need to.

2. **Pick *one* metaprogram pattern where you seem to be towards one end of the spectrum.**

3. **Identify someone at work who you're having difficulty motivating or communicating with.**

   Attempt to identify that person's pattern in the metaprogram you chose in Step 2. Use any of the techniques outlined in the preceding sections on the six metaprograms – or use the guess-and-test method outlined in 'Practising trial and error'.

   • If the other person's pattern seems to be towards the opposite end of the spectrum than yours, then – hey presto! – you have at least one reason you're not working together well.

   • If the other person's pattern seems to be similar to yours in the metaprogram you're working with, try a different one until you get to a metaprogram where you and the other person are running notably different patterns.

4. **Experiment with using the words and phrases that target a specific metaprogram pattern.**

   See the preceding sections on each of the six metaprograms for specific words and phrases.

5. **Notice how well you seem to be communicating with the other person.**
   How much easier has influencing become with this person?

Now you are getting some practise, keep on experimenting with other patterns – and other people! You may find it easier to tell some people what you are doing, and they won't then be phased by any of your questions. Where you wish to be more subtle, it may not be appropriate to ask the questions but to use you other detection methods instead - including guess and test!

# Chapter 8

# Choosing and Anchoring Positive Emotions

*O*ne of the key differences between humans and the rest of the animal kingdom is the amazing breadth and complexity of emotions that people experience. These emotions enrich lives, guide choices, and, of course, make life quite complicated.

At work, as in the rest of your life, your emotions influence what you do and say. Your feelings determine how well you work, how quickly you learn new skills, how you perform in challenging situations, and how you relate to others.

In certain cultures, that of the UK for example, displays of extreme emotion in business are frowned on. Shouting, crying, and even too much laughing can be 'just not how we do things around here'. Yet whether you make them obvious to the world or tend to hide them, your emotions influence what you do and say.

You may think that feelings have no place in the modern organisation. But working well with people who are not like you, or individuals who bring out negative feelings in you, is a challenge. If you feel angry, irritated, inadequate, or unappreciated, you can't do your best job or be at your most influential. Performing well in testing situations is hard if you're not feeling confident, motivated, or upbeat. So at work, your success depends very much on how your emotions are *working for you,* rather than against you.

If having more choice in how you feel when you need to influence others sounds useful to you, then this chapter's a good place to begin understanding and optimising the power of emotions.

# Tuning In to Your Emotions

You know when you're experiencing an extreme emotion. On these occasions you may feel:

✔ Very happy – even elated

✔ Furious with rage

✔ Extremely excited

✔ Incredibly nervous

When your emotions aren't quite so extreme and vivid, you may not pay much attention to them. Yet they're still really important, as they influence how you behave.

Most people spend a lot of time on 'autopilot', letting their unconscious mind, with all its values, beliefs, patterns, and emotions, fly the planes of their lives. Things can be a whole lot better when you take charge and start piloting yourself.

## Feeling those feelings

The preceding sections describe emotions as feelings; in fact, I use the words interchangeably. This is for a good reason. How do you know you're experiencing an emotion? Emotions are pretty much always connected to a *feeling* in your body, even if you don't realise it.

Noticing what's happening in your body helps you be more aware of how you're feeling. After you begin recognising emotions and noting that you're having them, you can choose to change your emotions if you want to.

Working with businesspeople, I can see that many people find emotional self-awareness challenging. Generally, paying attention to emotions is something that people are not trained, or even encouraged, to do. Education systems put a lot of emphasis on learning how to think. In many cultures, feelings are not often discussed, especially in business. So is it any wonder that really understanding your feelings and moods, and the impact they have on you and others, is a skill that many have to develop?

So get in touch with the emotions you're feeling – right now. Think about what's going on inside you at this very moment. Read through the following questions and then close your eyes for several moments while you ponder your answers:

✔ How are you breathing? Fast or slow? Shallow or deep?

✔ Are your muscles tense or relaxed?

✔ Does your body feel comfortable? If you have any discomfort, where is it?

✔ How do you describe your mental state? Alert or tired? Open or preoccupied?

Go through the questions above from time to time to work out exactly what you're feeling. Consider copying the questions or typing them up and sticking them up in your car or at your desk. Keep asking yourself the questions until they become second nature to you and you begin to know what your body's experiencing at any time.

After you become more sensitive to your body, you can begin to spot really unhelpful feelings. These feelings represent negative emotions – such as irritation, frustration, or anger – when they pop up. For example, you may have a colleague you find difficult to work with at times. Perhaps her communications style is much more confrontational than you like. By listening to your body, you may notice that your shoulders become tense just before an interaction with this colleague, as if you're bracing yourself for a fight.

## Changing how you feel

As a fully functioning member of the human race, you probably already have a number of ways to manage your emotions at work. You may use some of the following approaches.

✔ **Positive self-talk.** To encourage yourself, you remember previous successes and boost your self-belief, despite your underlying anxiety. As I said in Chapter 2, this may require you to sit up and notice what you've not been noticing, and reminding yourself of the good things you have achieved, small and large. This technique actually works in many situations.

✔ **Repetition.** For many people, gaining experience over time is a way of removing, or at least reducing, negative emotions. For example, you may feel very anxious the first time you have to speak to a large group of people. But after months and years of doing this, repeated exposure to the same thing makes the activity more familiar and more manageable. Repetition isn't a guaranteed success strategy, though. Many revered stage actors still report stage fright after decades of theatre work.

✔ **Suppressing emotions.** Doing your best to ignore or not pay attention to emotions can work for some – for a while at least. After all, this approach is what the British 'stiff upper lip' is all about! The challenge with suppressing emotions is that the underlying feelings are still there and can lead to stress later.

✔ **Using food, stimulants, and other substances.** Some people use cigarettes to calm, caffeine to boost, alcohol to relax, food for comfort, and so on. These substances can provide relief from bad feelings, but the relief's short-lived – and of course often leads to other problems.

All of these are ways of handling your emotions, and some may be more effective than others. NLP provides you with techniques that allow you to *choose* your emotions (see the following section, 'Choosing Your Emotions') and make long-lasting changes when you want to.

# Choosing Your Emotions

I've met many people who say, 'I don't like giving presentations' or 'I'm not good at presenting'. These same people have had presentation skills training and, on the face of it, appear to have the resources (in this case, the *skills*) to do the job well. What they're missing is another crucial resource – the right emotional state.

In Chapter 3 I describe the major principles of NLP, including:

> People have all the resources they need.

So for people who need to *feel* differently to give a convincing and memorable presentation, *choosing* how to feel, and finding the necessary resources to make that happen, can lead to a huge transformation in performance.

Imagine having control over your emotions. What might be possible if you could choose your state for any occasion? For example:

- ✔ When giving an important presentation to a large group, you choose to feel **confident** rather than **nervous.**
- ✔ When having a disciplinary meeting with a team member, you choose to feel **assured** rather than **stressed.**
- ✔ When a customer cancels a major contract, you choose to feel **calm** rather than **distressed.**
- ✔ When you hear unfavourable feedback on your performance, you choose to feel **curious** rather than **angry.**
- ✔ When you find out you failed to get a promotion, you choose to feel **optimistic** rather than **disappointed.**

Sound too good to be true? Well, NLP has an emotional power tool known as *anchoring* that can help you make these types of changes to your emotions, as I discuss in the following section.

## Discovering anchors

In NLP, *anchoring* enables you to identify triggers – what specifically leads you to feel a certain way – and then set new triggers to create different feelings.

Various experiences set off emotions all day long:

- ✔ When you see the face of someone special, you're likely to have a good feeling.
- ✔ When you hear a particular tone of voice, you may tense up and feel anxious.
- ✔ When you smell a whiteboard marker, you may transport yourself back to an important meeting you attended last week.

The above are all anchors – they're external stimuli that lead to a response. A *response* can be a feeling or emotion, or a behaviour, but whatever form a response takes, it's most likely to be automatic. Do you automatically respond to a bleep or icon on your PC by switching to read the latest e-mail to arrive? Emotional responses are often even more automatic!

Many anchors occur naturally, just like that feeling when you see the face of someone special. Others you set and respond to all the time, mostly without knowing you're doing it. You create some anchors as a result of one traumatic event, but you build up most over time through repetition.

Anchors can be positive or negative, in that they can transport you to good feelings or bad. In the following sections, 'Figuring out the emotions you want' and 'Setting new anchors', I discuss how to identify and set useful anchors for yourself, the kind that can help you perform at your best and achieve your goals.

Anchors – either naturally occurring or self-created – are most effective when they're:

- ✔ **Distinctive:** They stand out and you can't confuse them with anything else.
- ✔ **Repeatable.** They're easy to do or experience again when you want to.
- ✔ **Strong.** You set them when you're having a really good experience.
- ✔ **Timely.** They're set at the moment when you're experiencing a feeling really intensely
- ✔ **Meaningful.** They work for you and you can trigger them whenever you need them.

## Figuring out the emotions you want

To begin setting positive anchors for yourself, consider some current situations in which you want to have a different emotion. Use Table 8-1 to get you thinking. As you consider each situation on the table, think about your negative feelings and then what you want to feel instead.

| Table 8-1 | Identifying and Choosing Emotions for Specific Situations | | |
|---|---|---|---|
| **Occasion/Situation** | | **My Current Feeling** | **How I Want to Feel** |
| Talking to someone very senior | | | |
| Being assertive in meetings | | | |
| Holding a disciplinary meeting | | | |
| Giving or receiving a performance review | | | |
| Presenting to a group | | | |
| Delivering bad news | | | |
| Giving instructions to a team member | | | |
| Another challenge | | | |
| Another challenge | | | |

## Setting new anchors

After you go through Table 8-1 and figure out what emotions you currently experience in a difficult situation and what emotions you want to experience instead, you can begin setting a new, more useful anchor. Your goal here is to set up an anchor that you can use time and time again in very specific situations. For example, if you frequently find yourself getting agitated by interruptions to your work, then finding a new way to feel when this happens will be very helpful to you.

Read through the entire step-by-step process that follows before you start. That way you don't have to interrupt the good feeling you're going to be generating in order to find out what you need to do next!

1. **Find a quiet place, free from interruptions.**

   For example, you may want to do this exercise in a meeting room at work or a quiet place at home. Be sure you can block out distractions and get as comfortable as possible in your chosen spot.

2. **Think of a positive state or emotion that you want to have when you choose.**

   For example, think about confidence, optimism, calm, or any other positive state or emotion. Focus on just one specific positive emotion each time you work through these steps.

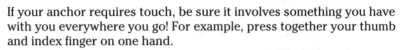

3. **Choose a suitable anchor for this positive emotion that you can easily use any time you need to.**

   The most effective anchors are distinctive, repeatable, strong, timely, and meaningful to you.

   Some possible anchors include something you can grip, touching a part f your body, or saying a particular word to yourself.

   If your anchor requires touch, be sure it involves something you have with you everywhere you go! For example, press together your thumb and index finger on one hand.

4. **Recall an occasion in the past when you had the positive feeling or state you want.**

   This past event may be a very different type of situation from the difficult situation you're encountering at work.

5. **In your mind, step back into that occasion and remember the experience.**

   See what you saw, hear what you heard, and feel what you felt. Relive the incident as fully as you can.

6. **As the good feeling that you want to have intensifies, set your anchor.**

   For example, press your thumb and index finger together while feeling the positive emotion you desire.

   Anchors are most effective if you start to set them as your feeling is getting very strong and then remove the anchor before the feeling starts to ebb away, as Figure 8-1 illustrates. Setting an anchor can take a bit of practice, so keep trying.

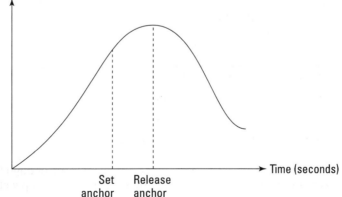

**Figure 8-1:**
Timing the
setting of an
anchor.

7. **Return to the present and shake off the memory.**

   Think about something completely different for a minute or two – like your plans for the weekend.

8. **Test out your anchor.**

   While you're still thinking about the weekend (for example), set off or *fire* your anchor. For instance, press your thumb and index finger together.

   What happens? Do you experience the good feeling you associated with your anchor?

   If so, congratulations! You now have a fantastic tool to take around with you anywhere you need it. Just fire your anchor and you'll have that positive emotion you need.

   If you didn't get the emotion you wanted when you fired the anchor, then there's just a little more work to do.

   - First, try again, making sure you are using the anchor exactly as you set it. For example, if you used your thumb and index finger together are you doing so in exactly the same place?

   - Second, if you still don't have success then go back to Step 5 and try the rest of the exercise again. Make sure that you are setting the anchor just when the feeling is intense, and before it starts to fade.

You can make changes to your anchor at any time. Maybe you' want to make it even stronger and use a new experience of the positive emotion. Maybe you find there's a slightly different positive emotion that would be more useful to you and you want to reset it using a previous time you have felt that way. All you need to do is carefully run through this exercise and you'll be able to choose to have a good emotion when you might have had a bad one.

Businesses are often frenetic, fast-paced, and taxing places to be. From time to time you may find unwinding after a long, hard day's work a real challenge. So set some feel-good anchors based on your senses to help feel more relaxed as soon as you come home. Some possible anchors include:

- ✔ The sound of a favourite piece of music
- ✔ The smell of fragranced candles
- ✔ A picture from a favourite holiday
- ✔ The experience of being in a particular place

Whatever anchor you choose, make sure it's strong enough to help you to create the state you need to enjoy your evening, sleep well, and awake refreshed.

## Hovercraft Harry

I spent some time with Harry, a coaching client, exploring how he felt when he was working at his best. He soon discovered that a metaphor worked easily for him. When Harry was working at his best he felt like a hovercraft, moving efficiently and quickly through the waves. Harry's hovercraft could turn and take a different tack, and go through the waves sideways.

As Harry talked about his hovercraft, I saw changes in him. He smiled, his eyes brightened, his face glowed with a little more colour, his gestures became more expansive, and he moved a lot in his chair. Harry didn't describe his feelings in words, but he knew he was experiencing a very different emotional state.

After our talk, Harry rushed to the Internet and downloaded a picture of a hovercraft. He put the image by his desk. It became an anchor; he only had to look at the picture to feel how he needed to in order to work at his best.

# *Building more powerful resources: Chaining anchors*

In some instances, setting a new anchor (see the preceding section, 'Setting new anchors') is enough to help you get the feeling you need in a challenging situation.

However, at other times you may need to bring up one feeling, then another and another in order to get through a difficult situation. In NLP, *chained anchors* are anchors that you link together to create a chain reaction. Each anchor is the trigger for the next. They allow you to move between one emotional state and another, one step at a time.

Say you want to move from anger to acceptance in a difficult situation. Making this change with a single anchor, when your anger's probably quite strong, may be asking too much of your system. Instead, you can move towards the state of acceptance through a chain of anchors. For example:

1. **Identify the current trigger that sends you into a negative emotional state.**

   For example. the trigger that sends you into an angry state may be something you see or hear or a sensation you have.

2. **Identify another feeling that you want to have instead of the negative emotion.**

   For example, rather than angry, you can feel surprised. Notice that surprise isn't acceptance (your ultimate goal), but is a potentially less volatile and negative emotion than anger.

3. **Use the anchoring technique that appears in the preceding section, 'Setting new anchors', to set a more positive anchor.**

   In this instance, take yourself back to a time when you were surprised. Relive the experience and get the feeling in your body. Anchor this feeling by touching your arm.

4. **Think of another state that may be useful in proceeding to your goal.**

   Perhaps you identify curiosity as a more positive and useful state than anger. Think back to a time when you were curious. Relive the experience and get the feeling in your body. Anchor this feeling by touching a different place on your arm.

5. **Think about your ultimate desired emotion or state.**

   If your final goal is acceptance, recall a time when you felt acceptance. Relive the experience and get the feeling in your body. Anchor this feeling by touching a third place on your arm.

6. **Take yourself back to the original, negative experience and go through your newly created chain of anchors.**

   For example:

   - As soon as you get the signal that leads you to feel angry, fire your first anchor (for surprise).

   - As the feeling of surprise increases, press the part of your arm that anchors your second emotion or state (curiosity).

   - And as curiosity builds, fire your final acceptance anchor.

There isn't any limit on how many anchors you can chain. However, whatever you decide to do needs to be practical and manageable. If you need to kick in your positive emotion fairly quickly, you probably don't want to have to fire a chain of 17 anchors! If this is a positive emotion you wish to be able to access when others might be watching, you'll want to fire your anchors discreetly – more difficult if you have a large quantity. Bear in mind that in this case you'll also want your anchors to be quite subtle, otherwise your colleagues might start to wonder what on earth you are doing!

Setting an effective anchor can take a bit of practice – and chaining anchors can take even longer. If at first you don't succeed, don't give up! After you establish a chain of anchors and are able to move through the sequence smoothly, fire the chain frequently and regularly. Over time, you'll build this chain reaction to become automatic.

Consider going through the chaining process with someone else – such as a colleague, friend, or associate who wants to experiment with setting anchors. When another person guides you steadily through the process, giving the instructions at each stage, it can help you to access and intensify your desired positive emotions. You may find that you will chain anchors faster and more effectively when working together.

# *Pulling out the heavy artillery: Stacking anchors*

Stacking anchors is quite straightforward after you understand how to set anchors (see the section 'Setting new anchors', earlier in this chapter).

In the sections 'Setting new anchors' and 'Building more powerful resources: Chaining anchors', I only talk about changing one state or feeling into a positive one. In some situations, you may need to do much more – stacking anchors is a good tool to turn to for this.

Consider the following example. Victoria has a difficult meeting coming up with a customer. The customer has made quite clear he's unhappy with recent service from her company. Victoria needs to be in a good state for the meeting. Specifically, she believes she needs to be:

- ✔ Curious
- ✔ Confident
- ✔ Calm
- ✔ Assertive

Victoria prepares for the meeting by reconnecting with, and anchoring, each feeling in turn (see the section 'Setting new anchors', earlier in this chapter). However, she uses the same movement and place on her body to anchor each one, which in effect *stacks* the various positive anchors. When Victoria fires her anchor prior to the meeting, she accesses a powerful set of resources all together, which helps her achieve a positive outcome to the meeting.

Stacked anchors are very useful for specific situations like the one described above. If you set a stacked anchor be careful where you use it – if you fire it in a setting where you don't need all of the same emotions you may be surprised at the results you get!

# *Removing negative anchors*

The problem with many naturally occurring anchors (see the section 'Discovering anchors', earlier in this chapter) is that they're really unhelpful. You have a lot more control over your emotions, behaviour, and the results you get when you can remove key *negative anchors* – those that immediately trigger you into a negative emotion such as annoyance – that hold you back.

The following sections offer a couple of approaches for removing negative anchors.

### Desensitising yourself

*Desensitising* requires you to get yourself in a neutral state first. It may help to close your eyes, breathe deeply and relax, so thing seems quiet and still. You are aiming for a calm, detached state where you are not having any strong emotions.

Then, you gradually introduce the problem in small doses, increasing its intensity until the experience isn't a problem, or at least is a much more manageable one.

One client of mine had a fear of spiders. About to travel to Australia on business, she was becoming very anxious about confronting poisonous spiders. At our first meeting I first introduced dome information about spiders, then some black-and-white pictures of Australian spiders, followed by colour images. We repeated this work in a second meeting, when she also watched a short video of a spider, first from the other side of the room, then a bit closer, then closer still. I continued to build up her exposure to spiders by emailing pictures and snippets until she managed a trip to the zoo to see some live spiders. She travelled successfully and didn't embarrass herself with her hosts.

### Collapsing anchors

Anchors *collapse* when you have two opposite feelings anchored, and you fire both anchors at the same time. Your nervous system just can't hold two conflicting states at once so becomes very confused. The good news is that all this confusion changes the negative feeling. If your positive feeling is the stronger of the two, you'll find you negative feeling collapsing into the positive.

Here's how you collapse two anchors:

1. **Think of a negative feeling you want to lose, and a positive replacement you want to have instead.**

    The positive feeling needs to be strong. You should aim for something stronger than the negative feeling. So if you want to counter lethargy with enthusiasm, make sure you can recall a time when you had unbounded enthusiasm for something.

2. **Remember a time when you experienced the selected positive feeling.**

    Re-experience that time. Use your memories and senses to create an intense feeling and anchor it. (See the section 'Setting new anchors', earlier in this chapter.)

3. **After re-experiencing the positive feeling for a minute or two, shake it off by thinking about something else, such as where you'd like to take a holiday, or try moving around for a minute or so.**

**4. Test the positive anchor to make sure it works.**

See the section 'Setting new anchors', earlier in this chapter, for more information on testing anchors.

If the new positive anchor isn't strong enough, find another time when you felt the selected positive feeling and continue building the anchor.

**5. Repeat Steps 2–4 for the negative feeling, finding a different anchor. Make sure your anchor is different to the one for your positive feeling. If you are using touch, press a different arm, hand, ear or whatever you choose.**

**6. Fire both anchors simultaneously.**

Hold the two anchors until you experience only a positive feeling. You may experience confusion along the way, perhaps for a few minutes or no time at all.

**7. Test out what happens now when you think about the negative feeling.**

Is the negative feeling still easy to access? If so, you may need to repeat Steps 1–6, making sure you anchor your positive feeling even more strongly.

**8. Imagine a future situation where you expect to have the negative feeling.**

As you think about that situation now, imagining what you might be seeing and hearing, how do you feel? What difference does this make to how you anticipate the situation?

## *Preparing for success: Future pacing*

When you want to have just the right state for a future experience, you can rehearse the event in advance by running an imaginary video in your mind. In NLP, this technique is called *future pacing*.

When you watch top-class athletes preparing for their sprint, jump, or throw, they're likely to be running mental videos of their hoped-for great performances. You can do the same in your professional life – and maybe find yourself climbing the corporate ladder in leaps and bounds!

Maybe you say that you're *not* looking forward to something. Chances are what you mean is that you *have* looked forward to something in your mind's eye and didn't much like what you foresaw. You may, for instance, imagine a forthcoming job interview and immediately find yourself anchored back into the last interview that went less than well. So you start to feel nervous, tense, and maybe defeatist – well before the upcoming interview happens.

*Circle of excellence* is a great NLP tool to use in anticipation of an important event. It makes sure that you can anchor all the feelings that you may need in advance, and then mentally rehearse the event with all those good feelings in place. You program your mind for success. What a great state to have!

You have to stand up and move around a little to do this technique, so you may want to find a quiet place without interruptions, such as a secluded room at work or some quiet space at home. Make sure you have a square metre or more to move in. Like all the anchoring techniques in this chapter, going through the following process with a colleague or friend can make the technique even more powerful.

1. **Think about an important upcoming meeting or event.**

   Choose something that you want to go really well. Identify up to three feelings you want to have in this situation. For example, you may be about to have a performance review with your boss and are feeling very anxious about her feedback. Maybe you'd like to feel optimistic, calm and self-assured instead.

2. **Stand up and imagine a circle on the floor in front of you.**

   Make the circle as large as you like in your mind's eye – as long as it's big enough for you to stand in.

3. **Remember a time when you had the first of the feelings you want.**

   See what you saw then through your own eyes. Hear any sounds and voices, and feel what you felt. Step into your circle with this feeling..

4. **As soon as the feeling is strong, anchor it with your fingers or hands.**

   See the section 'Setting new anchors', earlier in this chapter.

5. **Step out of your circle and shake off the feelings you now have.**

   Walk around and think of something else for a couple of minutes or more.

6. **Repeat Steps 3–5 for each feeling you want, stacking these resources on top of each other.**

   See the section 'Pulling out the heavy artillery: Stacking anchors', earlier in this chapter.

7. **Think about your future event and step back into your circle. Fire your anchor. Imagine the situation.**

   Notice what's changed and how you now feel.

# Generating Positive Feelings in Others

People set anchors for each other in lots of ways, without even realising they're doing this. A voice, a word, a face, or a particular facial expression induces different states in others. You may find yourself reacting to a person without even knowing much about her, just because they trigger an anchor in you.

Have you ever noticed that names can trigger feelings in you? Get introduced to someone who has the same name as someone you dislike, and you may find yourself battling with a negative feeling when you only just met this new person!

Sometimes you haven't even set the anchor yourself, but you fire one that someone or something else set long before. I've met people who react very badly to a particular tone of voice, which takes them straight back to the feeling they had when being told off by a parent or teacher. All this is out of conscious awareness but can generate a powerful negative reaction.

Locations can provide anchors too. When something great or bad happens in a particular place, being in that location again may trigger the original emotions. In business people have many meetings to discuss the same initiative or problem, yet see few signs of progress. Ever noticed how in regular meetings people tend always to sit in the same places? After the people involved get stuck with something, they stay stuck from meeting to meeting, anchored into this unresourceful state.

So creating anchors that are useful for others is a positive thing to do – for yourself, your co-workers, and your organisation. The following sections offer several techniques for anchoring others.

In business, you need to be constructive as well as creative when anchoring others. Anything else is manipulative – and funnily enough, just doesn't seem to work. Remember that anchoring is a natural process – you are setting anchors in others whether you intend to or not. So why not make them good ones?

## Providing a positive anchor for someone else

You can set up useful anchors for other people in a number of ways. For example, in a one-to-one session, you may coach a colleague through the anchoring process to develop some positive anchors for a forthcoming event, or as a general state. See the section 'Setting new anchors', earlier in this chapter.

Alternatively, you may not want to be so explicit. For example, if you're in a meeting and you think you can achieve your mutual objectives better if a colleague accesses a particular state, then you can work discreetly to set some anchors for that person.

Here follows some different approaches you can use for anchoring a feeling in another person, or even several at once.

1. **Prior to a meeting, select a subtle anchor that you plan to use.**

   Some appropriate and effective anchors you may use with others include:

   • **Space.** If it's the kind of meeting where you can move around, sit or stand in a particular part of the room. For example, you could stand up by a white board, if you've been sitting, or take a seat, when you've been standing.

   • **Words, phrases, and metaphors.** Use a word or phrase that you're unlikely to use elsewhere in the conversation, It could be anything, as long as it makes sense in the context. It could be positive words such as 'excellent', exceptional' or 'astounding'. Alternatively you might use a metaphor such as 'volcano', 'singing' or 'clockwork'.

   • **Posture or a movement.** Do something that you don't normally do in this kind of discussion (such as stretch your arms out).

   • **An image.** Use a picture, diagram, or illustration that you can draw or point to on a wall, desk or screen .

2. **Prior to your meeting, work out what emotion or feeling you want to anchor in your colleague.**

   Appropriate emotions or feelings may be something like:

   • Confidence

   • Excitement

   • Curiosity

3. **Link an anchor from Step 1 with a feeling or emotion from Step 2.**

4. **Whenever you see your colleague(s) demonstrate the desired emotion, use your selected anchor.**

   You need to use the selected anchor a number of times – probably at least four.

5. **Next time you think your colleague needs this positive feeling, fire the anchor.**

   If firing the anchor doesn't work, repeat Step 4 until you build a strong enough anchor and fire the anchor again.

Alex, one of my coaching clients, was lacking in confidence. A purchasing manager with considerable responsibility in a large hospitality provider, Alex put almost all her colleagues on a pedestal. As a result she felt overawed and intimidated and didn't recognise or value her own skills and contribution to the business. Alex was timid in meetings and completely overworked as she took on more and more projects in the hope of being recognised. Instead, what Alex's colleagues saw was a nervous, stressed individual who didn't seem able to get through her workload.

During the course of our very first coaching session, I discovered that Alex was a fan of extreme sports and spent her holidays taking major risks. Her next trip was to spend two weeks learning how to be a cowgirl in the USA. As Alex talked about her wild leisure pursuits her whole state changed. Rather than being nervous and apologetic – as Alex was when she discussed work – she held her head high, smiled and described how confident she felt when pursuing her activities. I smiled too, nodded a lot and just said "Wow! A cowgirl." a couple of times.

When our conversation returned to Alex's difficulties in the workplace, and her voice and body language all went back to the anxious, struggling Alex, I said: 'Yes, you do have a lot of issues. *And*, you're a cowgirl . . .'. I didn't have to finish the sentence. Alex laughed, changed her posture and started to speak with confidence again. She then started to reflect on her work successes, and talk about those with confidence. She gradually realised that she had a lot to offer, and by thinking about the out-of-work Alex, she could start to feel more confident. And all that was without me telling her anything about anchoring or what I had done with her.

What you are doing is quite supportive, and after all, a naturally occurring process – people set anchors with each other unconsciously all the time So even if your colleague gets a sense that you are doing something to help him have a more positive feeling, he is not likely to be concerned. If he really doesn't want to change how he's feeling (occasionally you may come across someone who feels most comfortable in a negative state), then he won't.

## Changing unhelpful anchors

People have anchored responses to other people. These automatic responses are of course outside most people's conscious awareness.

However, you may notice that in meetings some people's ideas are always listened to, while others' are dismissed despite their quality. Those who seem to get heard most may well have good anchors with others in the team.

By extension, other people's responses to you are sometimes anchored. Triggering a positive emotion in someone else is really helpful. Working with and influencing that person is easier. If some kind of negative anchor has been inadvertently set up, though, things may be more difficult.

When you become aware that a relationship at work isn't going as well as you want, think about how you want the other person to feel when she's dealing with you. As you use the techniques in other chapters of this book to improve your influence, watch out for an occasion when you improve your rapport and the other person seems to be in a good state. Set an anchor (maybe a word, smile, gesture, or movement) and repeat this anchor again when you can. You're soon able to develop a strong enough anchor to collapse the previous unhelpful one. For example, if a colleague has experienced a negative feeling whenever she sees you arrive in her office, find an opportunity to set an anchor – maybe a big smile and gesture with high praise of some work she is proud of. Next time you walk in her office smile and use the gesture.

I once reported to someone who had a few stock sporting phrases that he used continually to motivate the team. These were phrases like 'Let's play hardball' and 'It's a game of two halves'. This was about the sum total of his attempts to support or motivate those who reported to him. He offered no help and was quick to criticise any one of us publicly when anything went wrong. The sporting expressions became negative anchors. My response was the opposite of what he intended. I became irritated, demotivated, and disinterested in working with him. I hadn't discovered NLP then, so I made the only change I knew how and found myself a new job as quickly as possible.

## *Anchoring groups*

After you explore anchoring yourself and another person, you can develop your own creative ideas about how to set positive anchors in a group – for the entire group.

The following anchoring techniques are useful when you're presenting to a group:

- ✔ Find a space on the stage or room where you don't normally stand, such as the right hand side or in front of the stage area rather than on it. Occupy this space only for any bad news that you have to deliver.

- ✔ If you have to speak after someone who's been giving bad news, or whose presentation wasn't well received, stand in a different position to her.

✔ Stand in different places to represent a timeline. Talk about the past while standing in one place, talk about the present in another, and move somewhere else to discuss the future. You can move people out of how they're feeling now into the more positive state you want them to have about the future.

✔ Suggest to the audience that they remember a time when they were successful (or motivated or confident or whatever emotion you want to create). Use your words to build and intensify that state, then set an anchor. See the section 'Providing a positive anchor for someone else', earlier in this chapter, for some ideas.

TIP

# Anchoring your outcomes

You can use anchors in many different ways to channel your emotions in order to positively guide what you do and say when influencing others. And don't forget – anchors help you to influence yourself too!

After you glean enough from this book to start making the great changes you want in your life and work, consider setting yourself an anchor for your outcome or objective. For example, you can use:

✔ A picture in a prominent place (the fridge, your screensaver, your notebook)

✔ A key phrase or word that you can say to yourself, write down, or put in a prominent place

✔ Even a copy of this book on your desk or bookcase!

# Part III
# Leading People to Perform

The 5th Wave                    By Rich Tennant

"I've always been impressed with Larry's ability to control his audience."

## In this part . . .

If maximising the performance and potential of the people you work with is your main concern, then this is the part for you. In these chapters I explain the value of emotional intelligence in inspiring and enthusing others, even those who pose particular problems. I also talk you through the business of constructing valuable feedback and show you how to make the most of coaching.

# Chapter 9

# Leading from Within: Managing Your Emotions

*L*eading others can be hard – especially when you're battling to manage what's happening in your own body and mind.

Leading comes from within. If you can lead yourself to be more effective, happy, productive, and satisfied, then you can be in a better place to do the same with others. You may say, 'But I'm not a leader. I don't have people working for me or reporting to me.' That's not how I see things. Your behaviour affects everyone you deal with at work, whether you officially lead them or not.

How you're feeling influences your behaviour – what you say and do in any situation. What your general disposition is, and what your frame of mind at a particular moment is, may seem to be out of your control. But just imagine how different life may be when you discover ways of managing how you're feeling, easily and effortlessly.

In Chapter 8, I look at how to choose particular emotions or feelings for dealing with certain challenging situations. In this chapter you can find out how to exert more control over your emotions and moods, thus improving your personal effectiveness and the effects you have on others.

# Experiencing Emotions in Business

Business depends on people, and humans are emotional beings, so plenty of emotion is running around in the workplace. Everyone brings moods and feelings into work. These moods affect how everyone works – what you think, what you say, and what you do.

Without doubt your behaviour at work affects your colleagues. They may respond well, badly, or indifferently, depending on:

- What you do or say (your behaviour).
- What they think you mean by what you do or say (their filters). People always consider behaviours through their own filters; go to Chapter 4 for more.
- What emotions they have themselves.

## Emotional intelligence

The term *emotional intelligence* has a history stretching back to the 1960s, but it only came into general use in the 1990s, following Daniel Goleman's popular books on the subject.

In *The New Leaders* (Time-Warner, 2003), Goleman and his co-authors develop a model of emotional intelligence based on the following four dimensions:

- **Self-awareness,** which includes being able to read your own emotions and recognise their impact, using your gut feelings to guide decisions, knowing your own strengths and weaknesses, and having a strong sense of self-worth.

- **Self-management,** which includes controlling your emotions and impulses, adapting to changing circumstances, and being ready to act and seize opportunities.

- **Social awareness,** which includes sensing, understanding, and reacting to another's

emotions; understanding social networks; working with politics at the organisational level; and recognising and responding to others' needs.

- **Relationship management,** which includes inspiring, influencing, and developing others; building co-operation; and initiating and leading change.

Goleman suggests that your ability to succeed in life is rooted in these four aspects of emotional intelligence, as much as your intellect or IQ. During my experiences at working with people in business, I too have noticed how people manage and use emotions to drive thought, decision making, and behaviour determines whether they have good relationships, excel at work, and feel fulfilled. NLP offers a range of practical tools to enhance emotional intelligence. I introduce you to many of these techniques that you can try out, in later sections of this chapter and also in Chapter 8.

A colleague's response to you has an effect on you, how you feel and then how you behave, which in turn has an effect on the other person and on and on and on. As Figure 9-1 shows, this pattern is cyclical. You can see how emotions, whether positive or negative, can easily start to intensify.

Given the cyclical nature of human interaction, emotions can become almost infectious. A whole team can share the same or similar feelings – quite quickly at times. Rapidly spreading emotions are great when the feelings are positive, such as:

- ✔ Enthusiasm
- ✔ Optimism
- ✔ Excitement
- ✔ Pride

But when the emotions are negative, like the following, they can be really damaging to business performance.

- ✔ Stress and tension
- ✔ Anxiety
- ✔ Demotivation
- ✔ Procrastination

When negative feelings prevail, everyone tends to become more obsessed with their own position. Relationships become strained and barriers are built. Within this environment, people don't work well. Indeed, prolonged negative emotion can also harm everyone's health and well-being, which leads to people taking more time off and, even worse, experienced employees resigning to find somewhere new to work.

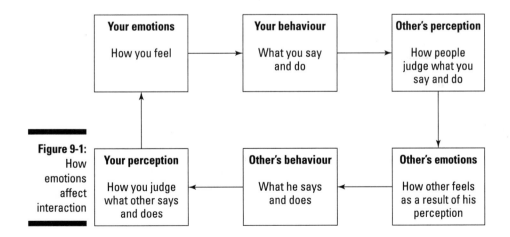

Figure 9-1:
How emotions affect interaction

**Your emotions**
How you feel

**Your behaviour**
What you say and do

**Other's perception**
How people judge what you say and do

**Your perception**
How you judge what other says and does

**Other's behaviour**
What he says and does

**Other's emotions**
How other feels as a result of his perception

# Realising the Impact of Your Emotions

People often talk about the *state* of things or people. On the news you may hear descriptions of the 'state of public services', the 'state of repair' of a famous building, or the 'state of health' of some celebrity. And never mind the old British favourite, the 'state of the weather'.

The word *state* is used to describe something's condition. Yet you may also use it in terms of people, saying someone's, for example, 'in a bad state' or 'in the right state of mind' or 'in no state to help out'.

When you use the word state, you're talking about the whole condition of a person – how he's thinking and feeling, in body and mind.

## Identifying your state

As you go about your daily life, you may notice when you're feeling absolutely on top of the world or in a particularly bad state. But you may *not* notice how you're feeling at all those moments in between the extremes.

Do you know what state you're in right now as you read this? Maybe you're feeling:

- ✔ **Curious,** wondering what exciting new things you're going to discover.
- ✔ **Uncertain,** feeling as yet unconvinced that this chapter can offer anything you can do to change your feelings in certain situations.
- ✔ **Intrigued,** anticipating finding out about handling emotions in yourself and others.
- ✔ **Impatient,** wanting to move on to something more active.

Whatever your state now – or at any given moment – becoming more aware of what's happening for you is the starting point to increasing your flexibility and having more choices.

When you feel good or the opposite, you may just describe yourself as 'in a good mood' or 'feeling out of sorts'. This kind of general description isn't very helpful for getting to know yourself. Practise putting more descriptive words to your feelings. When you are feeling good, is that because you feel happy? Optimistic? Satisfied? Energetic? Many different types of good feeling exist. Practise reflecting on what kind of emotion you have so that you know exactly what you're feeling. You can even tell others. For example your opening statement at a meeting might be: 'Good morning. I am really excited about what we are going to discuss today.' Table 9-1 describes some emotions you may experience at work and explores some subtle variations.

| Table 9-1 | Describing Feelings |
|---|---|
| *Category of emotion* | *Specific feelings* |
| Annoyance | Irritated, frustrated, exasperated, resentful, displeased, angry, aggravated, enraged, bothered, furious, infuriated, outraged, indignant |
| Pleasure | Happy, joyful, delighted, satisfied, excited, proud, grateful, fulfilled, relieved, contented, comforted |
| Fear | Worried, anxious, nervous, panicked, concerned, frightened, apprehensive, uncertain, dreading, terrified, inhibited |
| Calm | Peaceful, composed, relaxed, tranquil serene quiet, still, cool |
| Shame | Guilty, remorseful, humbled, embarrassed, disgraced, indignant mortified |
| Confidence | Certain, secure, assured, self-possessed, poised, assertive, self-believing |
| Unhappiness | Disappointed, sad, desperate, hurt, lonely, distressed, miserable, depressed, dejected |
| Lack of interest | Bored, tired, weary, demotivated, apathetic, indifferent, turned off |
| Interest | Enthusiastic, excited, optimistic, curious, attracted, fascinated, absorbed |
| Surprise | Shocked, amazed, disbelieving, in awe, astonished, incredulous bewildered, in wonder, admiring, horrified |

To effectively describe and know how you're feeling, spend some time thinking about how you felt in the past. The following exercise helps you explore past emotions in more depth:

1. **Take a few minutes to reflect on the last few weeks at work. Think back to the feelings that you have experienced (use Table 9-1 to remind yourself of different types of emotions.)**

2. **Write down each emotion you can recall having.**

   Group these emotions into 'good' feelings and 'bad' feelings. This is just your judgement, not anyone else's. If you think an emotion is useful to you at work, include it as a 'good' feeling. If an emotion seems to get in the way of you working effectively, put it in the 'bad' group.

If you have identified some feelings which you can't categorise, make a third category, called neutral.

What percentage of your time do you think you spent having good feelings?

What percentage of your time do you estimate you experienced bad feelings?

How do you feel about these percentages?

3. **Decide the percentage split between good and bad emotions that you want to experience in the future.**

Set yourself a target for each of the next three months to work steadily towards your goal. For example, you may determine that a reasonable goal is to increase the amount of time you spend having good feelings by five percentage points over each of the three months.

## *Noticing your impact*

After you spend some time identifying your emotional state (see the section 'Identifying your state', earlier in this chapter), consider how your state affects your performance and your colleagues.

What do your co-workers notice most about you? If people at work were to describe the state they think you present most of the time, what one word are they likely to use?

- Serious
- Humorous
- Happy
- Grumpy
- Intense
- Energetic
- Calm
- Aggressive
- Enthusiastic

Is the state you identify one you want to be in and be known for? Is this a useful way for people to perceive you? If not, then think about making some changes. Take a look at the section 'Building Better States', later in this chapter, for more information.

# Detecting internal conflict

Much of this book focuses on using NLP techniques to reduce *interpersonal conflict,* or conflict between two or more people. This section considers how to notice and work with the conflicts that you sometimes experience *inside yourself,* otherwise known as *intrapersonal conflicts.*

Sometimes you may be experiencing conflict without really being aware of its impact. That is, you're unaware until you start to pay attention to your body. Your body may well be storing the signs – maybe tense shoulders, a sore head, or an uncomfortable feeling in your stomach – that give you clues that something's not so good.

Examples of conflicts of emotions you may experience include:

- ✔ You feel compelled to stay late at work to finish something important, yet you really want to see your children before bedtime.

- ✔ You're excited at the prospect of retraining for a new career, but are dreading losing income while you do it.

- ✔ You're motivated to accept a promotion for the higher salary, but resent giving up the fieldwork you love.

Pay attention to the discomfort caused by such conflicts, because they can have an adverse effect on how you perform at work, as well as on your health and happiness.

In my work coaching business people, the two biggest sources of internal conflict are:

- ✔ **Work–life balance:** Working long hours, travelling, doing e-mails in personal time, and the like all add to a sense of being overwhelmed and to conflict with personal values and desires.

- ✔ **Being in the wrong job:** Many people are carried along on the wave of a career that they choose misguidedly or simply fall into. Their current careers may not fit their natural talents and personality, yet they try hard to make things work, while feeling dissatisfied in the job.

If you find yourself in one of these situations, you're probably struggling to maintain a good, positive state. The solution lies in doing one of the following:

- ✔ **Change how you think about the situation so that you can feel differently.** One way of doing this is explained in the 'Finding new meaning: reframing' section later in this chapter.

- ✔ **Change the situation.** A useful place to start would be to set a goal or outcome for what you actually want. Head to Chapter 16 to find out more about how to do this.

# Building Better States

In this section, I explore how to manage your everyday state (as opposed to creating certain emotions and feelings for particular events, which I cover in Chapter 8). Here I suggest things you can do to make quick and easy changes to how you're feeling. By making these changes, you can improve relationships and increase your success – as well as just feel good more of the time!

## Changing your physiology

Because your mind and body are connected, if you make changes to your body, your mind surely changes too.

Next time you're feeling down, pay attention to your body. Is your head down? As I explain in Chapter 5, when most people are closely engaged with their feelings they tend to look down. Most likely that's where the phrase 'feeling down' comes from – and of course when things improve, you say they're 'looking up'!

So, if you're feeling down:

- Look up.
- If you can, stand up.
- Lean back and open your chest by pulling your shoulders back.
- Move, if possible. Go for a walk or do something energetic, like running up the stairs, jumping on the spot or practising your favourite sporting pastime if you have one. Even a minute or two of doing this will make a difference.

Do you ever feel really stuck in a problem at work? Maybe you need to write something, and the words just aren't coming. Maybe you want to design something new, but you seem to be going around in circles. Or you have a problem that keeps coming back time and again, and nothing seems to change it. Try going for a walk – or if you're inclined and you have the opportunity, a run, swim, or workout. The changes that exercise creates in your body alter your state and free up your mind to be more productive. Try it and see!

If you are in a meeting with others, and get that same sensation of being stuck, find a way to get people moving. Ideas include:

- Declare you need a comfort break or a trip to get refreshments.
- Suggest that you all adjourn for 15 minutes and come back

- ✔ Start asking people to stand up t write individual contributions on a white board or similar.

- ✔ Be bold enough to announce that you believe things are not progressing and it would be good for everyone to stand up and change seats with someone else!

## Noticing the positives

When you aren't feeling in a great state, it's easy to to pay attention to all the things that are going wrong and give little credence to the stuff that's going right. So next time you're feeling down, list all the good things that are happening. Work hard at this.

If necessary to boost your list , think of the smallest positive things, such as:

- ✔ My journey to work was trouble free.

- ✔ Three people said good morning to me as I arrived today.

- ✔ My workstation is neat and tidy.

After you have a list, relive these good experiences. In your mind, see what you saw, hear what you heard, and make sure you allow your body some time to feel some pleasure at these positive events.

You can revisit positive experiences at any time of the day, until the process becomes second nature. You can make the experience even more intense and enjoyable by modifying your internal pictures, sounds, and feelings (more on this in the later section 'Changing Your Emotional Responses').

## Looking after yourself

You probably already know certain things that make you feel better. It may be more sleep, more exercise, less caffeine, healthier food, more relaxation, or something else. On the surface, all these things seem easy. In reality, if you're under pressure at work and don't feel good, you can find making such changes quite difficult.

After you read this book – even just a chapter or two – you'll know that you can make all the changes you want. As soon as you have a well-formed outcome or objective (more on this in Chapter 16), you can choose the NLP approach that you believe helps you most to build your flexibility and create the differences in your life that you want.

## *Finding new meaning: Reframing*

Humans are good at giving meaning to things they hear, see, or experience. This skill is really important. After all, if you don't know that an insistent loud alarm means fire, you don't know to evacuate the building when you hear it.

However, on some occasions, the meaning you give to something is less useful.

For example, I had a client, Julia, who complained that her colleague Bill was always late for meetings with her. For Julia, Bill's tardiness meant he didn't respect her or value her time. She was getting increasingly angry about this and then being irritable with Bill in the meetings. Julie and I considered some alternative meanings to Bill's behaviour, which in NLP is called *reframing*:

- ✔ Bill was a poor time manager and actually didn't get to *any* meetings on time.

- ✔ Bill was so customer focused that he always dealt with customer issues before leaving his desk.

- ✔ Bill believed that any phone call was a prospective new customer, so he always answered his phone on the way to a meeting and handled the call, which made him late.

- ✔ Bill didn't have a watch.

- ✔ Bill's experience was that most meetings started late in this organisation and therefore turning up late was the right thing to do in this culture.

- ✔ Bill heard the irritability in Julia's voice in the past and thought this meant she was irritated by too many meetings without a break, so by coming later, Bill was doing her a favour.

We could have gone on, but we didn't. Rather than confront Bill right now, Julia decided to try *reframing* the situation. She remembered that Bill was very conscientious and customer oriented, which was an equally good meaning for his lateness to lack of respect for her. As a result, Julia's state of anger and irritation towards Bill diminished.

You can reframe events according to the context or circumstances in which they happen – when, where, who else and any other background factors. Think about the weather – well, the British seem obsessed with it! The sun comes out and the day's gloriously hot. What does this mean to you? What does it mean to someone else?

✔ If your business makes its money selling ice cream, sunny weather means good sales.

✔ If you're a water supply company and reserves are running low, sunny weather means unhappy customers, lost water revenue, and higher costs as you impose usage restrictions.

✔ If you're about to head to the coast for a holiday weekend, sun means a fun time.

✔ If you get stuck in an overcrowded underground train with no air-conditioning, sun means extreme discomfort.

So sunshine can be good or bad, depending on what it means to you at that moment.

Next time you find yourself upset by something that happens, think about what meaning you're giving the incident that leaves you feeling bad. Then try some reframing and see what difference that makes to your state.

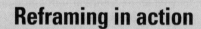

## Reframing in action

At a recent coaching meeting, I was working with Geoff on how 'not to lose it' when things didn't go his way at work.

When he reflected on what happened in his body when he was having this emotion (see the section 'Identifying your state', earlier in this chapter), he connected his feeling to an incident that happened only that morning on his way to work. In a dense crowd of people waiting to get on to a busy rush-hour underground train, Geoff stepped back to allow passengers to get off the carriage. A woman behind him suddenly started to speak angrily to him, asking him what his problem was and why he was messing about. Geoff said he felt his whole body tighten, his throat constrict, and his heart start to pump quickly as he turned to counter the accusations and aggression he was receiving.

Geoff acknowledged that he'd been feeling stressed and in a bad mood ever since. He then reframed the experience. He decided that the woman must be under intense pressure and feeling very stressed to have acted so unnecessarily badly. We brainstormed some possible explanations: maybe the woman was about to lose her job, was feeling unwell, or had just had a particularly unpleasant argument with a loved one. Whatever the problem, Geoff realised that the confrontation was *her* problem, not *his*.

As I watched Geoff physically relax and start to smile, he said, 'I'm really happy that I'm not having *her* day. And I'm certainly not going to let her stress spoil *my* day.' Within a few moments, his response to the whole event had changed and he was once more positive about his day.

Many years ago I was a manager in a company that decided cutbacks were necessary due to poor sales. Redundancies were planned, and I had to lose one of my team. I felt very bad about saying goodbye to a loyal and hard-working colleague, especially when he had a young family to feed. A year later I bumped into him at a conference. He had a new job with much more responsibility and opportunities for progression. He was very happy and told me, 'Redundancy was the best thing that ever happened to me.' His redundancy was completely reframed for me, and I felt completely different about the experience.

# Changing Your Emotional Responses

Because how you feel, act, and react is guided by your thinking, exploring what other changes you can make to your inner world to manage your state can be worthwhile.

As Chapter 5 explores in some detail, you experience the world through your five senses. You use your senses – visual (sight), auditory (hearing), kinaesthetic (feeling), olfactory (smell), and gustatory (taste) – to bring your memories to life, as well as to create and imagine new possibilities. Seeing, hearing and feeling are the predominant senses, also known in NLP terns as *modalities* – the mode or means by which things come in to, and are held by, the mind.

You can recall the face of someone special in your mind's eye, hear your own inner voice as you talk to yourself, and feel excited about an upcoming event. These are internal experiences, happening in your mind. You're not living the experience right now. So, what you see, hear, and feel isn't exactly the same as a real-life event.

Smell and taste are also used in storing memories, but not in all cases. In this Chapter I concentrate on how to change your state at work through working with remembered images, sounds and feelings. However, once you understand the techniques you can use them similarly on smell and taste.

When you describe your pictures, sounds and feelings modalities to someone else, you need to add some details and qualities to make the experience richer to the other person. For example, is the image you recall in colour or black and white, framed, with other things around it, or panoramic (filling your entire field of vision), moving or still? A sound may be loud or quiet, high or low pitched, human-made or something else. A feeling may be strong or weak, in one part of your body or another. These distinctions are called *submodalities*.

The following sections look at how these details affect you, your feelings and behaviour. I also show you how to make changes to manage your state more effectively.

## Programming your remote control

Submodalities define how you give meaning to your memories. For example, if your work was ridiculed by a superior in front of a group of colleagues, you may feel humiliated. When you remember that event, you may immediately see the face of the person talking about your work, and smiles on the faces of your colleagues. You may hear the words that were said and even a few sniggers of laughter. If those faces are right in front of your eyes in your memory, bright, in focus and large, and the voices are loud and clear, you are likely to still have very strong feelings of humiliation every time you remember. This memory means constant ongoing feelings of shame and humiliation. If the images and sounds you remember are more distant and less clear, your experience of that memory, and the meaning you give it, can be very different.

What's really interesting is that you can take control and change your submodalities. By varying the submodalities of a memory, you can make a distinctive change to how you feel about it.

You can think of this technique as being a remote control for your thoughts. Your internal representations may be digital, by which I mean you can turn them on and off. For example, a picture can be moving or still, colour or black and white. Other submodalities are analogue, meaning you can slide the controls up and down, like volume or brightness.

Practise using your emotional remote control with the following steps and see what differences you can make:

1. **Think about a very enjoyable experience you've had (at work or elsewhere).**

   Remember everything you can about the experience. Step right into it.

2. **Notice what senses you're using.**

   Do you have any pictures? Hear sounds? Get a feeling? Are smells or tastes part of the experience?

3. **Intensify the experience. Make it better. Feel it more deeply.**

   What did you do to change the experience?

   Did you make the picture closer, brighter, more vibrant? Did you turn up the volume or soften the voices? What did you do to any feeling? Did it move further or deeper into your body? Did you make it stronger?

This technique gives you a brief experience of how to make some changes through playing with your submodalities. As you went through the preceding steps, you tweaked your recording of a memory, altering it subtly yet powerfully.

Imagine how useful this can be to take away the effects of a really bad experience or something you're anticipating as unpleasant. And consider how much pleasure you can have from strengthening good experiences. Check out the following sections for more.

## Accessing memory qualities

To help you get more in touch with the submodalities of your memories, you need to think about all the possible finer distinctions – such as whether your pictures are still (like snapshots) or moving (like video clips), or you hear things clear and loud, or muffled and quiet.

The sections that follow give you some questions to ask yourself about the qualities of your different submodalities.

Although smell and taste can have very powerful effects on emotions, for the purpose of explaining how to use submodalities in business I concentrate on the visual, auditory, and kinaesthetic senses. After you understand the principles though, you can also work with the other two senses when they're an important modality of a memory.

### Visual submodalities

Many different attributes define the quality of the pictures you see in your mind's eye.

When you recall a visual image, think about the following categories and ask yourself the related questions to determine an image's characteristics.

- ✔ **Association**: Are you associated or dissociated? Are you seeing the picture as if through your own eyes, or do you see yourself in the picture? (Flip to the section 'Associating and dissociating', earlier in this chapter.)

- ✔ **Location**: Where's the picture in space? How near or far from you is it?

- ✔ **Size**: Is the image large or small?

- ✔ **Colour**: Is the image coloured or black and white?

- ✔ **Movement**: Is it a still picture or a movie?

✔ **Speed:** If moving, is it fast or slow?

✔ **Clarity:** Is the picture bright or dull? Focused or blurred?

✔ **Structure:** Is the image flat or in 3D?

✔ **Frame:** Is the image framed or panoramic? Is it in a border with space around it, or does it fill your field of vision?

 Take some time to think through some different memories, good and not so good. Explore the qualities for the visual elements in each different memory, and then ask the following questions:

✔ What patterns do you notice?

✔ Are you associated with good memories and dissociated from bad (or the other way around)?

✔ Do the things you feel bad about have similar qualities – and are they the same or different to the things you feel good about?

 After you're aware of any patterns that occur, you can very quickly move to change things by focusing on these specific visual submodalities when you're feeling bad.

### Auditory submodalities

Like images, the sounds you hear inside your head also have certain qualities.

When you recall an auditory sound in a memory, think about the following categories and ask yourself the related questions to determine a sound's characteristics.

✔ **Location:** Where do you hear the sound – inside your head or outside?

✔ **Distance:** If outside, where is the sound? How far away? Near or close?

✔ **Volume:** Is the sound loud or soft?

✔ **Tone:** Does the sound have a tone? Is it harsh, or rasping? Soft or mellow?

✔ **Clarity:** Is it a clear or muffled sound?

✔ **Pitch:** Is the sound high or low pitched?

✔ **Rhythm:** Can you hear any rhythm?

✔ **Continuity:** Is the noise continuous or intermittent?

✔ **Kind of sound:** Is it a voice, music, or some other sound? If a voice, whose voice?

When you identify a pattern of submodalities in the things you hear inside your head, try changing the experience by playing around with these sounds, changing things like volume, pitch and location and notice how this changes how you feel.

### Kinaesthetic submodalities

Like images and sounds, the feelings attached to your internal experience also have qualities.

The following are some questions to help you discover more about what's happening in your body.

- ✔ **Location:** Where in your body do you have the feeling? Head? Shoulders? Stomach?
- ✔ **Intensity:** How intense is the feeling? Strong or weak?
- ✔ **Size:** Does the feeling have a size? Big or small?
- ✔ **Shape:** Does the feeling have a shape? If so, what kind of shape?
- ✔ **Pressure:** Can you feel any pressure? Light or heavy?
- ✔ **Temperature:** Is the feeling hot, warm, or cold?
- ✔ **Texture:** Is any texture associated with the feeling? Rough or smooth?
- ✔ **Movement:** Does the feeling stay in one place or does it move around?
- ✔ **Duration:** Does the feeling last or is it short-lived?

Once you've noticed feelings in your body associated with various memories, you may notice that there are some commonalties or patterns. Again you can start to experiment with you body to make some changes. For example, if you detect tenseness in parts of your body, make a conscious effort to breathe deeply and relax tense muscles.

## Fine-tuning memories to change experiences

How you remember things and the effect that memory has on you often have much more to do with a few *critical submodalities* than what actually happened.

What I mean is that changing some of the qualities of a memory makes no difference to how you feel. while changing others can be more critical.

You need to experiment with a few memories to find out what your critical submodalities are. Consider a couple of scenarios that illustrate this process:

> **Scenario:** Sasha had a little too much to drink at an office party. She lost her inhibitions and asked the managing director to dance. In her inebriated and over-enthusiastic state, she toppled them both over on the dance floor. Sasha was mortified. Months later, she keeps recalling the incident, seeing the look of horror on the MD's face as he struggled to stand up that night. The picture of his face is close, very large and clear. She can hear the music playing. She then feels numbness in her head and a tightening in her stomach.

To find a more positive way to deal with the memory, Sasha needs to change the submodalities – how she is remembering it. For example, she can try to turn the music off. If this doesn't seem to alter how she feels, she can move on to the MD's face. When she pushes the face further away, making it smaller and reducing the brightness, she finds that her stomach eases and her head feels much better. Over time, she remembers the incident far less often and even has a philosophical attitude to this piece of history.

> **Scenario:** John doesn't get on well with his boss. Whenever he thinks about her, he sees her face then hears her voice in his head. She's pointing out what he's done wrong. Sharp, shrill, and loud, the voice talks into his left ear incessantly. Energy drains from his body, and he feels lower back pain whenever he's scheduled to meet her.

John can work to change the modalities associated with his boss's voice in his head. First he moves it further away, to sound more distant. Then he changes the pitch, so it's lower and easier on his ear. Next he dials down the volume, until he can barely hear it.

Now when John thinks of his boss, he stills sees her face but the voice – the really powerful part of the memory for John – is barely discernible. He's lost all the bad feelings in his body. John feels much easier when around his boss and is now able to work on improving their relationship.

Think of an experience you've had – at work or elsewhere – that you're feeling bad about, and maybe have been for some time. Life will be better when you can leave this experience behind and stop having these negative feelings. Then take the following steps:

1. **Remember the incident.**

   See what you saw at that time, hear what you heard, and get in. touch with the feelings that this memory gives you.

2. **Look at the picture or images you have. Change the picture, one sub-modality at a time.**

   Use the list of visual submodalities from the previous section, 'Accessing memory qualities', to prompt you to check each possible change you can make. Once you have tried each change, return the image to how you first remembered it.

3. **Listen to the sounds you can hear associated with this experience. Change the sounds, one submodality at a time.**

   Use the list of auditory submodalities from the previous section, 'Accessing memory qualities', to help you identify changes to make. Following each change, make sure you revert the sounds to how you originally read them in your mind.

4. **Feel all the physical sensations in your body resulting from remembering this experience. Change the feelings, one submodality at a time.**

   Use the list of kinaesthetic submodalities from the previous section, 'Accessing memory qualities', to guide you. Once you have made each submodality change, return each feeling to how and where it was at the start of the exercise.

5. **Remembering which of the submodalities you changed made the most difference (the critical submodalities), make these changes again, only this time don't change them back.**

   Notice how your feelings about this bad experiences have now altered. You may even find yourself thinking 'What bad experience?'!

## Associating and dissociating

You can turn your feelings up or down by altering how you relate to a memory. Ask yourself if you experience the memory as if you're reliving it or as if you're viewing the experience from elsewhere.

- ✔ When you see a past event as if you're looking out of your own eyes, you're *associated* with it.

- ✔ If you visualise yourself in your picture, as if you're looking at a photo or a home movie, then you're *dissociated*.

When you associate yourself into a picture, you usually find that your feelings are much stronger. This experience is helpful when you want to *increase* the intensity of a positive experience, but associating can make a negative experience considerably worse.

Sometimes people find associating with an experience very difficult – and sometimes dissociating with an experience can be hard as well. Yet both ways of relating are very useful when you want to have more control over your emotions.

The following exercise can help you test how well you dissociate:

1. **Think of a situation you're unhappy about at work.**

   Reflect on the situation as you usually do. Notice the critical visual, auditory, and kinaesthetic submodalities in how you think about it For example, you may find that altering the tone of an internal voice, or changing an image from colour to black and white, make a significant change to how you feel about the experience. Find more on this in the preceding section, 'Fine-tuning memories to change experiences'.

2. **If you aren't already, make sure that you're associated with your memory of the situation.**

   Try to see the situation through your own eyes. Does the experience seem more intense?

3. **Imagine yourself seeing and hearing the situation from the outside, in a dissociated state.**

   Set up the memory as if you're looking at a photograph of yourself or watching a movie in which you're the star.

   What has changed in your experience of the memory? How do you feel about the situation now?

Like all the techniques and tools in this book, the preceding may take a little practice before you master it. So give yourself some time and come back and try the technique again later if you need to. It's worth persevering. You can't change history but you can change how you organise your memories. Letting go of any unhelpful feelings you have, left over from bad experiences, frees you to be more resourceful and take much more positive actions in the future.

## *Making good use of your inner voice*

We all have an internal voice, and controlling that voice when it gives you a hard time isn't easy. Think for a moment about how you generally talk to yourself. Is your inner voice kind, encouraging, and upbeat – or do you tend to be self-critical?

You can try changing the talk from negative to positive, but a negative inner voice can be a hard habit to break. And of course, when you do something that you truly regret or that transgresses your values, talking things up is pretty hard.

You can have more say in what's happening with your inner voice after you're aware of its submodalities. Ask yourself the following questions about your inner voice:

- **Location:** Whereabouts do you hear the voice (Behind you? In one ear? Far away or near? )
- **Whose voice:** Is it your voice – or does it sound like someone else? If someone else, is it someone specific?
- **Volume:** Does the voice sound loud or quiet?
- **Tone:** Is the tone encouraging or warm, critical or scathing?
- **Pitch:** Does the voice sound high or low pitched?
- **Content:** Is the voice talking about you or others? What is it saying?
- **Time:** Is the talk about the past, now, or the future?

After you know more about your self-talk, experiment with what you can change about it. For example, what happens when you turn the volume down? How does changing the tone from critical to supportive help? What happens when you change the voice and you hear your words sounding like they're spoken by Donald Duck rather than you?!

Experiment with sliding the controls on the submodalities of your inner voice when it's overly critical. And do the same with that voice when it's working with you, by dialling everything up to be louder and more intense. Notice the difference that doing this makes to your state.

ANECDOTE

# Picture-perfect presentations

Craig, a client contract manager I coached, wanted to be confident in front of his main contacts at the client organisation, a financial services company. This was a major contract for Craig's company, and he was solely responsible for supporting the client.

Craig had to present to the group of 5 client staff regularly, but each time, he got flustered and tongue-tied during the presentation and then waffled endlessly when answering client questions.

Craig explained that he prepared well for each presentation, making sure he had all the facts and anticipating difficult questions. However, as he walked into the room he remembered the facial expressions of the group at a particularly difficult meeting in which he had shared bad news. This image was bright and strong, just in front of his eyes. As Craig saw this image, he started to feel all the nerves and bad feelings associated with that previous experience. Not a great place to begin a new presentation from, even though he had a positive message to share!

Craig decided to make some changes to the submodalities of his memory. He imagined himself just about to start a meeting and saw a picture of the faces. First, he toned down the brightness of the picture. Then he gradually moved the whole scene further away and to the left in his field of vision. Finally, he made it black and white. Craig started to feel better now that this unhelpful picture was hardly visible. He then remembered an occasion when the client group were all smiling and nodding. Craig then brought this picture up close and large, so it almost filled his field of vision. He saw it very clearly, and made the colours bright. He immediately felt calmer, confident and even slightly excited about the future meeting.

Just before Craig arrived for his next client meeting, the old picture came to mind. This time, he practised what he had done in coaching, and changed the brightness, colour, and location of the picture. He then remembered his bright, colourful picture with the entire group of clients smiling, and nodding. He brought this picture very close and made it large. Craig then felt confident, presented well, gave a good impression, and created a really positive meeting.

# Chapter 10

# Inspiring and Motivating with Artfully Vague Language

· · · · · · · · · · · · · · · · · · · · · · · · · · · · · · · · · · · · · · · · · · · · · · · · ·

· · · · · · · · · · · · · · · · · · · · · · · · · · · · · · · · · · · · · · · · · · · · · · · · ·

*Y*ou may have noticed how politicians and leaders inspire people with their words (well, some politicians anyway!). You may well have been enthused by passionate and articulate speeches.

But do you ever notice, when you think about the content later, that all those wonderful words don't really contain much detail or information?

Being able to inspire and engage people is one of the key requirements of modern-day leadership. Whether you're leading from the top of an organisation or you need to persuade, influence, and guide colleagues from a lower position in the hierarchy, *you can't not influence.* (I explore this principle in more depth in Chapter 3.) So why not influence in a way that's positive and motivational?

In this chapter I reveal the secrets of linguistic dexterity to help you inspire and motivate others — in one-to-one communications, informal meetings, and in formal presentations.

# Engaging Hearts and Minds: The Milton Model of Communication

Research into communication suggests that words form only 7 per cent of the total message when you communicate, with your voice tone and body language taking the lion's share (more on this in Chapter 4).

However, that 7 per cent still makes a big impression and directly affects the results you get. And this power doesn't only lie in the words themselves. How you structure or phrase what you say can be just as important as the actual words.

## Modelling a powerful influencer

When Richard Bandler and John Grinder, the originators of NLP (see Chapter 1), first began researching and modelling exceptionally successful influencing skills, they heard about a therapist, Milton H. Erickson, who was known to get outstanding changes in his clients. Erickson was a leading practitioner of hypnotherapy at the time. Take a glance at the sidebar 'Meet Magnificent Milton' for more on this influential man.

Bandler and Grinder spent a considerable time observing and listening to Erickson working therapeutically with individual clients. They discovered that Erickson was really effective when speaking in a way that they described as *artfully vague*. By being vague, Erickson was allowing his clients to take the meaning from his words that worked for *them*. Being vague in this way was a real strength, Erickson's speech was full of a number of linguistic tricks, but three types in particular stood out:

- ✔ Deletions (see the following section, 'Leaving stuff out: Deletions')
- ✔ Distortions (see the following section, 'Making your own interpretation: Distortions')
- ✔ Generalisations (see the following section, 'Compiling patterns: Generalisations')

Additionally, Erickson used a few extra, similarly subtle tricks ('Employing other powerful patterns', later in this chapter, gives more detail) and included a lot of stories (flick over to 'Metaphorically speaking: Stories', also later in this chapter) in his communication.

# Meet Milton H Erickson

Milton H. Erickson (1901–1980) was a renowned psychotherapist. He is considered by many therapists the most influential hypnotherapist of all time, achieving fast and meaningful changes in his patients . His unconventional approach to psychotherapy gave rise to what he named *brief therapy*. The name says everything. Erickson helped his patients to make changes and resolve their problems in a relatively short amount of time, particularly compared to most other therapeutic techniques being used at the time.

The heart of Erickson's work relies on *trance,* a naturally occurring phenomenon through which a therapist can talk to the unconscious mind. But rather than trance being artificially created, as you may have seen in stage hypnosis, Erickson believed that people naturally went into trance throughout the day – by engaging in activities such as reading, listening, taking exercise, or even just waiting for a train.

Erickson was largely self-taught and developed some of his techniques through his own life experiences. In particular, he developed ways of overcoming a range of adversities, including extreme polio-induced paralysis which he contracted aged only 17. A wise and skilful man, Erickson was the founder of the American Society for Clinical Hypnosis and held fellowships with many eminent psychiatric and psychological associations.

Erickson's methods inspired Richard Bandler and John Grinder to systematise critical ideas from his work as part of NLP. Thanks to Bandler and Grinder, many more people have come to utilise Erickson's genius in tools that help them create change and communicate more effectively – in all areas of life, not just one-to-one therapy.

Through his artful vagueness, Erickson achieved several effects including:

- Bringing about a trance (I reveal all in 'Creating a receptive audience: The nature of trance').

- Directly accessing the unconscious mind (influencing that part of the mind that is outside of our awareness but is driving much of how we think, act and react - more about this can be found in Chapter 4).

- Having people's unconscious minds make sense of what he was saying by filling in all their own specific details to fit with their own thinking.

Erickson's verbal dexterity led to powerful changes for the client in therapy, where major issues, phobias and unhelpful patterns of thinking were resolved.

Like many aspects of NLP, Bandler and Grinder were able to study the excellent skills of an outstanding influencer in one context and create a model that others can use in a wide array of situations, including business. This is known as the *Milton Model,* in honour of Erickson.

## *Creating a receptive audience:*
## *The nature of trance*

How many times have you been in a presentation and found that your mind has wandered and you've missed a few minutes? This experience is what NLP practitioners call *trance*. In fact, you're likely to experience this slightly absent state many times a day.

Trance can come on in many situations, including:

- ✔ When driving
- ✔ In meetings
- ✔ When reading
- ✔ While listening to a conference call
- ✔ When sitting on a train or bus
- ✔ When sitting at your workstation

Generating trance in your audience through language patterns is a key aspect of the Milton Model. In this state, your listeners become much more receptive to your words.

If the idea of trance alarms you, let me reassure you: it doesn't give you the power to make your boss cluck like a chicken (and only you can decide if that's a good thing or not!).

Going into trance – or eliciting trance in others – is something everyone does frequently. You just may not realise it! Trance isn't a state in which you are passive – you are totally in control, and most certainly not under another's influence. This misconception – and understandable fear of trance – comes from the use of stage hypnosis.

The Milton model is a tool you can use when you want people to be able to construct their own sense of what you are saying so that it will work for them. By mastering those techniques employed by Erickson, you too can use the structure of what you say – and what you don't say – to take someone into trance and help him fill in the details that work for him. I'll introduce you to Milton language structures in the later section 'Pulling the Right Words out of Your Hat'.

I train groups of people in organisations in leadership, influencing and other key skills. At the start of a training day I present a précis of what the delegates will learn about, and the benefits they will receive, from attending on that day. I will talk for around four to eight minutes giving this brief introduction. To summarise a day into a few minutes, before attendees have had the experience, I delete, distort and generalise the information. By the time I finish I usually have a group of faces staring at me, whilst still processing what I have told them. When I check whether anyone wants further clarification or has specific questions, I usually get blank faces. The individuals in the group have each made their own sense of my words and have answered their own questions. They are in trance!

## Skimming the surface or going deeper

When you formulate ideas, analyse information, and draw conclusions, you use what's known in NLP as the *deep structure* of your experience. The deep structure contains thoughts and ideas that are not actually related to language. To express these thoughts you transform them into words, gestures and movements. This transformation requires you to *delete*, *distort* and *generalise*- more on these in the section 'Pulling the Right Words out of Your Hat' - your thinking so that your communication is quite short. What other people hear is just the *surface structure*.

To understand how deep and surface structures work in practice, consider the following.

Imagine that your boss tells the team: 'We're not allowed to expand the team despite the extra workload, so we have to find ways of working smarter.' This statement is a real blow to you and your teammates because you're all working flat out and pretty smartly already. However, your boss is describing what he thinks using just the surface structure.

What's *behind* your boss's statement is the deep structure of his thinking. He knows that budgets are tight. He requested extra headcount six months ago and was refused. He believes that his director doesn't value this team. He resents this director, as she beat him to the job, and he's decided they can't work well together.

The deep structure of thinking incorporates all the myriad aspects of your experience as you filter them (read more about filters in Chapter 4). Your deep structure includes:

- ✔ Beliefs
- ✔ Attitudes
- ✔ Values
- ✔ Emotions

Often, to understand what someone else is really saying, you need to dig into her deeper structure. Good questions allow you to get more information and go from someone's surface structure to her deeper structure. In Chapter 12 I discuss the *Meta Model* and *Clean Questions*, two techniques that you can use to discover more specific information.

Surface structure is actually what makes conversation possible. After all, if you explain all that leads you to every opinion or idea, you never get anything done!

Although communication based on surface structure has much of the detail removed, understanding and using surface structure to your best advantage provides a truly powerful communication tool.

In fact, the Milton Model works well when you *don't* want people to have all the detail. Instead, you want your listener to make her own sense of what you're telling her. You speak from the surface structure, and others filter what they hear through their own personal experiences, beliefs, and patterns. This process makes your words more appealing: it builds rapport and it engages people emotionally.

See the section 'Pulling the Right Words out of Your Hat' for more on *how* to use the Milton Model and Milton language. Go to the section 'Choosing to Be Artfully Vague', later in this chapter, for more on *when* to use these techniques.

## Engaging the Emotions

Milton language allows you to make suggestions to people without getting caught up in the details which their conscious minds will wish to analyse and discuss. These suggestions can be used to create a particular feeling or state in another person, or indeed, a group of people. Consider the following two scenarios:

**Scenario 1:** A member of your team is anxious about a forthcoming presentation she has to give. She runs your through her PowerPoint slides in advance, and as you discuss it you use Milton language to build her confidence. For example, one of the things you may say is: 'And as you talk through this slide really well you may notice some of your audience starting to nod in agreement.'

Notice how different this is to saying: 'Don't be nervous. As long as you prepare well you'll do a fine job.' Your team member is now consciously engaged in the subject of her anxiety and will start to rationalise why she feels nervous, explain how preparation for previous presentations has not helped and report on several occasions where she hasn't done a fine job or presenting at all. The Milton language *suggested* instead that she would be talking through a slide really well and that the audience would agree with her point. A lot less to analyse and contend.

**Scenario 2:** Having launched a new invoicing system the IT department is facing a barrage of complaints. Customers are receiving inaccurate invoices. Users in the accounts department are experience various problems and system delays. Now the Managing Director has got involved and demanding that the system is fixed quickly, or removed altogether. As project manager for the system you meet with your exhausted, overwhelmed and dejected team.

You use Milton language to make suggestions to encourage and motivate them: 'We can make this work. As we get on top of things by the end of the week, complaints will subside and you'll notice people really like the system'. You're emphasising the capability of the team ('*can*'); you suggest that the team will al get on top of things, and by the end of the week; you introduce the possibility of people (implying the complainers) will soon like the system.

Contrast this with a more specific attempt to energise the team, which might sound something like: 'This will be fixed, but only if we all pull together to solve the problems. Here is the plan of activity I have devised to ensure that user problems will be fixed by Thursday and accurate invoices are issued to customers on Friday. Don't worry about the reputation of the departmcnt. I'll let the MD, accounts people and customer managers know the plan.'

# Pulling the Right Words out of Your Hat

You probably already use some of the words and phrases found in the Milton Model (see the preceding section, 'Engaging Hearts and Minds: The Milton Model of Communication'). So congratulations! You already have the skill to be vague – at least sometimes. I'm not talking about being obtuse or so tired or preoccupied that you don't express yourself clearly. Rather, life is just too short for you to express each specific detail in everything you want to talk about.

The more you become aware of the different ways of being artfully vague, the more effective you are in creating the results you want. In the following section I focus on the main patterns, all of which I find very powerful in business. You may find that you already use some of these patterns – and you may discover some that you don't use regularly.

Whatever the case, as you read through the following sections, realise that you have a great deal of choice in terms of which words and phrases you use in order to generate the positive response you want. Use the power of vague language wisely. Vagueness can be confusing or leave people believing that your thinking is superficial. Use the following techniques and patterns consciously when you believe they will be useful.

Pay attention to the types of pattern in the following sections, rather than to their sometimes cumbersome names. Developing your influencing skills is more important than being able to define exactly what you're doing.

## *Leaving stuff out: Deletions*

When you *delete* information from what you say, you allow listeners to go inside themselves and use their own experiences to fill in the gaps.

You're not being lazy or careless. Instead, you're *choosing* to leave out key information because you want your listeners to ask themselves questions and create their own answers.

Several types of deletion exist:

- ✔ **Simple deletions** are statements that have something important missing.

  For example, the statement 'We're going to succeed' doesn't specify exactly who is going to succeed, at what, when or where.

  Listeners are left to decide for themselves what the specifics are.

- ✔ **Comparative deletions** are statements in which the point of comparison is deleted.

  For example, the statement 'Our internal systems are better' doesn't point out what the systems are better than.

  Listeners must identify their own points of comparison.

- ✔ **Nominalisations** are statements in which action or process words (those good old *verbs* or 'doing words' from your school days) are used as if they're nouns.

  For example, in the observation 'Communication isn't good', the word *communication* is a thing (a noun), but it involves a range of activities – none of which you go into detail about.

  Listeners are required to fill in the gaps for themselves.

✔ *Unspecified verbs* create statements where the details of the action are undefined.

For example, the goal 'We're going to delight our customers' sounds positive – but you aren't saying how specifically you plan to delight them or how your customers' delight may look and sound.

Listeners must supply these details.

✔ *Unspecified referential indices* (yes, that's a mouthful!) basically means the object in a statement isn't specified. Instead of mentioning a specific problem or issue, you substitute *it, them, they,* or *that.*

For example, the statement 'It may continue to be challenging' acknowledges that a problem exists – but doesn't outline what the problem specifically is.

Identifying the problem is left up to listeners.

## *Making your own interpretation: Distortions*

*Distortions* happen when people filter their experiences and notice or remember certain things according to their own map of the world, rather than the reality of what happened. (Chapter 4 has more on filters and maps of the world.)

Here are some types of distortion you can use to good effect:

✔ *Cause–effect distortions* claim a direct relationship between two events, using words such as 'makes' or 'means'.

For example, 'Seeing this month's figures will make you optimistic for the rest of the year'.

Here there is a suggested direct relationship between seeing one month's results and feeling optimistic for the year. The person is not having attention put on any other feelings, or any of the possible factors that could affect the year's performance. The unconscious mind is being influenced to feel optimistic as a result of the month's figures.

✔ *Implied cause–effect distortions* suggest a cause-and-effect relationship between things when no direct relationship exists. These distortions often include words like *as, when, since, before,* and *after.*

For example, 'As you evaluate the options you can feel confident in our excellent service.'

- ✔ **Simple conjunctions** link otherwise unconnected statements and imply some connection. These distortions use words such as *and, with,* and *plus.*

  For example, the statement 'This year we're lowering costs and we're improving sales' lumps together two (and most likely separate) business goals. However, by joining the statements into one sentence, listeners tend to link the two ideas into one broader, more dynamic initiative.

- ✔ **Complex equivalences** imply that two different experiences are related and even give them the same meaning, however illogical.

  For example, 'We have the support of the CEO. This merger is the best thing that ever happened to the business' is actually two separate bits of information. But stating them close together can make listeners believe that the CEO is fully behind the merger.

- ✔ **Lost performatives** involve value judgements but don't specify who judged or on what basis.

  For example, the statement 'Our service is highly respected' feels good – but who said it?

- ✔ **Mind reading** happens when you claim to know someone else's internal experience.

  For example, when you begin a discussion with 'You're probably wondering what I'm going to tell you today', you imply that your message is important to listeners – so important they even start thinking about the conversation before you began to talk.

It may be tempting to associate these various distortions as deceptions or even lies! Let me assure you that this is not a technique for deceiving or manipulating people. Listen carefully and you'll notice statements containing distortions like this all around you, every day. You do it too! It's a natural process of communication, as you transform your deep structure thinking into some words to talk to others. Consciously using distortions to good effect, rather than not realising what and how you are distorting – which may be really unhelpful – gives you the chance to positively influence others.

## Compiling patterns: Generalisations

To make sense of your experiences, you have to generalise. How can you get in and out of a room if you don't have a general idea of what a door is – what it looks like and how to operate it?

With the Milton Model, you choose to generalise in order to engage your listeners' unconscious minds. In this way you can more effectively engage with people whose specific patterns of thinking you aren't aware of (see Chapter 4 for more on this) groups of people with differing patterns, and when you don't want the details to get in the way of in principle agreements.

Common generalisations include:

- ✔ **Universal quantifiers** are words such as *always never, everyone,* and *no one.* Including these words in your statements can make your message seem stronger and more credible.

  For example, while you can't prove a statement like 'Things always work out for the best', saying this to a discouraged person can be reassuring and positive.

- ✔ **Modal operators** are words such as *can't, must, should, need, ought, can,* and *have to.* These words pump up the intensity of any of your action words.

  For example, the statement 'We must pull together and make this happen' is more than merely telling people what to do – it's a call to action and perhaps even dynamic change.

- ✔ **Presuppositions** are assumptions or things that can just be taken for granted by the listener.

  For example, 'We'll be celebrating when we hit the target' suggests that there is no doubt that the target will be hit - it's a given.

## Employing other powerful patterns

In addition to deletions, distortions, and generalisations, Milton relied on other verbal techniques to communicate with his listeners effectively.

- ✔ **Embedded commands** send an instruction directly to your listener's unconscious mind – without explicitly telling your listener to do something.

  For example, when you tell someone 'Your confidence will increase as you get more experience', you're embedding the command that the other peson will grow in confidence over time.

- ✔ **Double binds** offer choices to listeners that are limited – and often skewed towards your needs or desires.

  For example, when you ask a customer 'Do you want to place your order today or tomorrow?' you're only offering two options – to order now or to order tomorrow. In reality, she can order next week or next month. She can even choose not to order at all.

- ✔ **Tag questions** are short phrases you add to the end of statements to invite agreement from listeners.

  For example, 'Our offices are very comfortable, aren't they?' leads your listener to agree with your assertion about the quality of your offices rather than evaluate the quality for herself.

✔ **Quotes** enable you to give a message – but wrap it up in essentially a mini-story about someone else. A quote can back up your point of view and encourage the listener to join you, as well as the person who supplied the quote.

For example, 'A customer told me yesterday that this is one of the best products she's ever bought' supports your sales message about your product with an additional, outside voice.

## Metaphorically speaking: Stories

Another approach to powerful communication that Erickson used – which also works very well in business – is story telling. Anecdotes and metaphorical stories are a great way of communicating with your listeners' unconscious minds and influencing how people think.

✔ **Anecdotes:** Real life stories about a similar experience, just like the anecdotes in this book. .

✔ **Metaphorical stories:** Metaphors are stories about something that has a similar structure or form as the message you want to convey, but a different content.

---

# Fighting for success

I was asked to work with a small firm of lawyers by Richard, their senior partner. He wanted his 40 employees - and himself - to work more effectively together and grow the business. He had big ambitions and needed to inspire the team to achieve them.

Richard had a metaphor for the organisation. He saw it as a powerful fighting ship, that travelled through the seas spreading peace and maintaining order, but ready at all times to go into battle. Employees all had important roles on the ship, manning the guns, maintaining the engine, and keeping everything shipshape. His role was to stand at the helm, steering with the help of his navigators and watchmen.

I helped Richard to share his metaphor with the team. I encouraged the team to question and challenge the metaphor. Once they made sense of it for themselves, the metaphor became part of the everyday language within the business. Requests for investment for training were explained in terms of needing more oil for the engine. Reviews of work allocation were discussed in terms of distribution of ammunition. New strategies were considered in context of destinations for the ship.

Eighteen months later the firm had increased its turnover by 31% and were preparing to buy out a competitor. The metaphor was a highly effective way of describing the type of operation he wanted to run in order to grow.

Business leaders are increasingly using metaphors and anecdotes to communicate. These language tools are particularly useful when you want to:

- ✔ Find a quick way to describe a complex issue.
- ✔ Bring a presentation to life.
- ✔ Teach something in a memorable way.
- ✔ Change how people are feeling.
- ✔ Reduce opposition.
- ✔ Gain buy-in to a new idea.

Metaphor truly allows your listeners to draw their own conclusions from what they hear and to translate these experiences back into the work place in a way that works for them.

Listen to the metaphors that people use regularly in their words and expressions at your work place. These images and stories can tell you a lot about how people think and even the culture of the organisation. Do you hear lots of metaphors that suggest fighting, battles, and wars? Or maybe sporting metaphors, involving competing, teams, and winning? Perhaps the metaphors are loftier and dreamy – shooting for the moon, reaching for the stars, and thinking big thoughts? Whatever the metaphor you can effectively use when you want to influence those that are using it.

## *Paying attention to three small words: Can't, try, but*

Although the preceding section focuses on more complex phrasing, small words can be very powerful communication tools too. Pay particular attention to:

- ✔ Can't
- ✔ Try
- ✔ But

Use these three little words wisely, as I outline in the following section, and you can have a great deal of influence. Careless use may lead you to results that you simply don't want.

### The can't can't go on

When you believe that you've explored all the options to make something happen, you may well want to resort to using the word *can't*. I hear it in businesses regularly:

✔ We can't hit budget this year.

✔ We can't get the funding for the new system.

✔ We can't do any more to increase sales in the short term.

✔ We can't deliver today's orders tomorrow.

When you want to encourage and inspire others, talking in terms of what *can* be done rather than what *can't* is so much more empowering (for them *and* you). So, revised versions of the preceding examples may be:

✔ Our figures may be lower than budget. We *can* still beat last year's results.

✔ We haven't *yet* secured the funding for the new system.

✔ We're working hard to increase sales in the longer term.

✔ We can deliver today's orders the day after tomorrow, and we're working to find a way that in future means we can deliver them tomorrow.

### No more trying

When you hear the expression 'I'll try to call you tomorrow', do you believe the other person's going to call you? It certainly isn't definite. The other person hasn't made a commitment to you. If she has, she says, 'I'll call you tomorrow.' In fact, you may even be surprised if she *does* call.

Using the word *try* certainly suggests that failure is possible – and implies that failure is acceptable. 'I'll try' is an easy thing to say and gives you a get-out clause if you don't do whatever you claim to be trying to do. Have you ever heard the following lines?

> We shall fight on the beaches.
> We shall fight on the landing grounds.
> We shall fight in the fields and the streets.
> We shall fight in the hills.
> We shall never surrender . . .

This is an extract from one of Winston Churchill's defining speeches during the Second World War. These words were highly empowering to the British people and all the Allied nations. They left no room for doubt. (Just imagine adding *try to* after each *shall* and see how weak the entire speech becomes.)

Notice whether when you're talking to yourself, you leave room for doubt or failure. Do you tell yourself you're going to try to get something done or try to do your best? Listen to your inner voice and change *try* to *will*. Pay attention to see whether achieving your goals becomes easier.

### Butting out

You probably hear the word *but* many times in the working day. Such a tiny little word – and you can forgive yourself for thinking that it's an innocent little word!

The power of *but* is in the fact that it undermines or contradicts *anything you say before it.* For example, if you hear 'I really like your report, but it doesn't include much about potential business in China', what part of the sentence do you pay most attention to? If you're like most people, you're much more concerned with the information that comes after the *but* – which is often the less positive part.

When you find yourself using *but,* think about the message you're actually giving: If you don't want to negate the first thing you say, use 'and' instead.

> **You say**: 'I hope to attend your meeting, *but* I have to visit a supplier today.'
>
> **Your colleague hears:** 'My visit to a supplier is more important than your meeting.'
>
> **Alternatively, you say**: 'I hope to attend your meeting *and* I have to visit a supplier today.'
>
> **Your colleague hears:** 'I have two important meetings and a dilemma. As a result I may not make your meeting.'

On the other hand, you can use *but* constructively to motivate someone. For example, the assessment 'We've had a difficult year, *but* profitability's now back on track' moves attention away from the negative (the difficult year) and towards the positive.

### Dumbing down the don'ts

Telling others, or yourself, what not to do is easy. Have you ever said anything like 'Don't forget to send that e-mail' – only to find that the message didn't get sent later? You hear parents use this phrasing often with their children: 'Don't spill that drink.' And guess what? Sticky juice everywhere in seconds.

Try out this little example: don't think of a blue elephant. No, I said *don't.* You did, didn't you? Giving negative instructions to the unconscious mind simply doesn't work. You can't *not* think of a blue elephant without thinking of it.

Read more about the power of *don't* in Chapter 16. For now though, be aware of whether you're using negative commands or instructions to others. Doing so may just get you the opposite of what you want.

Pick a day when you're going to be listening to lots of different people. Keep a checklist on a scrap of paper or in a notebook. Count how many times you hear the words *can't, try, but,* and *don't.* The next time you have a busy day involving several meetings or telephone conversations with others, do the same exercise and notice how many times *you* use these words. As you become more aware of how you *try* to eliminate *but,* you *can't* fail to choose different language. *Don't* be amazed by what you achieve.

# Choosing to Be Artfully Vague

You may find that reading about the Milton Model raises your curiosity about what can be achieved with it. And that means you'll develop your skills more quickly. With greater insights, your skills will grow. You know that leads to more success at work, don't you?

People find the Milton Model language patterns are easy to use once you remember to use them when you need to. The way to master the Milton Model is practise, practise, practise.

Did you notice anything unusual about the two paragraphs above? Did you make sense of them? This was the Milton Model in action.

Read through the first two paragraphs in this section again, and work out how many different types of pattern you can spot and what they are. Table 10-1 has examples of all the Milton language patterns. Or check out the section 'Pulling the Right Words out of Your Hat', earlier in this chapter, for more information on any Milton-inspired language choice.

Chapter 12 offers the flip-slide of the Milton Model – the Meta Model. While the Milton Model is all about creating vagueness, the Meta Model breaks down vagueness and helps you acquire more detailed information when you need it.

| Table 10-1 | Artfully Vague Language to Inspire |
|---|---|
| *Pattern* | *Example* |
| **Deletions** | |
| Simple deletion | You'll notice things changing. |
| Comparative deletion | The system is going to get faster. |

| Pattern | Example |
|---|---|
| **Deletions** | |
| Nominalisation | Relationships are suffering. |
| Unspecified verb | We can find a way. |
| Unspecified referential index | They are supportive. |
| **Distortions** | |
| Cause and effect | |
| Implied cause and effect | When you hear from the CEO. you're going to feel more positive. |
| Simple conjunction | We're intending to make changes and maintain our success. |
| Complex equivalence | Communications will improve. Sales will to rise. |
| Lost performative | Our people are valued. |
| Mind reading | You must be concerned about performance. |
| **Generalisations** | |
| Universal quantifier | Everyone's on board. |
| Modal operator | We must improve efficiency |
| Presupposition | It's going to be a hard year |
| **Other patterns** | |
| Embedded command | You may find yourself working longer hours. |
| Double bind | Can you see me now or later? |
| Tag question | It's a great company isn't it? |
| Quote | News reports say that work–life balance is an issue. |

Over time you may find yourself becoming more confident at knowing when to be artfully vague, with whom, and in what situations.

In general, when you want to engage, intrigue, inspire, or motivate people, the Milton Model of artful vagueness is your ally.

Some – but certainly not all – examples of times when being artfully vague can be useful include communicating:

✔ With groups

✔ With large audiences

✔ To marketplaces

> ✔ One to one
>
> ✔ In e-mails, letters, and reports
>
> ✔ In advertising
>
> ✔ With yourself

The following sections cover these situations in greater detail.

Many benefits come from using language inspired by the Milton Model, including:

> ✔ Getting people into a receptive state to hear your message.
>
> ✔ Generating and engaging with emotions.
>
> ✔ Avoiding direct imposition of your thoughts and opinions.
>
> ✔ Giving others the opportunity to develop their own options.
>
> ✔ Empowering others.

## *Working with groups*

When you have a room full of people to talk to, every person in the group is likely to be different – different needs, different maps of the world, different filters, different priorities, different beliefs, and different patterns of thinking (to mention just a few of the big differences!).

Finding one specific message that can convince or energise all these different people is rarely going to happen. Milton language gives you a way to connect with the whole group, regardless of individual differences or the type of meeting (delivering training, making a motivational speech, giving a presentation, and so on).

Milton language is commonly used in public speaking, particularly by politicians. Listen carefully and you hear expressions such as: 'People are ready for change. We will deliver on education and health', 'We believe in a good standard of living for everyone', and 'The economy is already in much better shape'. Notice the deletions, distortions and generalisations in these statements. And how about one UK political party's anthem in the late 1990's: 'Things can only get better' – leaving the electorate to make up for themselves which things might get better, and better than what!

# *Advertising*

Much successful advertising depends on deletions, distortions, and generalisations. (See the section 'Pulling the Right Words out of Your Hat', earlier in this chapter, for more on each of these Milton language tools.)

You've probably seen and heard thousands of slogans and advertising claims, such as:

'Washes whiter'

'Just do it'

'20% less salt'

'Higher definition'

'Smoother and creamier'

'You know it makes sense'

Although all of these slogans feel good and seem positive, none is very specific. So take your cue from advertising and marketing masters. When you want to influence large audiences, whatever the medium, the more vague you are with your language, the more effective you are in engaging the unconscious and creating the effect you want.

Do take care, however, with your advertising-inspired language. You must make sure that you don't delete too much. I've seen and heard many campaigns where the audience has to work too hard to work out what the brand or product is! For example, the following are genuine advertising slogans:

- ✔ We make it happen
- ✔ Excellence through total quality
- ✔ Where people matter

Each of the above slogans is vague - so vague in fact that they could mean almost anything for just about any or every brand! Just thinking about the first one, 'we make it happen', there are many deletions. It doesn't say *who* makes it happen. *What* is made to happen. *Why* does something needs to happen?

## Putting it in writing

Artfully vague language is equally useful in written business communications – sometimes. You may find yourself writing quite a lot at work: reports, e-mails, letters, training manuals, briefing notes, brochures, and more.

So before writing something important, ask yourself:

✔ What am I trying to achieve with this writing?

✔ Do I want to inspire or engage someone emotionally?

If your answer's yes, think about how vague you need to be for your writing to make sense to your reader. In contrast, if you want to generate a specific action, avoid the Milton Model and use more specific language instead (go to Chapter 12 for more).

## Motivating one to one

Much of the focus in this chapter is on using artfully vague language with groups and wider audiences. You can also use Milton language very constructively in one-to-one situations, where you're looking to:

✔ Motivate

✔ Build confidence

✔ Coach

✔ Gain agreement

Next time a colleague needs some encouragement to do something, think carefully about what you can say that is vague enough for her to connect and respond positively to. Make sure your words don't sound too contrived by practising the kinds of things you might say using Table 10-1 from the section 'Choosing to Be Artfully Vague'. Here are a few possibilities:

✔ 'You are nervous about it and you will make a great success of it'

✔ 'Everyone thinks you're the right person to do this job'

✔ 'You should realise that you've been specially chosen for this'

✔ 'You may find that once you get started it's much easier than you think'

## *Motivating yourself*

The words you use to others can also have a great influence on *you*. The generalisations, distortions, and deletions that you use with your co-workers and employees can work against you – or for you.

So, listen to your self-talk as well as how you talk about yourself to others. When you tell yourself 'I can't start my own business' or 'I can never learn this', think about the impression you're giving your unconscious mind.

On the other hand, you can encourage and empower yourself with artfully vague statements such as:

- ✔ 'I can do this.'
- ✔ 'Things are getting easier.'
- ✔ 'As time goes by, I'm going to enjoy giving feedback (or whatever job task) more.'
- ✔ 'I made a mistake but I've learned from it.'

# Chapter 11

# Giving Feedback to Fuel Improvement

*T*he success of any organisation depends, at least in part, on the performance of the people who work in it. What you think, say, and do within your work place is critical to getting the job done.

For people to work at their best – and to continue to become more capable and skilled – they need to know what they're doing well and what they need to improve.

As I explore in Chapter 3, you receive feedback continually through your senses. Indeed, feedback encompasses everything that happens as a result of your actions. It comes in many forms including:

✔ Other people's responses and reactions to you.

✔ Things that are automatically measured, , such as sales results.

✔ Things that have been produced, so can be seen, felt or heard – such as designs, reports, programs, products, and so on.

However, in the world of work, *formal feedback* – a manager's or supervisor's verbal or written responses – can take greater importance in people's minds than other forms of feedback. In this chapter I look at how to give such feedback easily and effectively, thus ensuring that people on the receiving end can make positive changes.

# Preparing to Give Feedback

I regularly meet people in various industries and at various levels who claim that the feedback they receive on how they're performing in their jobs is less than adequate. Common issues include:

- ✔ Receiving feedback only on things they can do better, never on what they do or have done well.
- ✔ Hearing surprising feedback once a year in a formal performance appraisal with no comments during the previous year.
- ✔ Getting no direct feedback at all.

Given that most organisations have performance management systems in place to make sure managers give feedback, why are people complaining?

The following sections explore some of the ways in which you can make giving feedback – including difficult feedback – more comfortable and easy for yourself and for those receiving the feedback.

Although this chapter concentrates on formal feedback sessions, much of you what you discover here can be used in those 'in-the-moment' situations where you find yourself giving feedback immediately after an event or completion of a task, or even as you pass someone in the corridor! Some of the ideas in the following sections are just as useful when you want to give positive feedback as well as when you are suggesting improvement.

## Appreciating the challenges of giving feedback

Giving feedback isn't particularly difficult for most people when someone's doing something well. In fact, you may get a lot of pleasure from being able to compliment and thank others for a job well done.

However, feedback can be much harder to deliver when the news isn't so good. You may find yourself more reluctant to give feedback to a colleague or team member – never mind your boss – when your message seems critical or negative.

You may postpone or sidestep giving tough feedback because:

- ✔ **You want to avoid conflict.** When you suspect that the person receiving your input may become defensive, challenging, or even aggressive, you may be reluctant to share your thoughts.

- ✔ **You're just too busy.** You may be working flat out and can never seem to find time to talk in depth with the other person.

- ✔ **You feel uncomfortable talking about someone else.** Perhaps you find discussing another person's performance personally testing, uncomfortable, or embarrassing.

- ✔ **You think feedback makes no difference.** If you gave feedback before and the individual just didn't change, you may think the entire feedback process is a waste of your already limited time and energy.

## Knowing how much feedback to give

Some people have a much greater need for feedback than others.

- ✔ **If you have a high need for feedback,** you are, in NLP terms, running an *external metaprogram* (see Chapter 7). This pattern of thinking requires input from the outside to judge your personal performance.

  People who run an external metaprogram measure their success through external means, such as comparing themselves to targets, but they also need to have direct input from others on how well they're doing.

- ✔ **If you have your own clear standards by which you judge how well you've done,** you're running an *internal metaprogram*. You may be less influenced by feedback from the outside.

In Chapter 7 you find out how to build your skill at spotting whether someone needs lots of feedback or not. If you haven't had time to master these techniques yet, just use the simple approach – ask: 'How much feedback do you like to receive?'!

If you appreciate and want feedback yourself, the chances are you give feedback to others. If, however, you have an internal metaprogram and don't really need a lot of feedback, you may not realise how important feedback can be to others. As a result. people with an internal metaprogram are more prone to forget to give feedback frequently and regularly.

If you run an internal metaprogram, you may find yourself frequently having to communicate difficult messages at annual reviews or when something major goes awry. You can make giving feedback much easier for yourself if you do it in little bits and often. With this approach, you can avoid surprises later down the road, as well as getting more experience of giving feedback regularly.

## Readying yourself

If you have concerns about giving specific feedback to someone, you're likely to prepare what you want to say in advance. Yet you may still worry that the individual may react badly, or that you may damage your relationship with him. In such a case, take the time to prepare your emotional state before you give the feedback.

The easiest way to feel bad about something before it happens is to run a mental rehearsal of the situation going badly. When you imagine things going less than well – guess what? – that's likely to happen! However, if you prepare yourself by *rehearsing success*, you can handle a potentially difficult feedback meeting much more effectively.

Rehearsing success is an NLP technique that can help you to prepare your emotional state and increase your chance of a positive meeting:

1. **Identify an upcoming meeting in which you need to give some tough feedback.**

   Some examples of tough feedback I've heard include 'Your performance is below expectations', 'You have worked very hard yet still haven't achieved the objectives we agreed', and 'Other people perceive you as uncooperative'.

2. **Imagine how the meeting may go.**

   Where and when will the feedback happen? Take some time to envision what you may see and hear from the other person.

3. **Recall a previous occasion in which you gave feedback and the process went really well.**

   Remember what you saw and heard in that meeting. Feel and enjoy that experience again.

4. **While you're still feeling all those good feelings, switch to thinking about your upcoming meeting.**

   Imagine that you receive a really positive response from the other person. What words do you hear? What do you see?

5. **Finally, thinking about this meeting ahead of you, how do you feel?**

   If you are now feeling more positive or optimistic about this meeting, you are now in a much better place to make it go well. Run this exercise again just before the meeting. If your feelings about the outcome are still not positive, repeat this exercise a number of times until you create the change you'd like.

By choosing your feelings in any given situation, you have a lot more control over how flexible you are. When you're flexible, you're more able to get the outcome you want, rather than the one you fear.

Chapters 8 and 9 offer a range of approaches for managing your personal state in challenging situations. Discover further techniques for creating new and effective ways of handling difficult communications in advance of a meeting in Chapter 13.

## Utilising the power of rapport

Giving feedback is easier when you have good rapport with someone. *Rapport* exists when the relationship between people has a certain, almost indefinable quality: a connection or alignment in the moment. You know rapport when it's happening – you can feel it.

Rapport is the foundation of good communication and creates conditions in which giving bad news or disagreeing with another's viewpoint is much easier.

Good rapport is essential to create the best setting for giving potentially difficult feedback. Effective use of rapport involves two aspects:

✔ **Building a relationship over time.** Building a relationship is more straightforward with someone who you relate easily to and who's more like you. But when you manage people and have to give them feedback, you don't typically get to choose only individuals you get along well with.

If you manage someone who you don't get along with so well, make time to work on that relationship. Find out more about what makes the other person tick. What's important to him? What's he interested in? Then use this information to create conversations and dialogue that help develop your relationship before you have to give any feedback.

✔ **Being in rapport while delivering your potentially difficult message**. Creating rapport in a feedback meeting makes a huge difference. Rapport keeps you both relaxed and constructive, and it eases the difficult things you may have to say.

Use what you know about the other person to make him feel comfortable. And mirror the other person's behaviour and verbal characteristics – match body posture, some word choices, tone of voice, and the speed at which he speaks.

Find out more about rapport – and the ways in which you build good rapport – in Chapter 6.

Making Feedback Meaningful I often meet people in organisations who tell me they know that they've been told to change, but they don't really understand what the change needs to be.

This phenomenon of giving less-than-useful feedback isn't restricted to inexperienced managers or poor communicators. One managing director I've coached, George, tells me that to make sense of feedback from his CEO boss he has to 'read between the lines'. When the CEO asks something like 'How are you getting along with Tony?', he means that he had heard that there has been some conflict between George and Tony's divisions and he wants it resolved!

People misinterpret feedback for two main reasons:

- ✔ **The language you use.** You must deliver feedback using language that suits your team member's patterns of thinking, speaking, and acting – rather than your own. For example, for someone who thinks in pictures, tell her: 'You'll have seen that every time you type a report for me you get it back full of corrections. I would like you to look through your work more closely, view the layout and spellings and show more attention to detail.' See Chapters 5 and 7 for more on identifying others' patterns.

- ✔ **The evidence in your description.** You must provide meaningful evidence of what exactly wasn't up to scratch, – what you saw and heard – and how you want a piece of work or a particular behaviour to look and sound in the future. For example, 'I am concerned about your level of customer care. I hear you speak sharply to customers on the phone and putting the phone down abruptly. I want to hear you using empathic words and a warm voice tone with complaining customers in the future.'

## *Tapping into other people's patterns*

Your personal experiences direct what you pay attention to and how you're likely to think, act, and react. As a result, no two people are the same. People have different patterns of thinking that play out in the way they speak to each other. You can read more about people's unique communication patterns in Chapter 4.

One important pattern to listen for is whether someone thinks more in pictures, words, or feelings (for more on this turn to Chapter 5) After you discover how to detect your own and others' thinking patterns, you can adapt the words and phrases you use in your message to help the other person hear and understand your feedback more easily.

Similarly, people often have distinct *metaprograms,* or patterns of motivation, which you can hear in their language (discover about these in Chapter 7). If you adapt the way you give your feedback to take account of the differences in your patterns, your audience can hear your feedback more clearly.

For example, if you're motivated by goals (a towards pattern) and your team member is motivated by moving away from problems (an away-from pattern), you may be inclined to give feedback such as:

> You need to keep your targets in mind to achieve the deadlines and get a positive response from Purchasing.

However, to connect more effectively with someone running an away-from pattern, you can present the same basic information but rephrase your feedback to a statement like:

> If you can stop missing the deadlines, you won't get the negative response from Purchasing, and you won't miss your targets.

## Being aware of the 'but'

If you have to give someone difficult feedback, you may well like to sandwich the tough information between the good things you want him to hear too. So you may start with something positive, move on to the more negative comments, and then wrap up by talking about something else he's doing well.

Be very careful when you present good, bad, and then good news. In particular, one small, powerful word can undo all your good work in providing the positive feedback – the word *but. But* plays interesting tricks on the mind. When people hear *but,* they hear and remember what you say *after* the *but* much more clearly than what you say before the *but.*

For example, you tell your employee:

> David, you ran the scheduling meetings really well in January and February, but in March you allowed everyone to discuss each point, so the schedule didn't get agreed.

Most likely, David's attention focuses wholly on his shortfalls in the March meeting, not on how well he did in January and February. He may become defensive, accusatory, and just shut down – all reactions that minimise the effectiveness of your feedback and the rest of the meeting.

By contrast, consider what David may remember when you present the same general feedback, without the *but:*

> David, you ran the scheduling meetings really well in January and February, and in March you allowed everyone to discuss each point, so the schedule didn't get agreed.

The only difference in the preceding example is that *and* replaces *but.* David is much more likely to notice the two pieces of feedback equally. The information feels balanced and is likely to lead to a very different – and probably proactive – reaction from David.

## Providing clear evidence

You know the importance of offering evidence when you're giving feedback. Yet often, many managers couch evidence subjectively or in ways that don't explain exactly what's required. For example, all the following bits of feedback lack adequate evidence:

> You need to be more confident in front of clients.

> You aren't assertive enough in meetings.

> You need to be more proactive.

> You have to manage the team better.

Feedback is designed to help people change. Whether you're trying to get someone to change a belief, build a new skill, or just think and do things differently, the best evidence comes from behaviour – what the person says and does.

Two important questions to ask yourself before you give feedback to someone you want to make a change are:

- ✔ **How do I know that this behaviour needs changing?** What do you *see* and *hear* in the other person's behaviour that tells you something isn't good enough? For example, you see this person arriving late for work every morning, and hear the same excuses about the train.

- ✔ **After changes are made, how do I know the situation *is* good enough?** What do you need to you *see* and *hear* to indicate that the person has made the necessary change? In the example, you'll see this person at her desk and ready to work at the expected time, just like the rest of the team.

Consider the following feedback example:

You need to be more confident in front of clients, Jane.

By contrast, an alternative version of the same feedback can take into account the two preceding questions and add supporting details and examples:

Jane, I want to see you smile at clients more and speak up in client meetings, particularly to tell them about the positive aspects of our product and service. When clients complain, you need to apologise for any problems they've experienced and assure them that you're going to resolve their issues. When they ask questions, you can actually reinforce your client relationships if *you* answer their questions, rather than deferring the questions to me.

ANECDOTE

## Just knowing what a change looks and sounds like makes all the difference

Lisa, a regional director for a clothing retailer, was thinking about firing one of her area managers. Although Gary was committed, hard working, and experienced, Lisa wanted him to change his working style, becoming less involved in small day-to-day issues and taking a more strategic view of his area. Lisa gave Gary this feedback on several occasions, yet to Lisa, nothing seemed to have changed.

When I coached Lisa, I asked her to think about what she wanted to see and hear from Gary. What would an improved Gary do and say to indicate that he'd shifted to working more strategically? Lisa devised a list of evidence that included:

✔ Gary spending more time in the office each week – and less time visiting shops to troubleshoot operational problems.

✔ Gary's direct reports, the shop managers, attending a training programme to improve their management skills and be better able to reduce operational issues, and more competent in handling them should they arise.

✔ Monthly reports describing the overall trends in Gary's area, rather than highly detailed lists of individual problems and staff issues at each shop.

✔ Hearing more innovative and creative ideas from Gary regarding efficiencies and new initiatives in team meetings.

I recommended that Lisa give Gary this far more specific, descriptive feedback. Things changed immediately. Gary started to develop and test new retailing ideas. He also took on board the need to change his monthly reporting style and Gary put together a schedule of training for his managers. Within six months he was making exactly the type of contribution Lisa was hoping for all along – and he was enjoying his job. A further four months later one of his concepts was rolled out over all shops nationally, reducing stock losses through theft by 21%.

When you get yourself prepared for giving this feedback, make sure you jot down a check-list of the specific evidence that you've noticed in support of your feedback, and the particular changes you want to see and hear. Then you'll have a few notes to make sure you get across all the points you want to make.

When setting someone a target for improvement, make sure you express it clearly, specifying what needs to be seen and heard. such as 'What other people need to see is . . . ' and 'What I want to hear when you're doing this differently is . . . '

# Ensuring Your Feedback Makes a Difference

Although sometimes you may want to, the truth is that you can't change others – only yourself. Through giving feedback, however, you're letting someone know what change you (or the organisation) need him to make in order to succeed.

Giving useful feedback on which someone can act and then supporting that person to adapt and improve is the best method of creating the conditions in which someone else can change.

## Directing attention to where change needs to happen

At work, any changes or improvements that need to happen are ultimately changes to behaviour. Yet sometimes feedback given is more about a person's identity than their behaviour. For example, you might tell a salesperson he need to be a 'go-getter', when what you are actually seeking is that he proactively calls new sales prospects.

A useful way of thinking about where and how feedback is targeted comes from Robert Dilts' NLP model for change, known as the *logical levels model* (find out more about this in Chapter 15). The logical levels model breaks down different aspects of the human experience and looks at where change can best be made to achieve the desired result.

Figure 11-1 shows an abridged version of the logical levels model that you can use to think about effective feedback.

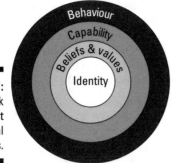

**Figure 11-1:**
Feedback
at different
logical
levels.

Figure 11-1 indicates four levels at which you can target feedback:

✔ **Behaviour.** What people say and do determines the success of their work. Throughout this chapter, I focus on ways to tell others what's working or what needs to change in their *behaviour*.

✔ **Capability.** Well-delivered feedback regarding people's behaviour often leads them to improve their *capabilities* or skills. For example, if you want Helen to write more convincing sales proposals, she may need on-the-job coaching or a specific training course. As her skills and knowledge increase, Helen will write differently and start to achieve the outcome you're seeking.

✔ **Beliefs and values.** People's beliefs and values drive their behaviour, but beliefs and values aren't usually obvious – sometimes even to yourself. Feedback isn't usually given overtly at the level of beliefs or values, unless you can explicitly notice from someone's behaviour that their values are very different to that of the organisation. You may choose to point this out, but don't expect people to change their values as a result of your feedback – only their behaviour.

✔ **Identity.** You may have heard or even given feedback at an identity *level*. You target this level in feedback that begins 'You are. . .'. Negative comments at identity level sound like:

- You are bossy.
- You are lazy.
- You are stupid.
- You are arrogant.
- You are slow.
- You are negative.

If you've ever had feedback at identity level, you know how unhelpful it can be. This feedback is inevitably very personal and goes to the heart of who you are – rather than just something you said or did. You may feel defensive, confused, hurt, or angry in the face of identity-level feedback. And even if you can muster the motivation to change, you probably have no sense of what you need to do or not do to change.

Of course, *good* feedback at identity level can be really effective. Positive comments ('You're a good manager' or 'You're an outstanding communicator') that link to your sense of who you are can be very personal and make you feel good about yourself, ultimately boosting your morale and performance.

If you want someone to make positive changes to their performance at work, direct your feedback to their behaviour – what they do and say – and how they can improve their skills and capabilities.

## *Making change stick*

Some people may still find it hard to accept and appreciate your feedback, even after you have prepared so well! Look and listen for clues in their communications. Nodding, smiling, and eye contact are often good indicators. You'll likely hear them talking actively about making the changes you're suggesting. If you aren't certain that they understand and are ready to respond to the feedback, ask them.

### Practising Breeds Success

When I coached Karl, a senior data analyst in a software development consultancy, he'd received feedback that he was failing to meet expectations. After I encouraged him to seek out more specific evidence, he was told that he was frequently missing deadlines, sometimes delivering incomplete work, and rarely initiating new projects. Karl identified that his desk was messy, his grip on his projects disorganised, and he was easily distracted by the mountain of emails that he received daily.

Through coaching, Karl decided to create a daily list of things to do, prioritised in terms of importance and urgency. He made a commitment to ensure he did at least two important pieces of work before he dealt with his emails each morning. Finally, he decided to tidy his desk and create files for each project he was working on. This was a quite different way of working for Karl, requiring him to take a more structured and disciplined approach. He found it a struggle at first but persevered. After six weeks Karl wondered how he'd ever managed to achieve anything through his previous disorganised way of working. Lists, a tidy desk and not considering non-urgent emails his utmost priority, all became second nature. His boss was delighted at the improvement in the quality, quantity and reliability of Karl's work.

After you give people feedback in ways they appreciate, understand, and respond to, then they know that they need to:

- ✔ Keep on doing something that's working.
- ✔ Make a change to something that isn't.

Maintaining good behaviours or taking on new behaviours requires practice. Over time, behaviours become habits. Any habit – whether good or bad – requires you to reprogram your mind and body.

 When you give someone feedback on what you want him to do differently, work with him on a plan to practise the new behaviours. Plan to give ongoing feedback as reinforcement and identify other sources of reinforcement such as feedback from others, better results, and tangible things such as items produced and important meetings attended.

# Receiving Feedback

The previous sections in this chapter focus on giving feedback. Although many managers spend a lot of time giving feedback, they also receive feedback.

 The next time someone gives you feedback, make sure it's meaningful to you so you can adapt with greater ease.

- ✔ **Check that you have enough information to explain any negative feedback.** If you're in doubt, ask the person giving the feedback, '*Can you provide more examples or information?*'

- ✔ **Check that the examples have evidence.** If an example seems unsubstantiated, ask, '*What have you seen or heard that tells you that?*'

- ✔ **Translate feedback from identity level to behaviour level.** (See the section 'Directing attention to where change needs to happen', earlier in this chapter, for more on feedback levels). Rather than getting upset, defensive, or angry with the other person, do your best to remain objective and neutral. Ask, '*What have you witnessed me doing and saying that leads you to describe me in this way?*'

- ✔ **Find out exactly what's required.** Don't guess how to respond to, or satisfy, feedback. Instead, ask the other person, '*What specifically do you want to see or hear me do differently?*'

 Preparing yourself to hear and handle feedback that you may not want to receive can be helpful. Mentally rehearse how you want to react to any 'bad news' so you can better manage your feelings and reactions in the moment. Work to get yourself in the most objective state possible, so you can question the feedback and find out what you specifically need to do.

# Chapter 12

# Coaching for Peak Performance

*A* common theme I hear when consulting in organisations is that people are always trying to do more with less. Expectations of employees are rising, while resources are limited. The fight to stay competitive drives this need to innovate continually to improve products, service, and processes.

In some organisations, this pressure leads to tightly managed, process-led approaches that focus on minimising errors and maintaining control. These management models have their roots in the days of heavy industry and manufacturing and the drive to control quality. Nowadays, however, these approaches tend to create workforces that lack motivation, initiative, and drive – and are often very stressed.

More forward-thinking organisations realise that supporting and developing people is as important as getting the job done, and in fact the job can't get done well unless people develop and grow their skills. These businesses put in place performance reviews, feedback tools, and training, and increasingly offer *individual coaching* between manager and employee on an ongoing basis.

In this chapter you discover how you can use NLP knowledge and techniques to coach others to improve their effectiveness. You also discover some valuable questions you can ask in order to find out more and make changes in coaching situations.

# Coaching for Change

*Coaching* is a highly supportive way of working with others. When you've set yourself the intention of assisting others to help themselves and have practised some of the coaching tools I outline in this chapter, you can coach friends, family, people in the community, or colleagues.

Coaching others to make changes and improve their performance can take some time. In the modern-day workplace, most people consider time a precious resource. You probably never seem to have enough of it!

The most progressive employers are working to integrate coaching into everyday company culture. Rather than formal coaching sessions offered intermittently as part of a development programme, coaching techniques and processes appear throughout the organisation. Key coaching behaviour – such as questioning and supporting others in order to create solutions to problems and to attain goals – becomes something that can happen at the coffee machine or in the corridor, as well as in structured sessions.

Coaching can be a really worthwhile investment and it doesn't always need to take a huge amount of time. In fact, you can use many of the questioning techniques I cover in the sections 'Questioning for Insight: The Meta Model' and 'Coaching Cleanly', later in this chapter, anywhere, any time, in any type of organisation – and as a result improve other people's thinking and results.

## Improving the performance of others

You can coach anyone:

- ✔ People who report to you
- ✔ Colleagues
- ✔ Mentees
- ✔ Even your boss!

Businesses generally only perform as well as the people working in them perform. If you're managing or leading others in some capacity, then coaching can allow you to get the most out of other people by:

- ✔ Building more effective relationships between you and those in your team.
- ✔ Using everyday experiences to help others learn.

✔ Encouraging self-motivation and responsibility.

✔ Giving others more opportunities to become independent and to cultivate the necessary skills for career progression.

✔ Helping team members to feel valued.

✔ Creating a more productive working environment for everyone in the organisation.

You can achieve much through coaching people throughout your working day, as well as in longer, more formal coaching meetings. You can use the coaching questions I introduce later in this chapter in your everyday dealings with people, particularly your team. You have the opportunity to coach when you notice some one is stuck, or they bring you a problem, or an issue comes up that you think they would benefit from thinking differently about.

NLP not only offers you an extensive range of models to use in coaching, it also provides you with a philosophy. The NLP philosophy is that your role is to create the conditions and relationships to support others so that they can grow their self-awareness, identify what they want, build their flexibility, and develop more choices of how to think, act, and react. Improving your effectiveness.

By devoting time to coaching others, you can create significant long-term benefits for yourself.

If you're in a position where others report to you, directly or indirectly, or you work in a team, coaching these people can have huge benefits for you. You may be tempted to put off coaching someone else because you're too busy or believe that a situation needs fixing fast. You may think to yourself, 'Doing it myself is just quicker and easier.'

Taking the time and making the effort to coach someone else can actually improve *your* personal effectiveness by:

✔ Delegating problem solving to the appropriate person or level.

✔ Supporting others to manage change and rely on you less.

✔ Enhancing your own questioning, listening, and communication skills.

✔ Developing your team members to work more effectively.

✔ Creating time to think strategically and work proactively.

✔ Reducing your own stress.

# Preparing to Coach

Before coaching you may find it worthwhile to take time to reflect on your role as coach. How does this role differ from others you may have at work, such as supervisor, manager, team member, or mentor?

Good coaches typically:

- ✔ **Build rapport.** Your coaching efforts are much more effective when you're in *rapport*. This sense of connection and trust fosters a more open and productive discussion. For lots of ways to build rapport, take a look at Chapter 6.

- ✔ **Listen and observe.** By paying close attention to the other person, you can discover what's important to her, identify where she may be stuck, and notice patterns of thinking that may be less than helpful to her in this situation. Chapter 5 has some great tips for this type of listening and observing.

- ✔ **Use a neutral tone of voice.** By adopting a calm, non-judgemental tone of voice, you can support someone and help her to feel safe in discussing issues and problems.

- ✔ **Have an open mind.** Allowing the other person to focus on what's important for her – not you – is essential. Instead of judging, ask open questions to help her find out more about what she's thinking by herself.

- ✔ **Facilitate rather than problem solve.** In a coaching situation, your natural instinct may be to say something like 'This is what I'd do.' Resist! Your job as a coach is to ask questions and guide the other person to develop her own solutions.

Keep in mind the key NLP principles I describe in Chapter 3 when coaching. NLP coaches use these principles to guide their one-on-one work with others. In particular, the following key NLP principles are particularly relevant:

- ✔ People have all the resources they need.

- ✔ If what you're doing isn't working, do something different.

- ✔ Choice is better than no choice.

When coaching others formally you must create the right conditions for them – an environment in which they can open up, be honest with themselves, confront personal challenges, and build the confidence and motivation to change.

In a formal setting, the coaching may have been requested by the other person. However, it may also be initiated by you or at the request of someone else in the organisation. In this case, make clear the positive intention of coaching, to support the other person's development or achievement of a particular goal.

If you are concerned about someone's reaction to your use of NLP techniques in your coaching, you may want to tell them in advance that's what you're doing. When I want to use an exercise that involves something unusual like moving around (I sometimes use the Meta Mirror exercise illustrated in Chapter 13 for instance), I check out that the other person is comfortable with trying something different first. Once you're confident in using NLP techniques, you may find there is rarely a need to explain that you're are coaching with NLP – it all becomes seamless!

This introduction to NLP coaching tools is not intended to give you all the knowledge you need to become a full-time coach. If that's your goal I'd advise you attend a coach training programme and read some specialist coaching books. Instead, the techniques I explore in this chapter are all easy to integrate – with a little practice – into your day-to-day coaching at work.

# Coaching with NLP

When using NLP to support people to make changes, you help them concentrate on the future, rather than directing their attention to past experiences that may have led to their current difficulties, NLP puts emphasis on the *outcome* – what you want, rather than what you don't want. Focusing on the outcome means change is created by working towards what is desired , and you don't even have to work out what the problem actually is.

Similarly, coaching is oriented towards goals and outcomes, which creates an easy fit with NLP techniques. Combining NLP thinking and tools with coaching can be extremely effective, enabling you to help someone else:

- ✔ Create self-awareness.
- ✔ Notice patterns.
- ✔ Build flexibility.

If you read through this entire book, you may feel spoilt for choice with useful NLP tools to use when coaching! Fortunately, in the following sections I summarise my favourites. These are the techniques that I have personally found most useful in my coaching over the years.

## Creating well-formed outcomes

Coaching is most successful when you make sure that the other person has a clear and well-defined outcome or goal. In NLP, a *well-formed outcome* is a statement that:

  ✔ **Is stated in the positive.** The outcome needs to express what someone wants, rather than what she doesn't want.

  ✔ **Is in the person's control.** The person must be able to start and maintain anything that needs to happen in order to achieve the outcome. Achieving the outcome isn't dependent on other people.

  ✔ **Is specific.** The outcome defines what the person wants quite clearly, including what she will see, hear, and feel when she achieves the outcome.

  ✔ **Has a context.** The person works out where, when, and with whom she wants this outcome.

  ✔ **Is supported by resources.** The person can access necessary resources, both internal and external, to achieve the outcome.

  ✔ **Has had its impact evaluated.** The person has considered how attaining the outcome affects other things and people.

One of the amazing things about the unconscious mind is that it doesn't distinguish well between what's real and what isn't. When you create a well-formed outcome and imagine how life is when you've achieved it, you begin to change the programming in your mind, and change starts to happen. Both your unconscious and conscious minds will spot opportunities that will help you to achieve your goal.

One key to using outcomes effectively is identifying the right outcome and then thoroughly defining and specifying it at the outset. See Chapter 16 for more about setting outcomes in business and ensuring that they are well formed.

As coach, your role is to make sure that whoever you are coaching has a well-formed outcome. You can question and encourage him through all the different elements of a well-formed outcome until you both believe that its robust and useful. Writing the outcome down clearly helps your coachee focus clearly on what he wants, and makes it easier to craft a plan of how to achieve it. I cover planning in more detail in the 'Coaching Cleanly' section later in this chapter.

## Playing with perceptual positions

In coaching sessions, my clients frequently want to discuss:

- Specific situations in which they feel stuck or unable to make a change.
- Particular work relationships that they are struggling with; these relationships seem to impede progress.

You can coach people through these types of problems by encouraging them to take on new and different perspectives, or *perceptual positions*.

The *meta mirror exercise* is a useful NLP tool for helping others assume different perspectives and perceptual positions. This NLP approach encourages people to act as if they are stepping into another person's shoes. The information and insights they glean from this simple exercise typically bring about subtle changes in thinking and behaviour, which can generate significantly different results. Find out all about perceptual positions and the meta mirror exercise in Chapter 13.

## Progressing through the logical levels for change

People often make changes to move away from problems or to achieve outcomes – only to become dissatisfied with the results they get. In these situations, they may have set an outcome but didn't make it well formed. Or maybe they just made the wrong change.

To ensure someone makes the right kind of change in order to attain an outcome, you can coach using the *logical levels model,* which suggests that people can make changes at six different, increasingly complex levels:

- **Environment:** For example, where you work.
- **Behaviour:** What you actually do while working.
- **Capabilities:** The skills and knowledge you bring to the job.
- **Beliefs and values:** What drives your decisions.
- **Identity.** Your sense of who you are at work.
- **Purpose.** The bigger reason for being at work.

In a coaching situation, you can help someone identify the most effective level or levels to make change in order to attain a specific outcome. You can find out more about the logical levels model and change in Chapter 15.

## Developing pattern awareness

At work, relating to and influencing others is critical to personal success. Many people I work with have outcomes that involve:

- ✔ Improving particularly important relationships at work. For example, someone's relationship with his boss, or a colleague with whom he needs to work closely.

- ✔ Needing exceptional influencing skills to inspire and persuade groups of people to do things differently.

NLP-based questions can help improve self-awareness and expand understanding of others' diversity. As I highlight in Chapters 5 and 7, people have a number of ways in which they *filter* experiences, which then affect how others think, act, and react. These filters lead to habitual ways of thinking, or *patterns*. By paying attention to what people do and say, you can develop the ability to identify others' patterns.

I coach teams to work more effectively together and to achieve team goals. I help team members understand their own patterns of thinking and behaving, and each other's, so that they can modify their behaviour and bridge their differences. This can transform the way a team works and the results the team attains.

Two particularly important patterns you can share with teams you're coaching are rep systems and metaprograms.

### Rep systems

The rep systems that various people in a team use can cause communication difficulties. As I explore in Chapter 5, you use your five senses to make sense of your internal world, just like you use them to experience the world outside of you. Generally, most people use one sense much more strongly than the others when thinking, creating, and remembering.

In NLP terms, this preferred system is a *rep system*. The primary rep systems are visual, auditory, and kinaesthetic.

Coaching people to understand which rep system they use – and to notice which rep systems others on their team use – can help a team behave more flexibly and accomplish what they want to have happen.

You can use the techniques I outline in Chapter 5 with a team. You can explain how to look for clues in people's eye movements and posture, and listen out for the sensory of words they are using. Breaking a team up into small groups of 2-4 people and have them do this for themselves usually creates some fun as well as developing skills and providing insights. Remember to let them know what to do with all this new information – how to adapt to work more closely with rep systems that are different to their own.

### Metaprograms

Many patterns drive our thinking, decision making, and actions. One set of patterns are metaprograms (see Chapter 7). *Metaprogram patterns* describe some of the key differences in what motivates people at work. Each metaprogram has two opposite patterns. Two people with patterns from each end of a metaprogram spectrum have very different ways of becoming motivated and may find it difficult to work with each other.

In this book, I cover six of the most useful metaprograms for a work setting:

- ✔ General/specific
- ✔ Proactive/reactive
- ✔ Toward/away from
- ✔ Sameness/difference
- ✔ Options/procedures
- ✔ Internal/external

You can use the specific questions in Chapter 7 to coach others to identify their key metaprogram patterns, in order to build their flexibility to influence others who have different patterns.

When team members understand some key metaprograms, and what pattern each of them are running, they appreciate how and why it is sometimes difficult to communicate and get on each other's wavelength. , Getting a team working together well, by understanding and responding to each other effectively.

When coaching a team in metaprograms, ask the questions outlined in Chapter 7 to them when in the group, or for some patterns, you may want them to work in pairs. Your goal is to get them to assess their own pattern for each metaprogram.

Once the individuals on the team have a sense of their own pattern for a particular metaprogram ask them to stand and organise themselves across the room in a line, or spectrum, of where they believe they fit for each pattern. Immediately the team members see who is most, and least like them in that particular pattern, as well as which members of the team operate at the extreme ends.

Make sure that you let team members know what to do with this information. There are no right or wrong patterns, just differences between patterns. Show the team the words and phrases they need to work more effectively with people who have dissimilar patterns.

## Managing emotional states

You know that managing feelings and emotions at work can be hard, particularly for some people. Emotional responses often get in the way of people or teams achieving what they want. Much coaching work revolves around responding effectively to unhelpful emotional responses to situations or other people.

Someone struggling to control her emotional state can get in the way of achieving an outcome – or indeed can become the outcome itself. In these circumstances, coaching can be really beneficial. For example, you can coach someone to:

- ✔ Change from a negative state or mood to a more positive one.
- ✔ Feel more confident or relaxed about an upcoming situation, such as a presentation or difficult meeting.
- ✔ Maintain calm in a situation of conflict.

Several of the NLP anchoring techniques I outline in Chapter 8 can be useful in coaching. With these techniques, you can help someone else to be far less debilitated by negative feelings and become far more resourceful in challenging situations.

The following sections cover two additional NLP tools to put in your tool kit for coaching: The Meta Model and Clean Language.

# Questioning for Insight: The Meta Model

People delete, distort, and generalise their experiences to create thoughts, memories, and ideas. The NLP Meta Model helps you go deeper into other people's messages to discover why they say or do things. Sound like a useful tool for coaching? You bet! The following sections explore using the Meta Model while coaching others.

## Skimming the surface – or going deeper

When people talk to each other, they tend not to give the detailed information that forms the backdrop to their thoughts. This is actually a good thing. After all, if you explain all the experiences, beliefs, and opinions behind everything you say, you never get your job done because you have so much to say.

Instead, people usually communicate just the *surface structure* of their experiences, rather than the *deep structure*. You can read more about this in Chapter 10.

Most of the time, communicating the surface structure is practical. Relying on surface structures keeps conversations manageable. And you can use specific types of surface-structure communications to engage others.

Of course, the surface structure is sometimes less useful – either for you or for others. You may want or need far more information from someone to comprehend her communications, such as when you need to:

- ✔ **Gain clarification** on instructions, directions, and expectations.
- ✔ **Reduce misunderstandings** that can lead to unnecessary conflict or difficulties.
- ✔ **Get far more information,** such as when interviewing for recruitment or market research.

Digging deeper beyond the surface structure can be highly valuable in coaching. The surface structure of thinking, the bit that people tell each other, is often the only part of thinking that many people are consciously aware of. The rest happens in the unconscious mind. When you want to make changes yet find yourself stuck, gaining insight into the tapestry of your thinking – including your deep structures – can bring new choices and remove limiting thoughts.

## Using precision questions

The *Meta Model* was the first NLP model that founders Richard Bandler and John Grinder identified and formulated. Bandler and Grinder based the model on observations of the language patterns of successful therapists.

The Meta Model provides a range of specific questions that you can use to explore the deeper meaning of what someone is saying. Through the Meta Model, you can rediscover lost thinking, jump-start stuck thinking, and inject fresh perspectives.

After you become familiar with the Meta Model and the kinds of question to ask to gather more information, use this tool with care. In truth, you can challenge probably anything and everything people say in a typical business meeting – deletions, distortions, and generalisations abound! But if you ask about everything you hear, you may not only extend the meeting many times beyond its original planned length, you may also alienate your colleagues. Choose your precision questions with care, and make sure you have rapport.

Also, keep your own outcome in mind (go to the section 'Creating well-formed outcomes', earlier in this chapter, for more on outcomes). If your outcome is to gain understanding for yourself or others, what bigger outcome can you achieve by challenging and questioning? Alternatively, if your outcome is to coach another person effectively, you can do this if you help her stay focused on her outcome.

### Recovering deletions

As Table 12-1 shows, you delete information in five main ways when you talk to others (or even yourself). I discuss deletions in detail in Chapter 4.

Asking specific questions based on the Meta Model can fill in important information gaps. You may notice verbs or action words that don't really explain much; or you may hear comparisons but be unsure of what's being compared.

The exact questions you need to ask depend on the kind of deletion that's happened (see Table 12-1). For example, if you hear the statement 'People aren't interested', you need to fill in some gaps to understand fully. Questions such as 'Which people?' and 'Aren't interested in what?' are essential.

### Investigating distortions

Sometimes other people just seem to get things so wrong. Your perceptions of what happened at a meeting, for instance, can be distinctly different from someone else's. Diverse ways of filtering experiences lead to different kinds of distortion of reality, or in NLP terms, *different maps of the world*. (Trip to Chapter 4 for more on maps of the world.)

The Meta Model includes four main categories of distortion. For example, you may come across someone making a connection between two things that just don't seem to you to be related. Or you may hear two different experiences given the same meaning, such as a manager (with a large ego!) saying, 'My team all hit target this month. I'm a good manager.'

Another form of distortion is mind reading, a skill that many people think they have! Have you ever said anything like 'The audience was really bored' or 'That director doesn't like me'? If you have that direct feedback, then you're right. Otherwise, you're mind reading!

Table 12-1 indicates four types of typical distortion, and the kinds of question that you can use to investigate and challenge these distortions.

### Refining generalisations

I always say that people make generalisations all the time. OK, I don't, but no doubt you get the point!

How often do you hear words such as *always, ever, never, everyone,* and *no one?* Meta Model questions allow you to challenge these generalisations. Just make sure you're in rapport, otherwise you may get a strong reaction to these types of challenge.

In Table 12-1 you find the main three categories of generalisation and example questions for investigating the assumptions and oversimplifications held within them.

| Table 12-1 | Meta Model Language Patterns | |
|---|---|---|
| *Patterns* | *Examples* | *Questions* |
| **Deletions** | | |
| Simple deletion | I'm confused. | About what specifically? |
| Comparative deletion | It's getting worse around here | What's getting worse? |
| Nominalisation | Team communication is poor. | How can we communicate more effectively? |
| Unspecified verb | I failed on that project. | How specifically did you fail? |
| Unspecified referential index | People are feeling pressurised. | Which people specifically? |
| **Distortions** | | |
| Cause and effect | He makes me angry. | In what way does he make you angry? |
| Complex equivalence | I don't have a degree. I'll never get promoted. | How does not having a degree mean you'll never get promoted? |

*(continued)*

**Table 12-1** *(continued)*

| Patterns | Examples | Questions |
|---|---|---|
| **Distortions** | | |
| Lost performative | Being late isn't good. | Who says it isn't good? |
| Mind reading | The others feel under-valued. | How do you know they feel undervalued? |
| **Generalisations** | | |
| Universal quantifier | Everyone says things have changed for the worse. Everyone? | Is there anyone who doesn't say this? |
| Modal operators | I should get my e-mails done every day. | What would happen if you didn't? |
| Presuppositions | I'm never going to get approval for this project. | How specifically do you know that? |

# Noticing musts, shoulds, need-tos and have-tos

Society, work, and home all have explicit or implicit rules, regulations, policies, and procedures that you strive, in the most part, to follow. Being polite to strangers, being at work by a certain time, or buying a train ticket for your journey are all rules of a kind.

People are also good at creating their own rules on top of all those imposed on them. Thoughts that start with words such as *should, have to, need to* and *must* have their place, but they can also become counterproductive when you put yourself under pressure with them, causing anxiety, frustration, and stress.

When coaching someone, I listen out for these types of words. It's ot uncommon for the person I'm coaching to have quite a pattern of these rules – and to use them to beat herself up!

Using Meta Model patterns to challenge the rules associated with imperatives can unleash a huge change in your thinking. Pay attention to when you use imperative words at work. Maybe you've heard yourself say something like:

> ✔ I should spend more time with my team.
>
> ✔ I ought to send minutes out after that meeting.
>
> ✔ I must read and reply to all of my e-mails.

The next time you notice yourself using one of these expressions, just stop and ask yourself one or more of the following questions:

> ✔ Who says?
>
> ✔ What happens if I don't?
>
> ✔ What happens when I say 'I choose to' instead?

Then notice how your feelings can change as a result of talking to yourself differently.

## Identifying 'them'

I don't know if you find the same, but in just about every organisation I've ever worked with that had more than a handful of employees, I've encountered an 'us' and a 'them'. ('Them' also masquerade as 'they'). I frequently hear things like 'They don't seem to have a plan' or 'We're all waiting for them to announce the new structure'. Sound familiar?

Abdicating responsibility for issues to an unnamed non-specific group of people, generally assumed to be senior in the business, is a commonplace occurrence. Using the Meta Model, you can define this as an *unspecified referential index*. Frankly, I just remember 'them' and 'they', and then I know what to ask! When you hear – or even make – such comments challenge them with this simple yet powerful question:

> Who specifically?

The person challenged then has to unpick her thinking – probably generalisations and assumptions she's holding – in order to answer the question. Trying to figure out who 'them' is inevitably leads to a change in perception and often to a new attitude and behaviour, which is far more constructive than continually moaning about 'them'!

I was recently coaching a senior director, Sahid. He talked about needing more strategic direction and guidance from 'them'. When I asked him specifically who he meant by 'them', we ascertained it was the board into which Sahid reported. With a little reflection, Sahid realised that he was not only in a position to request what he felt he needed from his boss, but that he should make constructive suggestions as to how to improve the business to his boss.. After all, Sahid is a very senior figure in the business. After he made this breakthrough in his thinking, Sahid took charge and started to work more closely with the board to create the strategy for his area of responsibility.

# Coaching Cleanly

One of the more recent of the continuing developments in NLP is clean language. Using NLP modelling techniques, James Lawley and Penny Tompkins examined the approach of renowned therapist David Grove to identify a model that can be replicated for similar success.

## Using Clean Language

*Clean Language* is not about removing expletives from your speech (although they aren't usually much help when coaching!). In Penny Tompkins' words:

> Clean Language is 'clean' because it keeps the facilitator from unwittingly introducing their assumptions, suggestions or metaphors into a conversation (no matter how well meaning these may be). When personal change is the goal, Clean Language invites a client's perceptions to evolve and change organically – one question at a time.

*Reproduced with the permission of Penny Tompkins, The Developing Company*

Clean Language offers another highly useful coaching technique for people to examine the deep structure of their thinking (delve into this in the section 'Skimming the surface – or going deeper', earlier in this chapter) The technique is called clean because it only uses a range of specific questions, known as *clean questions,* and the words and phrases of the person being coached.

Some key principles for utilising Clean Language in coaching include:

✔ The coach does not bring her own ideas or opinions to the coaching.

✔ The coach follows the other person's lead in terms of what the other person pays attention to.

✔ The coach doesn't introduce words or assumptions that the other person has to make sense of.

✔ The coaching session is not a two-way conversation. Instead:

- The coach repeats back key words and phrases heard.

- The coach only uses clean questions (see Table 12-2).

Only use a combination of the words of the person you're coaching and the clean questions. If what you say doesn't sound grammatical, don't worry, it will still have the desired effect on the person you're coaching, as I explain in the following section.

### Developing an outcome

As I discuss in the section 'Coaching with NLP', earlier in this chapter, the starting point for coaching is always to look to the future and work on a desired goal or outcome. The clean question for creating an outcome is:

What would you like to have happen?

Often people are stuck with a problem that they want to get away from, but they haven't yet worked out what exactly they want. If you don't get an outcome expressed in the positive, the follow-up clean question is:

What would you like instead?

The following dialogue shows this technique in action:

Coach: What would you like to have happen?

Paulo: I want to stop missing deadlines.

Coach: You want to stop missing deadlines. What would you like instead?

Paulo: I want more time to plan.

After you have an outcome – something specific that someone wants, rather than what she doesn't want – use further clean questions to find out more. Two clean questions are:

What kind of [word or phrase from outcome]?

Is there anything else about [word or phrase from outcome]?

You can repeat the preceding question several times, until you get the answer 'No'. Here's how Paulo and his coach's conversation may go:

Coach: What kind of plan?

Paulo: Thinking, preparing, and organising my work.

Coach: Thinking, preparing, and organising. Is there anything else about plan?

Paulo: Yes, I want to be more proactive.

Coach: You want to be more proactive. Is there anything else about plan?

Paulo: With a plan, I can start to improve the way we do things.

Notice that the coach asked a question that's not grammatical: 'Is there anything else about *plan*?' You may be forgiven for thinking this is a bit odd! However, you can also spot that Paulo answers the question. This is because the coach is using Paulo's word. Paulo used it as a verb – a doing word. So the coach could only say 'plan' or 'planning'. But, Paulo didn't say 'planning' so the coach mustn't either. This is Clean Language at work!

After you spend some time asking clean questions about the outcome and discover more information, you can then check the wording of the outcome by asking the clean question:

> Given what you know now, what would you like?

In a coaching session, this question may go something like:

> Coach: Given what you know now, what would you like?
>
> Paulo: I want to work proactively.

Notice that Paulo changed the wording of his outcome compared to what he initially stated as his goal. Responding to his coach's clean questions helped him find out more clearly what he wanted.

If the person still isn't sure of her outcome at this stage, ask more questions to help her get clarity. Ask the 'What kind of . . . ?' and 'Is there anything else about . . . ?' questions about a variety of words and phrases that she uses. Then find out if she can define her outcome yet by asking the 'Given what you know now, what would you like?' question.

In the example in this section, notice that the coach repeats some or all of Paulo's answers. When you repeat back another person's words, you help her think more deeply and access more of her unconscious experience – at this stage to get a better articulated goal or outcome.

### Action planning

After you help people you're coaching find out more about their outcomes, you can support them to devise action plans – what they are going to do to achieve the outcome. Specific clean questions to generate action plans include:

> What needs to happen for you to [outcome]?
>
> Is there anything else that needs to happen for you to [outcome]?

Make sure that you repeat all the words used by the other person to define your outcome in these two questions where I indicate 'outcome'. Repeat the second question until you get to a firm 'No' from the person you're coaching. Then, list back all the actions that the person came up with and ask this second question one more time. You may be amazed at how often something else emerges!

This is not *your* action plan – it's the other person's! Despite all your knowledge and experience, resist any temptation to make suggestions or give advice. You may think something essential is missing from her person's action plan. Keep it to yourself! This style of coaching is all about getting people to create their own changes and achieve goals their own way. If something critical is missing the other person will realise at some point and adapt her plan.

Once the other person is satisfied they have a complete action plan, you have just two more clean questions to ask:

> What's the first thing that needs to happen?

> Can you [answer to last question]?

After you know the other person can initiate the first step, she has a usable action plan. Once she takes the first step she is on her journey to achieving her outcome. If she needs to prioritise the other steps in her action plan, she will.

Consider the following example between Paulo and his coach (see the section 'Developing an outcome', earlier in this chapter, for more of this coaching conversation):

> Coach: What needs to happen for you to *work proactively*?

> Paulo: I need to clear my desk and manage my e-mails.

> Coach: Is there anything else that needs to happen for you to work proactively?

> Paulo: I need to say 'no' more.

> Coach: Is there anything else that needs to happen for you to work proactively?

> Paulo: I need to coach my team to take on more.

> Coach: Is there anything else that needs to happen for you to work proactively?

> Paulo: I need to give priority to planning.

Coach: You need to clear your desk, manage your e-mails, say 'no' more, coach your team to take on more, and give priority to planning. Is there anything else that needs to happen for you to work proactively?

Paulo: No.

Coach: What's the first thing that needs to happen?

Paulo: I need to coach my team to take on more.

Coach: Can you coach your team to take on more?

Paulo: Yes.

When you're using the questioning technique to create an action plan, write down the other person's answers – at least key phrases and words. You need this to be able to repeat everything back to the other person, so she can check that you've covered everything and then choose a first step.

### Motivating

After you develop an outcome ('Developing an outcome') and create an action plan ('Action planning'), the only task left is to ensure the other person has sufficient motivation to get started. The final question you need to ask is:

When [outcome is achieved], then what happens?

In the Paulo/coach example, the approach may sound like:

Coach: When you work more proactively, then what happens?

Paulo: I start to improve the way we do things.

Coach: When you improve the way you do things, then what happens?

Paulo: My team and I get much better results.

Coach: You get better results. Then what happens?

Paulo: I'm really satisfied with my work and very happy in my job.

In the example, Paulo discovers that he doesn't simply want to stop missing deadlines, which is where he started (see 'Developing an outcome'), but he wants to work more proactively, which ultimately improves his satisfaction with his work and enables him to enjoy his job.

Keep asking the 'Then what happens?' question until the other person struggles to come up with an answer or starts to repeat herself.

# Coaching quickly

Using clean questions for coaching means you can coach someone in as little as five minutes to develop an outcome or an action plan. In fact, Mariette Castellino and I created the 'five-minute coach' model to support coaches in business to coach effectively both briefly on the job and in a longer, formal session that lasts up to 45 minutes.

The clean questioning approach I outline in the section 'Using Clean Language', earlier in this chapter, forms most of the five-minute coach model. Table 12-2 summarises the technique and essential clean questions.

| Table 12-2 | Extract from the Five-Minute Coach Model |
|---|---|
| **Coaching purpose** | **Clean questions** |
| Creating an outcome | What would you like to have happen? |
| | What would you like instead? |
| Finding out more about the outcome | What kind of...? |
| | Is there anything else about...? |
| Choosing the final outcome | Given what you know now, what would you like? |
| Action planning | What needs to happen for [outcome]? |
| | Is there anything else that needs to happen for [outcome]? |
| | What needs to happen first? |
| | Can you [do first thing]? |
| Motivating to change | When [outcome], then what happens? |

© Lynne Cooper and Mariette Castellino. Reproduced with the permission of Marietet Castellino and Lynne Cooper, Amicas

You can find many more clean questions in *Metaphors in Mind* by James Lawley and Penny Tompkins (The Developing Company Press, 2000), which also explains how Clean Language can be used in conjunction with metaphor to help people make changes to their thinking and achieve their goals.

# Discovering Clean Language

In the mid-1990s, NLP trainers James Lawley and Penny Tompkins came across the work of a highly innovative and exceptionally effective therapist, David Grove. Lawley and Tompkins wanted to dig deeper into how this talented man was facilitating amazing transformations for his clients. Like many who have contributed to the world of NLP, they used their NLP skills to develop a model of Grove's therapeutic strategies – what it is that he actually said and did with his clients to get results.

Lawley and Tompkins' book *Metaphors in Mind* (The Developing Company Press, 2000) explains the concept and structure of *Clean Language questions* to help an individual develop a metaphor representing how they are thinking, and then work further with this metaphor to create change and achieve a goal.

Until Grove's death in 2008, Lawley and Tompkins continued to model his evolving creative approaches to individual change – including the concepts of Clean Space and Emergent Knowledge, which are available through the Web site www.cleanlanguage.co.uk.

The clean approach to change is now used extensively in business, including in coaching, team alignment, interviewing, feedback, and leadership development, as well as in other fields such as education, parenting, and therapy.

# Chapter 13

# Handling Difficult People

· · · · · · · · · · · · · · · · · · · · · · · · · · · · · · · · · · · · · · · · · · · · · ·

## In This Chapter

▶ Improving your most challenging work relationships

▶ Moving forward in stuck situations

▶ Having more influence with multiple stakeholders

· · · · · · · · · · · · · · · · · · · · · · · · · · · · · · · · · · · · · · · · · · · · · ·

*O*rganisations thrive on people and their ability to communicate and work together. Yet working together isn't always easy. Sometimes:

✔ People understand issues differently.

✔ People don't have the same beliefs about a problem or opportunity.

✔ People have their own goals, which put them in conflict with others.

Whatever the cause, you've probably experienced – and may continue to experience – challenges with particular people in your working life.

In this chapter I look at some NLP approaches for gaining insights into these difficult work relationships and introduce essential strategies to create more flexibility in difficult situations – techniques that can help you get the results you want.

## Meeting Some Difficult People

In my work with organisations, I've certainly come across many examples of people who might be described as difficult. However, rather than labelling a particular person as difficult, I find it much more helpful to focus on difficult relationships – and relationships always involve more than one person.

Difficulties between people can seriously frustrate progress and success in the work place, leading to:

✔ **Conflict and disagreement** between individuals, teams, or groups.

✔ **Unproductive relationships** in which one person – or both – doesn't feel the other hears or understands them.

✔ **Stuck situations** in which decisions aren't made – or if decisions are made, they aren't properly put into practice.

✔ **Blaming the other party** when things go wrong or aren't achieved.

✔ **Secrecy,** where people have little confidence or trust in each other and end up withholding useful information from each other.

✔ **Avoidance,** where people just ignore thorny issues and don't deal with them until they become serious problems.

The situations that result from difficult relationships tend to affect everyone concerned in a negative way – and frequently people outside the relationship are negatively affected too.

The behaviours associated with difficult relationships can become very unproductive. Some of my clients struggling with particular individuals have described the other person in at least one of the following ways:

✔ Passive

✔ Aggressive

✔ Difficult

✔ Demotivated

✔ Unproductive

✔ Unhelpful

✔ Disinterested

Keeping people motivated, enthusiastic, and committed – especially when they're experiencing this kind of difficulty or being labelled with negative states of mind such as those listed above – can be an uphill battle. In the following sections, I present several ways to make the going easier, and working relationships more effective.

# Working with People You Just Don't Get

To achieve change in a business relationship that you're struggling to make work, you have to do something different. I explore a number of basic principles behind NLP in Chapter 3, and one that particularly applies to difficult relationships is:

If what you're doing isn't working, do something different.

If another person's seriously getting in the way of you making something important happen, you've probably already tried several alternative approaches without success. Now's the time to consider something new.

## Gaining new perspectives

As well as focusing on the structure of people's thinking and their use of words, John Grinder and Judith Delozier, two of the original developers of NLP, also discovered another way in which good communicators and influencers are successful: Good communicators and influencers can experience a situation from different perspectives, or *perceptual positions*.

As with many of the NLP techniques I discuss in this book, moving into different perceptual positions to get a different viewpoint on an issue is something you probably already do some of the time.

For example, good marketers emphasise the benefits of their products, focusing on what their customers are keen to have, rather than what excites the marketers. Excellent presenters imagine what their audiences see, hear, and feel and develop a presentation accordingly. The best customer service people anticipate how customers may react, particularly to bad news.

You also hear phrases in the work place and elsewhere every day that indicate appreciation or understanding of someone else's perspective:

'I see your point of view.'

'I hear where you're coming from.'

'I'm really pleased for you that. . .'

'From a completely objective standpoint. . .'

Despite being able to take on others' perspectives, every so often you still find yourself stuck in a groove with someone with whom you just don't communicate well. Often this stuck feeling is because you've become firmly stuck in your own point of view.

Getting another perspective, for example by temporarily imagining you have taken on another person's map of the world (venture further into this in Chapter 3), can create the subtle changes needed to unlock a tricky relationship. The following sections explore how.

## Recognising different perceptual positions

Three main perceptual positions can be taken. Exploring each of these can be helpful when you're faced with a difficult relationship. The three perceptual positions are conveniently called *first, second*, and *third position:*

✔ **When you're in first position,** you see through your own eyes, hear through your own ears, and have your own feelings. This position's like being in your own shoes. What you're interested in and care about, what you believe and what you want to achieve drive how you think and what you do and say.

✔ **When you're in second position,** you've essentially stepped into another person's shoes. You think about the situation as if you were that person. You may have some knowledge of that person – but you may also have to guess some of his thinking.

However, when you step into second position, you are the other person for that moment. Whatever he's doing or saying that you find challenging in first position seems normal after you're in his position.

✔ **When you're in third position,** you can stand back and observe the situation. From here you can see and hear yourself in first position, as well as the other person in second position. From this detached standpoint, you don't get caught up in the emotions of either party. Instead, you notice what's happening and think about things objectively.

Being able to move between these three positions at will in your mind gives you information on what to do and say next. This is a valuable skill in many business communications, including:

✔ Negotiation. For example, you may be being locked in discussions over new office premises that are just what your organisation needs. You want a lower rent and the lessor won't reduce it.

✔ Customer service. Imagine a customer calling in mid-winter to get an appointments being available for five days.

✔ Advertising. You may have a very loyal customer base, happy with what they've been buying from you over the last five years, when you launch a new improved version of your product.

✔ Handling grievances. Often complex and emotional, grievances might include someone claiming he's being bullied by his boss.

✔ Communicating change. Company executives are about to announce a restructure, including job losses, whilst their positions are secure.

✔ Selling. Many customers find themselves faced with a barrage of features they don't need or – in this electronic age – understand. A mature lady wanting a mobile phone for emergency purposes may not be interested in camera and mp3 features.

✔ Product and service development. Developing the most efficient dry cleaning service that only opens between 9.30am and 5.00pm is unlikely to meet many customers' needs to drop off and collect on the way to and from work.

✔ Labour relations. An organisation that takes into account the thoughts, needs and perspectives of its workforce will gain more cooperation and productivity, and can prevent serious disruption to output.

## Choosing the best perspective

At work, you may find that you spend most of your time in one of the three perceptual positions (see the section 'Recognising different perceptual positions', earlier in this chapter). Being aware of which position you prefer can be useful – particularly if moving into another position could help you to deal with certain challenges.

Table 13-1 describes some occasions during which you benefit from being in a particular position, as well as when it may be less valuable to you.

| Table 13-1 | The Effects of Different Perceptual Positions | |
|---|---|---|
| | *When Spending Time in One Position Is Useful* | *Possible Consequences of Too Much Time in One Position* |
| First position | For setting your own outcomes and goals and for being assertive | You lack understanding of others' ideas or feelings. |
| Second position | For understanding others' behaviours and feelings | You meet others' needs at the expense of your own. |
| Third position | For thinking objectively and removing emotions from decision making | Others perceive you as unemotional and uncaring. |

Over the next week, reflect on the conversations and discussions you have had at work. Notice which of the three positions you seem to spend the *least* time in. Ask yourself:

✔ Do I spend much time in my own shoes thinking of my own wants and needs?

✔ Do I spend much time empathising with others and imagining what it's like for them?

✔ Do I detach myself and think objectively about matters?

During the following week or two, practise thinking through issues and relationships from this less familiar position so that it becomes easier to do.

# Making Changes to Tricky Relationships

In 1988 NLP innovator Robert Dilts created an exercise to help people to make shifts in tricky relationships through exploring different perceptual positions. This approach can be used in any relationship where difficulties exist, whether at work or elsewhere. A shortened version of Dilts' technique, which he called the *meta mirror*, follows.

You get the best result from the following exercise by physically moving around. Not only do you need a bit of space, but you may want to make sure others can't see you – they may wonder if you've gone a little crazy! Consider going through this exercise in a quiet room at work or at home.

1. **Choose a difficult work relationship that you want to improve.**

2. **Use pen and three sheets of blank paper to create signs that label the three positions, as indicated in Figure 13-1.**

   Place these on the floor, with some space between them (at least two metres).

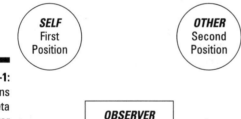

**Figure 13-1:**
Positions for the meta mirror exercise.

3. **Step into the SELF (first) position.**

   Imagine that the other person in your difficult relationship is standing in the OTHER (second) position spot. Imagine you are having your next important interaction with this person.

   Ask yourself:

   • What am I experiencing?

   • What do I see and hear?

   • How do I feel about the situation?

   You'll now be having some of this experience, as if it were really happening. Once you've answered the questions in your mind, you're ready for the next step.

**4. Move to stand in the OTHER (second) position.**

Now act as if you're the other person in your difficult work relationship. Really step into his shoes. Imagine you're looking at yourself standing in first position – only the person standing in first person is another person.

Ask yourself:

- What am I experiencing?
- What do I see and hear?
- How do I feel?

Take as long as you need to create the experience as if you were the other person. once you have answered the questions in your mind, move on to the next step. Once you've answered the questions in your mind, you're ready for the next step.

**5. Move to the OBSERVER (third) position.**

Imagine you see two people – one standing on the SELF position, the other standing on the OTHER position.

Look at the two people in this relationship and notice what's happening between them. Stay objective about that 'you' over there as well as the other person.

Then, as the independent *observer*, ask yourself these questions:

- What do I notice?
- What seem to be the sticking points of this relationship?
- What can that 'you' over there in first position do differently?
- What different attitude can that 'you' in first position try out to change things?

Take as much time as you need to answer these questions. If you get several answers, you might even want to write them down so you remember to try them all out.

If you struggle to come up with answers to the questions, don't give up! Keep on thinking. If inspiration still doesn't come then move to another – *fourth* – position. From this position you can view 'you', the other person *and* the observer. You'll find that yet another perspective will likely give you the information and answers you are seeking.

Once you've answered the questions in your mind, you're ready for the next step.

6. **Return to the SELF (first) position.**

   Think about trying out the changes you came up with in third position. Think as if you're putting those changes into place.

   Imagine the other person reacting to your changes. Ask yourself:

   - What am I seeing and hearing from the other person now?

   - How does this feel now?

   - What's changed?

   Once you've answered the questions in your mind, you're ready for the next step.

7. **Step again into the OTHER (second) position.**

   Imagine the 'you' in first position having made the changes you came up with in Step 5.

   As the 'other' person, ask yourself:

   - What am I seeing and hearing from the other person now?

   - How does this feel now?

   - What's changed?

8. **Go back to the SELF (first) position.**

   Having implemented all the changes you came up with in Step 5, and noticing the difference this is making to the relationship, ask yourself:

   - How does the situation feel now?

   - What's changed?

After you've tried out this exercise, discovered some changes you could make to the way you approach this colleague, and feel differently about the relationship, then put it into practise! Before you next speak with that person, reflect on all that you found out through the meta mirror exercise. Notice how things are different, whether subtly or dramatically, in the relationship.

Once you are familiar with this technique you'll find you can also do it in your mind as well as by physically moving in space. So when you need to get more insight into a difficult relationship whilst in the middle of a conversation, mentally run through the different positions. You may be amazed at what you find out and the difference you can make in the moment.

A colleague and I had great difficulty communicating. After I discovered perceptual positions, I decided to run through the preceding exercise to explore our relationship. By stepping into her shoes, I discovered that behind her often aggressive outbursts, my colleague seemed to be very insecure and uncertain. She was also quite lonely at work (and at home), which may have affected her moods. In third position, I saw that I'd started to become very dismissive of her ideas – and indeed of her. So I made the change to think of her as a vulnerable and sensitive person who needed supporting rather than ignoring. Over time our relationship changed, her aggression dropped, and we achieved much more together than ever before.

Relationships involve two people and are really the responsibility of both. Wouldn't it be great if you both had the same desire and skill to make the relationship work well? Unfortunately that rarely happens. And, you can't change the other person to make them less 'difficult'. However, what you can do is to be more flexible, using the meta mirror exercise to discover some new approaches.

# Looking for the Positive Intention

One of the key NLP principles I discuss in Chapter 3 is:

Examining the positive intention that is driving people to do or say something – whether it's you or someone else – helps you gain more insight into, and understanding of, a difficult relationship.

1. **Think about a difficult situation that exists between you and somebody you interact with through your work**.

2. **Make sure you have a quiet interrupted place where you can move around a little – at work or elsewhere.**

   Use pen and three sheets of blank paper to create signs that label the three positions, as indicated in Figure 13-1.

3. **Step into the SELF (first) position. Ask yourself:**

   What am I doing and saying to this other person?

   What does doing and saying these things do for me?

   What is my positive intention?

4. **Step into the OTHER (second) position.**

   Think as if you are have stepped into the shoes of the other person. Ask yourself:

   What (in this position) am I doing and saying?

   What does doing and saying these things do for me?

   What is my positive intention?

5. **Move into the OBSERVER (third) position.**

What do you now know from here about the positive intentions behind the behaviour of these two people towards each other?

Now you know this, what difference does it make to how you are thinking and feeling about the relationship?

What might you do differently as a result of this change in thinking and feeling?

# Bringing Change to Political Situations

Difficulties between people that impede progress in the workplace are unfortunately not just restricted to one-to-one relationships. No matter what size of organisation you work in and its level of bureaucracy, you almost inevitably come across situations that involve a number of parties who end up completely stumped in making progress.

You have more than one person to influence in these political situations. Each person is a stakeholder in the matter and has his own goals – and potentially some hidden agendas too.

I've seen many different examples of political situations in organisations, including:

- ✔ Making organisational changes
- ✔ Agreeing budgets
- ✔ Developing new products
- ✔ Introducing new systems
- ✔ Merging divisions or businesses

To move forward in such situations – without over-compromising your own position – you can use perceptual positions to give you more insights into the other people involved and then make changes accordingly.

## Stepping into stakeholders' shoes

David Grove, a therapist who achieved remarkable results helping people to make change, promoted the idea of moving around in space to get new perspectives. Physically moving can actually help people to achieve challenging goals. Grove's approach, further developed by James Lawley and Penny Tompkins, is called *Clean Space*.

Working with many organisational leaders facing complex matters with multiple stakeholders, my colleague Mariette Castellino created the following exercise, using the core principles of Clean Space. You can use it when you are running -or are contributing to – a project that has become stuck or where your voice doesn't seem to be being heard.

Like the exercise in the section 'Making Changes to Tricky Relationships', earlier in this chapter, you may prefer to find a place with some privacy in which to go through this exercise. Find a space a large enough to walk around and stand in a number of different positions, as indicated in Figure 13-2.

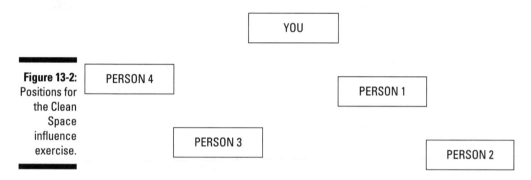

**Figure 13-2:** Positions for the Clean Space influence exercise.

1. **Identify a complex work situation that involves more than one stakeholder, in which you want to have more influence.**

2. **Take a piece of blank paper and write your name on it.**

   Place the paper on the floor.

3. **Write the name of each of the other people involved in the situation on an individual piece of paper (you may group people together if you can only influence them as a group – for example: 'advisory board', but focus on individuals as much as possible).**

   Place these other pieces of paper on the floor, in relation to yourself. Leave some space between each. You need to be able to see each of the other positions clearly from the other positions. Figure 13-2 is an example of how you can place various people for a situation, but you'll know which positions they should be in for you and this situation.

4. **Stand on the piece of paper that represents you.**

   Look around the room at the other pieces of paper. Ask yourself:

   • What do I know about the situation from here?

   • Is there anything else I know about the situation from here?

   Ask yourself this second question three times, or until you reach a 'no' whichever is the soonest.

**5. Move to another piece of paper, representing the position of another person.**

You're now stepping into his shoes. Ask yourself:

- What do I know about the situation from here?

- Is there anything else I know about the situation from here?

    Ask yourself this second question three times, or until you reach a 'no' whichever is the soonest.

**6. Move through the remaining pieces of paper, standing on each.**

In each position, step into the person's shoes. Ask yourself the same questions:

- What do I know about the situation from here?

- Is there anything else I know about the situation from here?

    Ask yourself this second question three times, or until you reach a 'no' whichever is the soonest.

**7. Find a new position in the space not marked by any pieces of paper.**

From this new position, look at all the other positions. Ask yourself:

- What do I know about the situation from here?

- Is there anything else I know about the situation from here?

    Ask yourself this second question three times, or until you reach a 'no' whichever is the soonest.

**8. Return to the position with your name on it.**

Look over the situations from your own position. Ask yourself:

- What do I know NOW about the situation from here?

- Is there anything else I know about the situation from here?

    Keep asking this question until your answer's 'no'.

Ask yourself one final question:

- Now that I know all of this, what's the first thing I need to do?

*Clean Space influence exercise reproduced with the permission of Mariette Castellino, Amicas*

I worked with Sally, a learning and development director of an information services provider. Her brief was to create and develop a pool of talent throughout the business. She developed a plan that required a 50% increase in the learning and development budget. As budget negotiations progressed, she met stiff resistance from some key members of the executive team, including the finance and sales directors, and a divisional head of operations. By using the Clean Space exercise outlined above, Sally gained a deeper understanding of the constraints and challenges of those who were resisting her bigger budget. She also noticed how she might be perceived by each of them in turn. As a result, she changed her approach, by tackling each of the Directors individually. She worked hard to build rapport (find out about rapport in Chapter 6) and to discuss the issues that she believed were most important to each director. Ultimately Sally influenced her colleagues to support a 40 per cent increase in budget, with a promise of more over each of the next three years.

## *Achieving greater influence through flexibility*

One of the NLP principles that I outline in Chapter 3 states:

> In any system the person with the most flexibility controls the system.

If a *system* is something that operates through the relationship of its various parts (see Chapter 3), then a complex situation with a number of stake-holders is a system, in which each stakeholder is a part. As one of several people in a situation where you want more influence, by having more flexibility you have greater influence. I'm not talking here about giving in to other people. Instead, you have more options in what you do and say to maximise your chances of achieving what you want. I talk more about flexibility, one of the four pillars of NLP, in Chapter 2.

When you're just one cog in the wheel of a complex or political situation, even a small amount of change on your part affects the system. For example, you may have been communicating with the three other people involved in a project at weekly meetings where everyone is present. You feel that your opinions and suggestions are being ignored. You decide to act more *flexibly* by meeting with each person involved on a one-to-one basis. You set an objective for each meeting and work to influence each person to hear and understand your views. At the next weekly meeting, things have changed. Those involved now have a broader perspective and they are listening to your thoughts and arguments.

As things change, keep repeating the exercise I describe in the section 'Stepping into stakeholders' shoes'. You get continued new insights and ideas from each repetition. For example, more stakeholders may emerge, the situation may change, and you may continue to discover new ways of influencing the system.

# Part IV
# Achieving Business Excellence

## The 5th Wave
By Rich Tennant

"In searching for a successful model of change for the business, I recalled how successfully punk rock changed the music scene..."

# In this part . . .

**W**ant to know how to use NLP to effect real business change? How to create a vision for your organisation that your colleagues will want to buy into? Step inside.

From identifying and developing well-formed outcomes to aspire to, through to modelling the ways of working which have brought others success, this part shows you how to use NLP to take your business performance to the max.

# Chapter 14

# Creating a Compelling Vision

· · · · · · · · · · · · · · · · · · · · · · · · · · · · · · · · · · · · · · · · · · · · · · · · ·

## In This Chapter

▶ Creating visions that engage and motivate

▶ Using metaphor to communicate vision

▶ Collaborating on metaphors

▶ Shifting beliefs in organisations

▶ Developing meaningful values

· · · · · · · · · · · · · · · · · · · · · · · · · · · · · · · · · · · · · · · · · · · · · · · · ·

*M*any companies have a defined corporate vision, as well as goals or objectives. Some businesses declare their values to the world. A number have mission statements.

When putting together visions and missions, leaders usually want to convey their beliefs and values, the quality of the contributions the business makes, and aims and aspirations for the future. Setting out these things for employees, customers, and other stakeholders is considered helpful in getting everyone on board and motivated to do her best. Yet so often, these things are perceived as 'just a set of words'. They're so bland that they have little or no effect on people.

 When crafted well, a vision enthuses and encourages people to strive towards achieving it. It portrays something to aim for that's desirable and aspirational – something that goes beyond simple financial goals like sales and profit. When leaders carefully construct, meaningfully explain, and actively demonstrate a company's vision and values, these beliefs can be very powerful.

NLP offers tools to develop powerful visions that truly engage and fire up employees. With NLP you can also determine the actual values of the organisation and define the evidence that shows the organisation working towards its values.

In this chapter I explore how to develop vibrant and compelling visions and express values in a way that everyone understands and can commit to.

# Crafting a Vision that Motivates

Senior executives frequently construct an organisation's *vision*. They often try to describe a company's reason for being and its goals for the future in a few sentences – or less. These statements pop up on the company's Web site or in its annual report. They're supposed to inspire employees, shareholders, and even the general public.

Most vision statements don't energise or excite people. In fact, in many organisations I visit, most employees can't even remember what the vision is. Why? These people haven't been involved in the creation of the vision and aren't motivated by the way it's communicated.

Some vision statements I've come across that fit into this category include:

- ✔ 'Our vision is to become the market-leading supplier of data to the marketing sector, with products and services that exceed customer expectations at all times.'

- ✔ 'Powered by innovation, guided by integrity, we help our clients achieve their most challenging goals.'

- ✔ 'We will be the leading components provider, recognised for operational excellence, customer service and commitment to safety; the choice for long-term growth, investment value and financial strength; and a company driven by the leadership, skills and diversity of its employees.'

These visions don't usually have any effect in the organisation as they are neither inspirational nor aspirational – they don't stir up passion or enthusiasm, and certainly don't give people anything exciting to aim for in the future. In fact, employees don't even notice them and they're more likely to turn customers off than impress them.

The following sections offer meaningful ways to create vision statements that truly affect and inspire people within and outside organisations.

## Tapping into all the senses

People become much more engaged by a vision when it's expressed as a rich, bright view of the future. An important clue is in the word *vision* itself. A vision must be a detailed picture, something you can focus on. Add in the rest of the sensory experience – what you hear and feel when you have this vision – and you have a statement that becomes enticing and attractive.

When you describe something in terms of the sensory experience you want people to have, it usually becomes much more meaningful and alive (turn to Chapter 5 to find out more about sensory descriptions). A well-described sensory-specific vision is motivating, at whatever level you intend it:

- ✔ Individual
- ✔ Team
- ✔ Organisation

The vision forms a dream of the future, something that ignites passion and enthusiasm. People can then connect to the vision, believe in it, and be excited about working towards it. Consider a few examples of vision statements that hit the mark a little better:

To create leisure and hospitality experiences that make people feel better - every time they visit us. – *Whitbread Group plc*

To create new value, excite and delight our customers through the best automotive products and services. – *Mazda Motor Corporation*

It's tricky to get much sensory specific language into such a short (and therefore memorable) statement, but not impossible. Here's an example:

To deliver the best in quality home furnishings to our customers, with a passion that can be seen and heard in everything we do.

Read through the vision statement of your own organisation or that of another company you do business with. Notice how many sensory specific words are in it (you can find examples of sensory language in Chapter 5). Does the vision inspire you or just leave you cold? If you were given the job of rewriting this vision, how might you express it?

## *Magnetising with metaphor*

You may not realise how much you and the people around you talk in metaphors. Whether a metaphor's a single word, a phrase, or a full-blown metaphorical description of something, metaphors continually run through our conversations, and those chats we have with ourselves. How often have you heard (or said) something like:

- ✔ 'He's getting on my nerves.'
- ✔ 'I'm in two minds.'
- ✔ 'This customer's a nightmare.'
- ✔ 'Let's get a grip of this situation.'

People don't mean these expressions *literally*. Someone isn't physically on someone else's nerves. You can't actually pick up and hold a situation. These statements are metaphorical.

With a *metaphor,* you describe something in terms of something else. Metaphors make communicating easier and faster and give away a great deal about the experience a person's having. For example, if someone describes a customer as 'having high standards' or 'being indecisive,' the speaker's probably having a far less emotional experience than the one who describes the customer as 'being a nightmare'.

Communicating your vision through metaphor is powerful. Unconscious minds absorb metaphors quickly and make their own sense of them, even when they're someone else's thinking. When you describe something metaphorically, visions come to life. Your words communicate something quite complex very quickly and easily. They hold and convey values. They have the potential to engage and captivate.

The section 'Generating a Meaningful Team Vision', later in this chapter, takes you though the specifics of working with a group to develop a metaphor that's powerful for each and every team member.

Listen out for implicit metaphors in the organisation you work for – or the businesses you work with. These metaphors express company culture, albeit out of conscious awareness. You may even hear people talking in the language of the metaphor throughout the organisation. Sporting metaphors are common, as are those that centre on combat. For example, when people in an organisation view everything as a fight, you may hear expressions like:

- ✔ 'We battle it out.'
- ✔ 'All guns blazing.'
- ✔ 'You need to fight for what you believe in.'

When you explicitly create a new metaphor, lining up the language and the culture behind it is important. The next section explains how to create a useful and meaningful metaphor, to which people subscribe. Once such a metaphor exits, what people do and say occurs within the context of the metaphor.

# *Generating a Meaningful Team Vision*

As well as a vision for the organisation, functional teams – project teams, departments, and divisions – benefit from having a vision that gets people excited. Rarely do such groups within businesses have their own clearly defined vision of what they aspire to achieve.

A team vision must be negotiated, agreed to, and aligned with, in order to ensure that everyone pulls in the same direction. It provides a context for decision making, prioritising, and planning. When everyone on the team buys into a vision, things start to change!

The following sections take you through the process of creating dynamic, metaphorically rich team visions.

One team I coached through the team vision process reported back to me nine months later that they had a much higher profile within their organisation, were operating more strategically, were working together more effectively, and were getting great feedback.

Developing a metaphor that everyone agrees to sometimes has its challenges! Ideally, you construct a vision with input from *everyone* concerned. When you're leading or participating in the creation of a team vision, make every effort to get the whole team involved in the discussion.

The process is based on the *Metaphors@Work* technique developed by Caitlin Walker, a skilful change facilitator. I've used it in a number of organisations to create group, team, and even corporate visions. Metaphors@Work has its roots in Clean Language and Symbolic Modelling, which you can read more about in Chapter 12.

This process works well when give some time. It's useful to be able to take up to a day, and is best done face-to face. Many groups find that using a meeting room off-site provides the opportunity for the best creative thinking, and of course, the avoidance of interruptions. It also helps to pose the first question of the exercise to the members of the group or team a few days in advance, so they have some time to consider their response before the meeting. Ask them to bring a visual (drawing, clip art, photograph, model etc) to the meeting to illustrate their metaphor.

Make sure that you have a good supply of paper – A3 and A1 size – and a good selection of marker pens in an array of colours, available for the meeting room.

1. **Ensure everyone in the group or team has created her own metaphor for the vision.**

   Remind people of the question they are answering: When this organisation (or team) is working ideally, that will be like what? Think of a metaphor.

   Give people a little time to talk through their metaphors in pairs or small groups an, allowing anyone who hadn't brought along a visual a little time to develop and draw this metaphor.

2. **Ask each member of the team to spend a few minutes sharing her metaphor with the rest of the group, using words or pictures.**

3. **After each team member has described her metaphor, the rest of the team members ask questions for around ten minutes in order to gain more insight into the metaphor and its values.**

Have team members use *clean questions* to discover more about each metaphor. In NLP, clean questions help you to access unconscious thoughts and build and enrich metaphors. These questions are considered *clean* because the questioner doesn't bring in her own interpretations of the metaphor. (See Chapter 12 for more on clean questions.)

Questioning for more information should be directed at using clean questions, with specific words that a team member uses to describe an aspect of her metaphor. Make sure each team member has a copy of these useful clean questions:

- What kind of [.....]?

- Is there anything else about [.....]?

- Where is [.....]? (And follow up this question with: Whereabouts is [answer to last question]?)

- Does [.....] have a size or a shape?

- How many [.....] could there be?

- Is there a relationship between [.....] and [.....]?

Insert the person's exact words in the clean questions. For example, if the metaphor is *A precision clock with fine cogs. All the cogs work together, well oiled, to tell the time reliably*, you might ask:

- 'What kind of *fine cogs*?'

- 'Is there anything else about *fine cogs*?'

- 'Where are *fine cogs*?'

- 'How many *cogs* could there be?'

- 'What kind of *precision*?'

- 'Is there anything else about *precision*?'

- 'Is there a relationship between *fine cogs* and *precision*?

It's important that you don't allow people to make criticisms, jokes, or suggestions about anyone else's metaphor. In fact, there should be no comment at all – just questioning using clean questions.

4. **After responding to clean questions, each individual decides what's really important to her in the metaphor.**

   Have each person refine her vision until she identifies a single must-have value from her own metaphor that needs to be presenting the final metaphor.

   This is most likely a word or short phrase, for example, 'quality', customer-centred' or good communications. Write each person's must-have value on a white board or similar, which everyone can see.

5. **After the team members have shared all their individual metaphors and extracted each of their key values, the team begins to negotiate a new metaphor for the vision.**

   This new metaphor needs to incorporate what's most important to each member. Some teams start with one of their members' metaphor and adapt it to ensure that is has characteristics that will mean the individual values of each team member are met. Others start from scratch and create a whole new metaphor to encapsulate the values. Either way, the process can happen very quickly, or take a few hours. If the group gets stuck, make sure you get them moving – changing places, going out for a short walk, or something similar, before reconvening. A shift in physiology helps to bring about a shift in thinking.

6. **Once the metaphor has been agreed, invite the team to draw the combined metaphor on a large piece of paper.**

   Use at least an A1 size sheet of paper. Often team members delegate the drawing task to one or two people. If so, make sure that everyone gives suggestions, and encourage eth addition of as much detail as possible to the picture.

7. **As the image is taking shape, check in with each team member that her own key value is represented in some way.**

   When the drawing's complete, ask whether everyone agrees with the overall metaphor. Have team members update and amend the image as necessary.

*Metaphors@ Work process reproduced with permission of Caitlin Walker, Training Attention*

When you have your well defined vision in metaphor, there are a whole range of things you can do to add energy and direction to working towards the vision:

✔ As a team, identify how you and others will know that you are moving towards the vision. What behaviours will be seen and heard by the team and others which indicate that the team is working ideally, or at least, aiming to do so?

✔ Develop an action plan to achieve the vision. See the section, 'Planning for action', later in this chapter.

✔ Some teams like to define the roles within the metaphor. For example, one team I worked with created a modern swing band as their metaphor. It was important to them to specify who played which role in the meta-phor – drummer, lead singer, guitarist etc. They then used the language of the metaphorical roles when talking to each other, saying things like – 'You're drumming a bit too loudly!' This team also identified what they needed from each other, in terms of the metaphorical roles, to perform at their best.

✔ Ensure everyone has a copy of the metaphor visual, and puts their copy where it can be seen frequently. A constant reminder to both conscious and unconscious minds will help to keep everyone on track.

✔ Consider how to communicate the vision (see the 'Conveying your vision' section later in this chapter).

✔ Keep talking about the vision. Put it on the agenda of team meetings. Use the metaphor to convey messages where it may be helpful. Review the metaphor – and update it if things are changing and evolving – on a regular basis.

# Building Commitment: Sharing Your Vision

As a team negotiates and creates a metaphor (see the section 'Generating a Meaningful Team Vision', earlier in this chapter), they start to buy in to it. Through working on the metaphor – its characteristics and details – each team member starts mentally to rehearse already having achieved that vision. That's the wonderful power of the unconscious mind.

When the vision is for a larger body of people, such as the whole business, it needs to be communicated in such a way that people understand it, believe it, and commit to it. If you can get other people involved in working with your metaphor, this can be very effective at gaining commitment (see an example in the sidebar, 'Merging with metaphor', later in this chapter. In a very large organisation it may not be possible to get everyone involved. Then you have to make a judgement as to whether your metaphor is the most straightforward and meaningful way to convey the vision, or whether it needs to be expressed in sensory specific business language, such that it's described with descriptions of what the vision looks and sounds like.

## A harmonious effort

I coached a team through the process of developing a vision for their division. (Flip to the section 'Generating a Meaningful Team Vision', earlier in this chapter, for more on this process.) Group members' various individual metaphors gave rise to a summary of words and phrases for must-have values, including:

- Connections
- Flexibility
- Quality and good results
- Highly skilled
- Purposeful
- Directed

Through their individual metaphors, the group members were able to convey some of their own meanings for these words, leading to a shared understanding of what was important to each other.

The team agreed a metaphor to represent their vision – a world-class orchestra. Their performance was strong, they were well conducted and well rehearsed, and they entertained their audience. Their range of music was broad, and many musicians played more than one instrument. Not every musician was required for every piece of music, so members had the freedom to come and go as necessary for a particular piece.

## *Conveying the vision*

Before you start communicating an important vision to others, put a plan together. Ask yourself the following:

- **What result do you want?** Start with your *outcome*, or goal. What do you want to have happen as a result of passing on the information?

  For example, your outcome may be to engage and motivate others to work towards achieving this vision.

- **Who needs to know?** Who needs to know your vision? And *what specifically* do they need to know?

- **What's next?** After the intended audience knows your vision, then what happens?

Whether you choose to use your metaphor or you find another way to draw people towards the vision, remember to use sensory language. A vision makes much more sense if you tell people what they're likely to see, hear, and feel. See the section 'Tapping into all the senses', earlier in this chapter, for more.

ANECDOTE

## Shifting stories

I worked with a team responsible for launching a change initiative in their accountancy organisation, including some leading-edge training and development opportunities. Some months had gone by and they weren't getting the results they hoped for.

They decided to negotiate a vision of the changed organisation in a metaphor – a Formula 1 race track. They saw their organisation as a high-quality, slick track with all the latest amenities. Only the best worked here. The track included the most skilful drivers, mechanics, and support team. The audience was agog at the thrills and risks.

This same team then developed a metaphor for how the organisation was at that time. They identified a group of safety-conscious Volvo drivers driving carefully along the inside lane of a motorway, 20 miles an hour under the speed limit.

The change team quickly realised that, metaphorically speaking, they were promoting their change programme with the language of the race track – very fast, different, exciting, and with a hint of danger. But the people they needed to influence wanted safety, security, and reliability. This realisation made all the difference. What they discovered through metaphor now directed what they needed to do back in the workplace. The team rewrote its brochures, posters, and presentations, with emphasis on the aspects of the new programme that offered the qualities their audience was interested in, downplaying what excited the change team – the innovations and differences. These fairly subtle changes led to the acceleration of buy-in to the change initiative and a huge increase in the uptake of the accompanying training and development programme.

Meanwhile, behind the scenes, the change team were inspired by their vision, and worked to achieve the high standards represented by their race track. They kept their metaphor very firmly to themselves though!

After you know the answers to the preceding questions and are ready to share the vision, make the opportunity for others to ask in-depth questions about the vision in order to gain their own understanding. Have an open mind about adapting and moulding the vision with feedback and ideas from those you're keen to influence. Remember, these are the people you want to engage with the vision.

TIP

Sharing your vision with people in metaphorical form is valuable – apart from when it isn't! Your customers may think you've gone mad if you tell them your company vision is to become an air force aerobatics team when you're supplying them with silicon chips or even deep-fried chips! If you wish to share your vision with your customers, it may be best to focus on the outcomes that affect them – what they can see, hear and even how they'll feel, when you are working to your vision.

# *Storytelling*

People have told stories throughout time, using myths, legends, and metaphors to communicate messages. Stories are just as useful today as they've always been. And you tell them all the time. After all, just telling someone about your day, sharing a humorous tale about something that happened to you on your way to work, and relating any incident you recall, is storytelling.

Given that you already have the skill to tell stories, the goal in business is to use stories purposely to add depth to your communications, allowing people to hear a story to help make their own sense of your message. A story is much more likely to engage a room of people you want to influence than a 50-slide PowerPoint presentation. Anecdotes, testimonials and case studies describing the benefits other people experienced from working with your organisation are all very powerful convincers for new customers.

You can tell many different kinds of stories, depending on your audience and message:

✔ Personal experiences

✔ Business anecdotes

✔ 'Tall' tales

✔ Humorous stories

✔ Metaphorical stories

When you use stories, prepare them in advance. Practise and rehearsal of a story will give you the cache to get all the important parts of the story in. It needs to do the job you want it to do, although of course, must sound fresh and new to your audience. Keep in mind the following when composing your story:

1. Keep it brief. Stories that can be told in a few minutes hold people's attention and give them enough information to be able to form their own meaning or understanding of them.

2. Remember simplicity is key. In a business setting, stories can lose credibility or usefulness if they become too complex, with different strands of plot and multiple characters.

3. Use sensory-specific language (see Chapter 5 for examples of this). Descriptions using the five senses make stories much more vivid for listeners.

4. Be relevant. Make sure your story is pertinent to your intended message, and not so obtuse that the listeners can't make the sense you wish them to make.

5. Have a range of characters in stories. Too many stories just about you *can* turn people off.

# The moral of the mountain

I once heard a newly appointed CEO speaking to the 40 most senior managers in his organisation. This leader had been employed by shareholders to 'turn things round' as they described it – which meant that they wanted him to make some drastic changes to move the business from making a substantial loss back into profit.

Anxiety about the future was rife throughout the organisation. People were fearful of redundancy and concerned about changes. Motivation and energy were low. The new leader needed to engage people – and quickly.

Within his presentation the CEO used a story about himself. It went something like this:

'A few years ago I realised I was feeling very anxious. I was running a business that had got itself into some difficulties. There was a lot of pressure, and no matter how hard I worked nothing improved. And then a friend asked me to join him to trek in the Himalayas. I laughed – I was unfit I couldn't even walk up three flights of stairs without completely losing my breath) , overweight and I certainly couldn't leave the organisation for a month. How would it survive without me?

'My friend explained more. The trip isn't for another eight months. That will gave you time to get fit. And surely you've got a competent executive team that can manage the business? If not you've got eight months to put that right.

'To cut a long story short, eight months later I found myself having the most memorable and life-changing experience of my life. It was demanding, it was exhausting, and yet it was absolutely exhilarating. I was walking in the Himalayas, seeing the most breathtaking views, and feeling totally different to how I had ever felt before. I felt at peace with myself – the pace of my life had slowed right down, as climbed cautiously and steadily to avoid attitude sickness.

'We made good progress on our trek until one day a member of the group fell ill. The altitude had affected him. He needed to go some way back down the mountain until he recovered. We were a team and had to stay together, so down we all want. Two days later, our team member recovered, we started our ascent again. Then another few days and the same thing happened to me. I had to go back down – and of course, the others did too. This became the pattern of our progress over the next 16 days. We stuck together as a group whether things went well, or they didn't. Eventually we reached our goal. My sense of elation, as we stood on the peak, looking at this beautiful mountain range stretching into the distance, congratulating each other on our achievements, was almost overwhelming.

'I now truly understand the importance of a good team, the need to stick together through the ups and downs, and that a steady pace is a great way to achieve your goal. This business isn't going to be profitable tomorrow, nor the next day. We will give ourselves enough time, as a team, to accomplish our goal and have the excitement and fulfilment of standing on our mountain top.'

Use stories to bring to life all sorts of abstract ideas or complex issues, including:

- ✔ Vision
- ✔ Values
- ✔ Innovations
- ✔ Bad news
- ✔ Technical information

## *Planning for action*

> *Vision without action is a daydream. Action without vision is a nightmare.*
>
> –Japanese proverb

Many people in businesses are so busy being busy that they've no idea where their busy-ness is taking them. In contrast, some organisations have expressed their visions, but don't appear to be directing much of their activity to achieving them.

After you have a clear, well-defined vision (see the section 'Generating a Meaningful Team Vision', earlier in this chapter), you need to move on to making that vision happen. If you're not sure where to start, then take the lead from the five-minute coach model I describe in Chapter 12. Based on this model, ask the team who developed the vision:

- ✔ What needs to happen for [vision]?
- ✔ Is there anything else that needs to happen for [vision]?

Repeat this second question until no further actions emerge, and then ask:

- ✔ What's the first thing that needs to happen?

After you answer this question, the seeds are sown, and people's attention is on the vision and the steps they need to take to start to move towards it.

Consider involving other people in the vision – perhaps developing it further or creating a complementary vision for a specific aspect of the business or department that dovetails with and supports the bigger vision. As you involve more people, you grab far more of the organisation's hearts and minds and are heading for success.

## Merging with metaphor

Three organisations were planning to merge and wanted make as smooth a transition as possible for all involved. My colleague Mariette Castellino worked with the three leaders to clarify what they wanted in the future organisation. Their metaphors were:

✔ A group of beehives

✔ A willow tree

✔ An Olympic team

Through exploring each other's metaphors, the leaders discovered more about what was important to each original organisation. They then negotiated a model for the future organisation: *Enlightened United Nations*, which incorporated all their key values. The leaders presented the metaphor to a cross-section of their managers. The managers in turn added details and refinements to the model, such as the role of ambassadors, export–import arrangements, and internal sharing of surpluses. This vibrant, evolving metaphor provided a common understanding and shared language for the vision of the merger. Issues were more easily explained to staff, clients, and suppliers. The merger went smoothly, employee resistance was minimised, and the new organisation quickly started to work effectively.

*Reproduced with permission of Mariette Castellino, Amicas.*

# Harnessing Beliefs and Values

As you may have read elsewhere in this book, everyone has beliefs and values, formed from your experiences though life. . Your beliefs and values are in the background, influencing what you think, say and do.

Beliefs and values drive and motivate people, including you. You put energy and other resources into what's important to you, and pay less regard to what's not important. These principles are intrinsic to how you operate and are likely to have been in place for a very long time, but you can change them.

Beliefs and values also pervade organisations. They become a part of everyone's thinking (at least the majority's thinking) and shape the organisational culture. Like personal beliefs and values, organisational beliefs and values may be outside of conscious awareness.

By observing and listening to what happens in businesses, you can identify a lot of the prevailing beliefs and values. For example, I've observed organisations that value activity more than output, and others that value the opposite. I've worked with organisations where people firmly believe you have to dress a certain way in order to be professional and others where the pervading belief is that being late for meetings is acceptable.

# *Working with beliefs*

Beliefs are very powerful. The things you decide are true – the facts of life – come from generalisations you've made over time, sometimes even a lifetime. Of course after you have a belief, you naturally look for evidence that supports it. Your attention goes to the information that backs up your belief, and you may delete or distort things that don't. (Take a look at Chapter 4 for more on deletions and distortions.)

Some beliefs are very empowering , others very limiting, depending on the situation. People hold on to their beliefs with some conviction, which is great when they're helpful beliefs but not when they aren't. Conflicting beliefs make relationships difficult, frustrate good team working, and limit creativity.

Supporting or empowering beliefs make achieving goals, being effective, and enjoying success possible. A goal is pretty elusive if you don't believe you can achieve it. Likewise, a company's goals and vision are most likely to be accomplished if they foster a climate of positive beliefs, such as 'We are the best at what we do'; 'We can achieve the target'; 'We can attract our competitor's customers'.. When leaders communicate positive, albeit artfully vague messages (more on those in Chapter 10), what may have seemed impossible becomes achievable.

Positive beliefs can be instilled in organisations with positive messages, particularly about *capability*, or what people *can* do. Messages you hear in organisations that are building positive belief include:

- ✔ 'We can do this.'
- ✔ 'We have the capability to turn things around.'
- ✔ 'This is a strong business.'
- ✔ 'You are the right people for the job.'

Beliefs can change. This is good news for organisations with a history of disempowering beliefs. If you're seeking to turn around a negative work culture, focus on developing capability. A perceived lack of capability influences what people believe they can do either individually or as part of an organisation. You can change this belief. You can help people discover they can do so much more with:

- ✔ Good NLP coaching (see Chapter 12)
- ✔ Meaningful feedback (see Chapter 11)
- ✔ An outcome-based focus (see Chapter 16)
- ✔ More flexibility (explored in many chapters in this book)

Being able to do more leads to greater achievements, changed beliefs, and more positive thoughts and actions.

## Energising with values

Your *values* are what's important to you. Values determine the choices you make in your life, including the work you do, the friends you choose, the company you work for, how you spend your leisure time, and so on.

Values are very personal. and unlike beliefs, have an emotional element. They give you a sense of purpose, particularly your *higher-level values*. These *higher-level values* are what really matters to you. Higher-level values are often abstract concepts such as:

- ✔ Security
- ✔ Freedom
- ✔ Making a difference
- ✔ Happiness
- ✔ Fulfilment
- ✔ Love

When your activities fully support your values, you're energised and driven for success. If what you do doesn't accord with your values, you're on the road to nowhere.

I sometimes meet people who are unhappy in their jobs. A short bit of probing later, and some conflict of values often appears. For example, the person may be motivated by caring for others yet is in an isolated technical role with little chance to make a difference to other people.

## Walking the talk

Talk is cheap, so they say. When an organisation has decided what its values are, it can all too easily get carried away putting them on posters, Web sites, stickers, and goodness knows where else. Actually being seen and heard *living the values* is much more difficult.

I've worked with several organisations that claim to value work–life balance yet give staff BlackBerries and send them e-mails at midnight. I once worked for an organisation that declared it cared about the environment, yet had over 100 sales and account management people driving between 40,000 and 70,000 miles each year in gas-guzzling cars. And I regularly come across companies that proclaim honesty as a value, yet allow rumours to circulate about restructurings and redundancies for months.

When the values expressed become more than a set of words – and have *shared meaning* for people throughout the organisation – this conflict of words and actions begins to disappear. Organisations must make changes to ensure that leaders in particular 'walk the talk' and continually operate to the explicit values, rather than those that are implicit in the culture. By setting an example, people at the top start to create the desired outcome and model it for all employees.

One of the ways to make it easier to implement and work to the values, at all levels of the organisation, is to work out what behaviours would demonstrate the value in practice. The following section, 'Knowing values when you see them', explains how to do this.

## *Knowing values when you see them*

If a set of values exists for an organisation, the million-dollar NLP question to ask is: *How do you know that these values exist?*

In the context of a value, how do you know when you're working to that value? You're looking for evidence, quite simply. You need specific examples of what working to the value looks and sounds like.

Rather than issuing a list of values and sticking it up around the building, you can describe values in terms of the behaviours that demonstrate them. Your aim is to have the entire organisation being guided by and working to the company's expressed values.

For example, I recently read the following value on a company's Web site:

> Our employees are renowned for their professionalism, and this has been key to our success to date. We expect them to present a professional image of the company when meeting clients and in the office environment.

But how do you describe and define *professional?* Your definition and mine are probably going to be different. So this company can benefit from explaining which behaviours demonstrate what it means by *professional*. Specially, when an employee presents a professional image, what do others see and hear that lets them know that's what she's doing?

To get values integrated into a business, involve people throughout the organisation. After you've defined and communicated the values, begin exploring what each value means for each area and each individual. And remember that the behaviours that define whether people are modelling the value are likely to be different for each role. For example, what do you see and hear from the staff restaurant manager? How about the customer service assistant? And what behaviours demonstrate the same value in the accounts department?

When defining how values affect each area or person in an organisation, ask these key questions:

- ✔ How do you know?
- ✔ What do you see and hear?

This information can then be used in a number of useful ways:

- ✔ Individuals, teams or departments can communicate to others in the organisation – and remind themselves – what they can expect to see and hear that informs them that this individual or group is working to a company value.

- ✔ Performance reviews for people can include an evaluation of how well the individual is demonstrating the required behaviours and therefore working to the organisation's values.

- ✔ When people know *how* to live the values, they can align themselves more fully to them, and the organisation reaps the benefits of the resulting energy. If people find the values in conflict with their own, they have the choice of whether to stay or go.

The internal communications process of an organisation can also play a part in emphasising the importance of the organisation's key values and how they're being utilised and implemented. Employee newsletters, briefings, gatherings and more provide the opportunity to share stories and recognise – and even reward – successes enjoyed by people embodying the values.

# Chapter 15

# Maximising Success through Change

. . . . . . . . . . . . . . . . . . . . . . . . . . . . . . . . . . . . . . . . . . . . . . . . .

## In This Chapter

▶ Thinking about change in a new way

▶ Helping yourself and others respond to and initiate change

▶ Aligning levels to make change effective

. . . . . . . . . . . . . . . . . . . . . . . . . . . . . . . . . . . . . . . . . . . . . . . . .

*P*robably the one constant that businesses and public bodies face in the 21st century is change. Change takes many forms, including:

- ✔ Expanding through more people, equipment, technology, locations, and so on

- ✔ Improving processes for efficiency

- ✔ Adapting to new market demands

- ✔ Downsizing through redundancies, closures, and mergers

- ✔ Reacting to competitive pressure

- ✔ Introducing new technology

- ✔ Reorganising people's roles, responsibilities, and reporting lines

- ✔ Merging divisions or businesses

- ✔ Moving, opening, and closing sites

- ✔ Responding to new regulations or legislation

- ✔ Implementing new guidelines or initiatives imposed by stakeholders

Sometimes change just doesn't yield the hoped-for result. People lose motivation and drive, valuable personnel can leave the organisation, and suddenly sales are falling and costs rising. Many organisations' change initiatives don't, in the end, seem to change much at all.

In this chapter I introduce a tool – the logical levels model – that can help you to think about change in a new way. You can use it to increase your success in making personal change, coaching others to make changes, and supporting major change within your team, division, and organisation.

# Leading Change

Leading people through change is one of the key challenges for business managers. Change takes time and effort and is usually costly. Costs are both direct – such as the costs of, for example, new systems, moving premises, recruitment, redundancy, and so on – and indirect, such as the cost of people working at less than peak performance due to the anxiety and stress of change, taking on new responsibilities or learning new ways of working. And when change initiatives don't have the anticipated effect, and achieve their goal, guess what? Even more change follows, at more cost to the organisation – and potential emotional cost to its people.

When I ask business leaders what got in the way of them making change or why they think the changes didn't lead to the expected results, I hear justifications such as:

> 'People here really don't like change.'

> 'We maybe didn't communicate well enough.'

> 'People think they've been treated badly.'

> 'Change is never easy.'

These perceptions, or *maps of the world* in NLP terms (find out more in Chapter 3), may be true. But what if you challenge them? The result may go something like this:

> **Business leader:** 'People here really don't like change.'

> **Challenger:** 'Really? If you offered to give them more flexible working hours, they'd probably like *that* type of change. Or if you offered everyone a chance to earn a 40 per cent bonus or guaranteed that everyone's working day was easier and more fun, they'd like those changes!'

The reasons business leaders offer up for slow or difficult organisational change are only part of the story. So what else is happening?

# Finding the Difference that Makes the Difference: Logical Levels

You can get a new perspective on what gets in the way of effective change by considering the *logical levels model,* created by NLP developer Robert Dilts. This model contains a number of different categories, or levels, at which change can take place, and a hierarchy which indicates the relationship between the parts – the *logical* element. Figure 15-1 illustrates the logical levels model. In an organisation, or even personally, the changes you and others make may be at one or more levels.

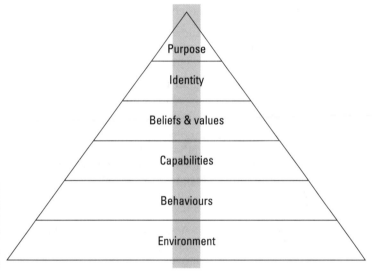

**Figure: 15-1:**
The logical
levels of
change.

Dilts proposes that change can happen at one or more of six levels:

- ✔ **The environment level** describes the situation. This level answers the questions *where? when?* and *with whom?*

- ✔ **The behaviour level** refers to what people say and do within the environment. It answers the question *what?*

- ✔ **The capabilities level** includes the skills and knowledge that direct people's behaviour in the environment. This answers the question *how?*

- ✔ **The beliefs and values level** encompasses those things that are true and important to people within the situation. They answer the question *why?*

✔ **The identity level** is people's sense of self or their roles. It answers the question *who?*

✔ **The purpose level** is about how people connect to something bigger than themselves. It answers the question *what for?*

## Navigating the levels

The hierarchy of levels indicates the relationship between each category. A few general principles apply to the logical level model:

✔ **Everything works well when the different levels are aligned.** All the levels are connected, so when they line up an individual., or organisation, can work most effectively.

✔ **Many more changes are made at the lower levels than the higher levels.** Think about it: the flooring in a work place is much easier to change than the company's culture.

✔ **If you make changes at higher levels, the levels below change.** By contrast, if you make change at the lower levels, any levels below are affected, but the levels above may or may not be. For example:

  • You attend appraisal skills training to improve your ability to review your team members' performance. At the next round of reviews, you have some new things to say and do (your behaviours). You may change your beliefs about the importance of performance reviews, but you probably don't change your sense of your role as the manager running the reviews.

  • You were working in a junior role in the accounts department. You decided to take training and are now a fully qualified accountant, and running a department. You have new skills and behaviours – and your environment may have changed (you're almost certainly not sitting at your old desk, for example). You now identify yourself as an accountant.

✔ **When organisations or individuals make changes, they are less likely to succeed if they don't make those changes at the most appropriate logical level.** For example, improving the working environment to improve performance is fine if the workspace is putting lots of obstacles to effective communications and efficient working. However, if the primary reason for underperformance is poor skills, then merely changing the environment is not going to have all desired effect on results.

The following sections examine the impact of change at each level in the logical levels model and highlight what you can – and can't – expect from making various types of changes.

# Adapting the environment

In your job, the environment level involves:

- **Where:** The physical place where you work – your surroundings. This level may include different locations, and if you travel, even the cars, trains, or planes in which you spend time while on business.

- **When:** Your general working hours – or the time you spend in specific meetings, at different locations, and so on.

- **With whom:** The colleagues, customers, suppliers, and anyone else you deal with at work.

Making a change to your environment is sometimes the *easiest* change to make, yet it isn't always the *right* change to make to achieve a different outcome. For example, a commonplace reaction when people experience job dissatisfaction is to leave the organisation and find a new position elsewhere. (Maybe you've done this yourself.)

If you choose to move to a role in another company that requires many of the same behaviours and capabilities as your previous job, the alteration in your environment may not be enough of a change to really make a difference. The cause of your frustration is most likely at a higher logical level, so soon you start feeling unhappy about your new position. You may begin looking for another position or environment, perpetuating the cycle.

However, changing your environment can be really influential. I've witnessed great positive shifts in the motivation and attitude of staff in several organisations with which I've worked when a cramped, old, tatty working environment is transformed and made attractive and comfortable.

Also, if you believe that you make a good contribution to a business in your current role, you may well believe that you deserve a decent work place. In this case, a good (or improved) physical environment is definitely in line with your other logical levels. If environment is important to you and the organisation invests money in it, you may also sense an alignment in your values and the company's.

# Changing behaviour

The behaviour level is everything you do and say – quite a lot of stuff then! The list of behaviours that you may use at work is very long, so here are just a few possibilities:

- Thinking
- Speaking

- ✔ Analysing
- ✔ Presenting
- ✔ Listening
- ✔ Typing
- ✔ Driving
- ✔ Designing

These behaviours and others closely depend on all your other logical levels. While your behaviour is what happens *on the outside*, the higher logical levels are all about what happens *on the inside*. And these higher logical levels involve your thoughts and feelings.

Behaviours can be habitual, so you may find that some of your behaviours are serving you well – and others less so. Becoming aware of what you're doing and saying is the first step to changing any behaviour. You can discover more about what you do as you start to pay more attention to yourself. It's also useful to seek feedback from others for further insights into things you habitually do or say that you just haven't noticed! From there you can identify whether a behaviour is actually in line with your higher logical levels.

For example, say you're working in the health service as a clinician, a role on which other specialists rely in order to do the best job of treating their patients. You want to make a difference to people's lives, so how does your arriving late for work every day (a behaviour) fit with your higher levels?

Always check that your behaviours, or the behaviours of a group you're leading, line up with higher logical levels. If you're struggling to change something you do, try thinking about it at the level of identity as well as behaviour. For example, if you want to interact more patiently with someone on your team (a behaviour), start to think of yourself as a patient and considerate person (an identity-level thought). Notice occasions where you've been patient and considerate in the past to reinforce this sense of identity. See the section 'Choosing identity', later in this chapter, for more on changing at the identity level.

You need to practise all behaviours, good and bad, for them to become normal or habitual. Start practising *today* the ones you want to become your habits.

## Expanding capabilities

The capabilities level includes skills, talents, and qualities. You probably know many of your capabilities, but you may not recognise others.

For example, as you read this book, you can reflect on the fact that you have the capability to read and understand English. You also have the capability to evaluate the ideas presented here, compare them with your own experience, and make decisions about which of the tools in this book you want to try for yourself.

These days most organisations refer to capabilities as *competencies*. The focus is on competency-based recruiting, appraising, and training to make sure that a job's done well. Focusing on competencies is a useful approach to making change and improving performance.

As the logical level model shows, you can gain new skills, but if they aren't in line with your higher levels – your beliefs, values, and sense of self – these new competencies aren't going to create lasting change.

## Fine-tuning beliefs and values

The beliefs and values level covers what you believe and what you value. Beliefs and values continually influence what you think, what you do and say, and how you feel.

The following sections explains more about your beliefs, and values, how these are subtly different, and where they come from.

### Beliefs

Your *beliefs* – about your job, your organisation, yourself, and others – are formed and reinforced from your experiences. Beliefs are those things that you've decided, fro you experience, are true or the way things are- – in your map or the world (more on this in Chapter 4).

So if in your early career you give one or two wooden presentations, you can easily begin to believe that you're a poor presenter. As time goes by and you get more experience talking to large groups, one of two things can happen:

✔ You keep the belief that you aren't a good presenter, which can result in you feeling and looking anxious, rushing through presentations, and not making eye contact (all behaviours) – or limiting your chance to build your skills (capability).

✔ Through practice, you improve your skills (capability) at engaging a group. You receive good feedback, and you eventually change your belief.

Changes in beliefs don't generally happen overnight. Instead, you may find that a specific belief or two gets fine-tuned over time. For example, you may once have believed that working in the evenings was best avoided, whereas you now have an exception – such as making calls and handling e-mails while on your journey home from work.

## Shifting values

Mike started off in his career as an ambitious, hard-working HR administrator, striving to build his skills and knowledge with the goal of eventually becoming a senior HR director. Mike had a sense of what his role would be, believed he could do the top job with enough experience, and knew that he was at his best when doing something that involved people and success.

Eventually Mike reached his goal and became HR director. After two years Mike realised that although his sense of purpose was still to help people and create success, his values were changing.

Helping organisations make money for shareholders while millions of people were starving in the third world no longer sat easily with Mike.

He valued other people's need for food and healthcare much more than he valued commercial success. Another year on and Mike's sense of internal conflict from doing a job that no longer fitted with his values brought him to the conclusion that he had to make a change. He resigned from his job and went to Africa to do voluntary work with a charity. After twelve months he returned home and secured himself a full-time management position in a major international aid charity. The move into the charity sector seemed life-changing for Mike – he was so enthused and energised by his work. He had made the necessary shift to align his logical levels following his change in values, and was much the happier for it.

Other beliefs change more dramatically. For example you may once have believed that the difficulties you experienced with another person were impossible to overcome. Now, after discovering some tips and tricks for dealing with difficult people in Chapter 13, you believe that you can do something to change the relationship.

### Values

Your *values* are, simply, those things that are important to you. What's important to you at work, and *how* important it is, drives your decision making and your actions. Unlike beliefs, there is an emotional element to values.

For example, if you value recognition for a job well done, you're more likely to give praise and recognition to others. If your boss doesn't give you that recognition when you think you deserve it, you're likely to become unhappy because one of your values isn't being met within the organisation.

Like beliefs, you may not be consciously, actively thinking about your values. They may be hidden away, running your decisions without you realising it. For example, you may find yourself getting some pretty tough feedback from your boss, who's noticed you've missed a string of important deadlines. You've been working hard to help a less-experienced colleague with an important project she's working on. Your value of helping others is so strong that it motivated you to support your colleague at the expense of your own performance – unconsciously driving your choice of what to work on.

Your values, like your beliefs, can change, but often over time. New experiences and more knowledge can fine-tune your values. as can change at higher logical levels. For example, I have met several female managers who valued putting their job ahead of their personal life. Doing the best job was important to them Their sense of identity shifted when they became working mothers. This change altered their values. They still wanted to do the their best job but no longer valued their work ahead of their personal life which included a young child. Becoming aware of change in your values can be an important trigger for change.

Changes in values can take place within a group of people too, particularly with increased awareness and sometimes aided by peer pressure. After much education by environmentalists and politicians and coverage by the media, much of the western world has experienced a rapid and continual shift in environmental values. Individuals, communities, and businesses are now changing their capabilities and behaviours to meet these more recently developed values. Changes include:

- Increased recycling
- New initiatives in environmentally friendly energy production
- Active lobbying to reduce deforestation

You can find out more about beliefs and values in Chapters 4 and 14.

## Choosing identity

Your identity level is based on your idea, or sense, of who you are. Your role in an environment often describes your identity in different contexts:

- At work you may see your role as an accountant, a sales specialist, or a leader.
- At home you may be a mother, father, brother, wife, daughter, and so on.
- In your community life you may be a volunteer, school governor, or football coach.

People often confuse identity with behaviour. At work people have asked me, 'Are you a driver?' At my identity level, my answer's 'No'. But what the person asking the question really wants to find out is whether I'm able to drive. The answer to that question is 'Yes'. For me, driving's a behaviour and a capability, but not my identity. However, someone professionally employed to drive most certainly describes himself as a driver.

A change in identity is probably the most radical change you can make – not least because the change affects all the logical levels below. A more senior role, a career change, or giving up work to become a full-time parent all involve certain changes to your sense of your role.

A key challenge for organisations is when changes are imposed on an employee at identity level that may create conflict for the person. If your sense of self is as a manager, with a purpose of helping others develop and a belief that this is the best contribution you can make, what happens when you get moved into a specialist role with no team?

## *Defining purpose*

The idea of your purpose level is maybe the hardest of the logical levels to grasp. Indeed, you may never have thought about it before. Consider:

- ✔ What are you here for?
- ✔ What is your contribution to your organisation, the world outside, and society at large?

If these are difficult questions for you to answer, then spend some time thinking about them. What makes your life worthwhile? If people are going to remember you for just one thing (and you can choose what it is), what may it be?

The answers to the preceding questions are very personal, but some responses from my clients include:

- ✔ 'To improve people's health.'
- ✔ 'To support others to be the best they can be.'
- ✔ 'To bring fun into the world.'
- ✔ 'To give my family the best chance in life.'
- ✔ 'To add new knowledge to human science.'
- ✔ 'To create freedom.'

These statements may not sound very specific, and certainly if you were helping someone define their goal or outcome, you might challenge them to define their statement in more depth. The vagueness of the language used to define purpose however can be important. There are probably limitless ways in which you might fulfil a purpose such as 'To improve people's health'. You can find your own way, one which fits with your sense of identity (such as doctor, dietician geriatric carer), your beliefs and values (for example believing in the power of alternative medicine or valuing the emotional needs of your patient), and your skills and capabilities.

In my experience many people find it quite challenging to define their purpose – particularly as it's not something they have ever put their attention on. Some people have old me their purpose has changed over time. Certainly I've noticed adjustments in people's expressions of their purpose and changes in the emphasis of an aspect of it.

An organisation that seriously considers its purpose often expresses it fully in its mission statement. Some organisations actively and very publicly express their purpose through their behaviours. The Body Shop, for example, carries out its purpose which in essence is to do good for the world, through its refusal to test cosmetics on animals, its approach to fair community trading in acquiring ingredients and its charity work.

# Aligning Levels for Change

Alignment of your logical levels at work helps keep you energised and productive. For example, let's consider that your sense of purpose is to teach others. You are a trainer (identity), you believe that the training you do makes a positive impact on individuals and the organisation in which they work (belief), you've the right skills and knowledge to do your job well (capabilities) and you run seminars and workshops (behaviours) in training rooms and conference centres around the country (environment). Your logical levels line up and you feel good.

It may be obvious to you when you're working in a situation where things are not aligned for you – maybe you are being asked to do things (behaviours) that are in conflict with your values. Alternatively, this misalignment may not be clear, but you have a sense of unease or stress that you just can't put your finger on. When you take notice of that feeling, and consider your position in terms of your logical levels, you may find that you need to make a change.

For change, personal or organisational, to be truly effective, all the logical levels need to be aligned.

## Looking to levels for personal change

Sometimes I describe this conflict as a heart-versus-mind issue. For example, you've been offered a promotion. Your mind says that the extra money that comes with the job is really nice to have. Your heart says the new role's likely to take you away from day-to-day contact with children, the aspect of your work that you most enjoy.

In logical levels terms, you can break down your sense of unease more specifically, look at how change may affect each level, and find out what needs to change to bring your levels into alignment.

So if you're in conflict over a potential job promotion, you can examine your logical levels like this: if you value the work that you currently do, believe it affects other people very positively and is helping others (which is key to your purpose), taking the promotion is going to cause you great unease. Knowing this gives you the chance to seek out other ways of meeting your needs for a bigger, more financially rewarding role – while still meeting your purpose and living and working to your values.

## Aligning different roles

One way to respond to change is to examine the various roles you play and seek alignment both within, and between, these roles.

Consider this example. You're offered a new job that involves a lot of travelling. It's an exciting job, you like travel, and it means great career progression. On the other hand, the new position requires you to spend a lot of time away from your spouse and young children. You have a dilemma.

In this case, you have two roles to align: your role at work and your role as a parent at home. To make the best decision in a situation like this, you need to examine very closely the higher logical levels for each role:

1. **For your work role, ask yourself the following questions:**

   • What are my beliefs and values?

   • What is my sense of self?

   • What is my purpose?

2. **For your home role, ask yourself the same questions:**

   • What are my beliefs and values?

   • What is my sense of self?

   • What is my purpose?

   Obviously, the questions in Steps 1 and 2 are challenging and deserve some time to address.

3. **After you have some answers, ask yourself the following questions about alignment:**

   • At the level of purpose, what factors are the same?

   • At the level of identity, does a relationship exist between one role and the other?

   • At the beliefs and values level, what is common or similar for each role? Are any differences major? Where are the conflicts, if any?

4. **Use all the information you uncover from this exercise to inform the decisions you take – and the changes you make.**

## Change at the wrong level

A coaching client of mine had a pattern of changing jobs frequently and was again feeling frustrated in her current job. Anita was a market research analyst, and a very capable one too. She believed that her work should drive key commercial decisions of the business and that her role was pivotal to developing strategy. Anita's purpose was to help the business make well-informed decisions in order for it to be successful. Anita's experience, in several companies, was that often senior management ignored her findings and recommendations.

Anita and I explored her frustrating situation through the logical levels model. During the discussion we realised that while Anita's capabilities in research were excellent, her ability to influence senior people wasn't so good. As a result, what she said and did to get her point across to the executive team didn't convince them.

As a result, Anita typically changed her job (her environment), when she needed to change her communications capabilities.

After our work together, Anita decided to stay in her current position for a while and work on improving her influencing skills (building rapport, and spotting and using others' patterns iwhen communicating with them). As she started to talk to and interact with people differently, her behaviours and capabilities became much better aligned with her beliefs and values, as well as her sense of self and purpose. Anita started to get the results she wanted – people listened to and respected her opinions and she became a trusted marketing advisor to the company's leaders.

Decisions of this nature that affect such important aspects of your life are not easy to make when a dilemma exists. At the end of the day it's a personal step, a choice that you have to make. Considering your options with the assistance of the logical levels model may certainly give you more insights and information on which to base your decision.

## *Aligning for organisational change*

To be effective, significant changes made to a business by its leaders must happen at the most appropriate levels, just like personal change (see the section 'Looking to levels for personal change', earlier in this chapter).

I've worked in businesses where senior teams have come back from an 'awayday' with a spanking new set of values to impose on staff. They ask the internal communications people to advertise these new values freely around the organisation. The executive may even have the marketing department promote the new values just as freely to customers and the world at large.

## Lofty vision, lost opportunities

A colleague of mine deals with the Children's Services division of a local authority. The organisation expresses its vision as: 'Working together to improve life chances and aspirations for each child and young person in [City].'

My colleague's experience of working with this organisation is that its staff didn't work well together at all – either internally or with those outside the organisation.

As a result, decisions were frequently delayed, and the organisation was often extremely slow

to fund essential services for some of the children in its care. In fact, it took 22 weeks to respond to a formal complaint that its own policy said needed to be addressed in four.

As a result, several children were not having their life chances improved. In this case, the behaviours and capabilities of individuals throughout the organisation were most certainly *not* aligned with purpose – with potentially disastrous results for vulnerable young people.

Unfortunately, these values are often just aspirational statements with little in place to put them into practice. For example:

'We are committed to excellence in all that we do.'

'Our employees are our most important resource.'

'We always aim to exceed customer expectations.'

These statements are what senior management want the company's values to be – not necessarily the values the employees are experiencing on a daily basis. If people from the top down don't 'walk the talk' and ensure the behaviours match the values, serious misalignment results. For example, stating that 'our employees are our most important resource' and then cancelling all training and development because of short term profitability concerns, causes a mismatch of values and behaviours. Employees determine the actual values from 'the walk', not 'the talk'.

Until employees understand what the organisation's values look and sound like in practice – and can find behaviours that match their own beliefs, values, and identity – then the buy-in for the values is extremely limited.

When an organisation's clear about its purpose, identity, and values, employees are much more able to decide if it's a place in which they can work well. When an individual's logical levels are in good alignment with those of the group or business in which he works, he's usually a happy and productive employee - and productive employees help create a successful business.

When an organisation's and an individual's levels are misaligned, sooner or later the individual feels the stress. In this case, the individual needs to:

1. **Notice that something's wrong.**

2. **Work out at which level the change needs to take place.**

   Ask yourself the following questions:

   - What do I do (behaviours)?
   - What are my capabilities?
   - What are my beliefs and values?
   - What is my sense of self (identity)?
   - What is my purpose?

   Then consider:

   - What does the organisation require me to do (behaviours)?
   - What capabilities does the job need ?
   - What are the organisation's beliefs and values?
   - What *is* the organisation (identity)?
   - What is the organisation's purpose?

   You may have to assess for yourself what the answers are for some of the organisational questions, as the answers may not be explicitly apparent.

   After you have some answers, ask yourself the following questions about alignment:

   - **At the level of purpose,** does any conflict exist, or is there room for your purpose within the organisation's?
   - **At the level of identity,** can your identity fit into the organisation's?
   - **At the beliefs and values level,** what is common or similar between you and the organisation? Are there any significant conflicts?
   - **At the capabilities level,** do you have, or can you acquire, the skills the business needs?
   - **At the level of behaviour,** do you do what is required by the organisation?

3. **Take action at the appropriate level.** If you want to be more energised, effective and satisfied at work, change needs to happen.

   If your job needs certain skills that you don't have, acquire them or resolve to change your job to one which used your capabilities. If you are not doing the things (behaviours) that you are required to, what's stopping you? Is it due to a conflict in capabilities, beliefs or values? If you have different values to the organisation, you'd so best to find a new employer. If the sole purpose of the business is to make money for the shareholders, and your purpose is to make a positive difference society as a whole – well, only you can decide if that purpose can be fulfilled in you current organisation. If it can't, and you're feeling unhappy at work, this is most probably one of the biggest causes. Consider making a change.

At whichever logical level you introduce a change, the levels below are affected. Levels above may, or may not, change. More change comes from a change at a higher level.

# Coaching Others through Change

When you're coaching, or just listening to, a team member or colleague who's talking through issues, you pick up some clues in what he says. How he says this can help you find out at which logical level the person's thinking.

A simple example is the phrase: 'I can't do that here.' Consider how just placing the emphasis on a different word alters the statement's meaning:

- ✔ 'I can't do that *here*.' This emphasis tells you that the environment is the issue.

- ✔ 'I can't do *that* here.' The focus is on behaviour.

- ✔ 'I can't *do* that here.' This phrasing suggests that there may be a capability problem.

- ✔ 'I *can't* do that here.' This statement is a definite expression of a belief.

- ✔ '*I* can't do that here.' This rendition indicates an issue around identity.

After you have an indication of the logical level at which the person's having the problem, you can start to help him to identify the specific level that's stopping him from doing what he's saying he can't do. Guide the other person, using the same techniques that I outline for you to use on yourself in the section 'Aligning Levels for Change', earlier in this chapter.

# Chapter 16

# Setting and Achieving Goals

● ● ● ● ● ● ● ● ● ● ● ● ● ● ● ● ● ● ● ● ● ● ● ● ● ● ● ● ● ● ● ● ● ● ● ● ● ● ● ● ● ● ● ● ●

## In This Chapter

▶ Defining outcomes

▶ Motivating yourself to achieve your outcomes

▶ Helping others to formulate achievable goals

● ● ● ● ● ● ● ● ● ● ● ● ● ● ● ● ● ● ● ● ● ● ● ● ● ● ● ● ● ● ● ● ● ● ● ● ● ● ● ● ● ● ● ● ●

*I*n business, a great deal of time and effort goes in to creating outcomes – goals, objectives, and targets. Whatever terms you use to describe them, most companies, divisions, departments, teams, and individuals are working towards some kind of outcome at any point in time.

The whole purpose of setting goals is to have something to aim for. In profit-motivated organisations, making money is a key component of success, so having objectives designed to ensure profitability is important. Indeed, setting objectives and developing plans is an approach that has, by and large, been proven to work. Yes, businesses don't always get planning absolutely right every time. An unexpected expansion in the market or an unforeseen rise in fuel prices may lead to over- or underachievement of a profit target. However, the goal usually sets a direction and an intention, focusing business activity.

Yet people rarely set *personal* goals, either in the context of work or elsewhere. You may know what you want – or what you *don't* want – but have you ever said these things out loud? And how good are you at achieving your goals?

In this chapter I explore *outcomes,* the NLP term for goals and objectives. An outcome is, quite simply, what you want. Outcome thinking is one of the four pillars of NLP (more on this in Chapter 2). Focusing on outcomes helps you to move from being stuck with your problems – those things you don't want – towards achieving what you prefer.

# Creating Well-Formed Outcomes

Are you one of those people who sets New Year resolutions, only to find that you're falling back into the same habits that you wanted to break by February? Well, you aren't alone. Most New Year resolutions, and in fact many of the goals that people set themselves, simply don't work. Maintaining new behaviours or striving for something different just becomes a struggle.

If you've been involved in setting business goals and objectives, you may well have come across the SMART model. SMART goals are specific, measurable, achievable, realistic, and timed. Although the SMART model is very useful, the NLP model for goal setting goes further. It includes more sensory-specific information.

The *NLP outcome model* has been developed based on the activities of people who are excellent at achieving their goals. The critical differences between outcomes that are likely to be achieved and those that aren't come down to the crafting of *well-formed outcomes*.

Figure 16-1 summarises the characteristics of a well-formed outcome, which I then explain in more detail in each of the following sections.

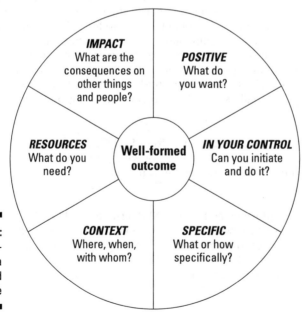

**Figure 16-1:**
The charac-
teristics of a
well-formed
outcome

When coaching clients I find time and again that when they take their goals and make them well formed using the NLP model, things happen and they make achievements. The following sections take you through the process of setting well-formed goals.

## Knowing what you want

When you set an outcome, you're programming your mind to achieve that goal. Consciously or unconsciously, you start to notice opportunities and possibilities around you that can help you reach your goal. So getting the programme absolutely right from the very beginning is an important step. Otherwise you don't achieve your outcome – and you may actually get something that you *don't* want.

The starting point for any outcome is to make sure you express it positively – *what you want to have*. Consider the difference between these two outcomes:

- ✔ I don't want to feel bored in my job any longer.
- ✔ I want a new challenge in my job.

Although the first statement doesn't include any overtly negative words (such as *no* or *not*), the statement clearly expresses what *you don't want*. Even more importantly, the first statement doesn't give any indication of what needs to replace the current situation. In metaprogram terms (see Chapter 7), you're expressing this goal in *away from* language, rather than *towards* language.

The difficulty with focusing on what you don't want is that in order to think about *not* having something, you need to think about that very thing. This puts your attention on what you *don't* want rather than what you *do* want. (Turn your attention to Chapter 10 for more on this.)

A focus on what they don't want is one of the reasons people struggle to meet outcomes like:

- ✔ I want to stop being short-tempered at work.
- ✔ I want to give up smoking.
- ✔ I want to cut out sweet and fatty foods to lose weight.
- ✔ I want to resist the temptation to open e-mails as soon as they arrive.

To change these desires into positive outcomes, you must concentrate on what you want, rather than what you need to stop doing or give up. To shift an outcome to the positive, ask this question:

What do I want instead?

When you honestly answer this question, your outcomes can shift to things like:

- ✔ I want to be more patient with others at work.
- ✔ I want to be fit and healthy.
- ✔ I want to be slim.
- ✔ I want to work more efficiently

Set yourself some outcomes for your work right now. Ask yourself:

What do I really want in my work?

Write down all the ideas that come to mind. Then consider some timescales for each idea. Perhaps you want to reach your goal:

- ✔ This month
- ✔ This year
- ✔ In the next five years
- ✔ By the end of your career
- ✔ Throughout your career

Look over your list of outcomes and check for words like *should*, *try*, and *must*, as well as anything suggesting what you don't want. An outcome is what you truly want, not what others want, or what you think you 'should' want. Any time you find yourself expressing what you *don't* want, ask yourself what you do want instead and spend some time getting the description right for you.

## Taking responsibility

When setting yourself an outcome, make sure that it's something you can actively do something about. You need to be able to initiate the outcome, keep it going, and make it happen.

So, for example, the outcome 'I want my team to take on more of my work' isn't under your control. You're relying on other people, in this case your team, to act by taking on the work. However, if you rephrase this goal as 'I want to coach my team to build the confidence to take on more responsibilities', you now have an outcome that is very much more in your control – and is therefore attainable.

Pay close attention to the level of control needed in well-formed outcomes. You need to have a fairly strong influence on the outcome, yet others can be involved. For example, if your outcome is to get promoted, of course other people are going to make that decision. However, you can still set yourself the outcome and work out exactly what you need to do to make that promotion possible.

> ✔ You can identify smaller sub-goals, such as acquiring all the necessary skills and experience for the promotion you want.
>
> ✔ You can explore ways of demonstrating that you're ready for promotion so the decision makers notice you.
>
> ✔ You can even build a business case for the creation of a new, more senior post that doesn't already exist.

All the preceding actions are things you can initiate and control, even through the final decision – promotion or not – isn't within your control.

## Defining the specifics

Anyone can come up with broad outcomes such as 'I want be successful' or 'I want more balance between my work and my personal life'. Unfortunately, such vague outcomes often don't work, as they don't hold specific enough information for you to aim for.

When you add specific detail into your description of the goal, you're more likely to get what you want – and maybe just as importantly, avoid getting what you don't want.

Consider the outcome: 'I want to earn a lot of money.' A reasonable outcome that many may share. However, how much is a lot? How do you know when you've earned a 'lot' of money?

To develop a more detailed and clear outcome, ask the following questions:

> ✔ How much money *specifically* do I want to earn?
>
> ✔ What do I see, hear, and feel that tells me that I've earned this amount of money?

When you ask these questions, you may discover details such as: 'I want to earn enough money to buy a spacious and comfortable home for my family, to retire early, and to travel to see the seven wonders of the world.' Already you're getting a much more vivid description of the goal, with more specifics and even some sensory information. You have a goal that you can imagine, dream about, and mentally rehearse. With further questioning, even more detail can emerge about what you may see, hear, and feel when you actually achieve the outcome.

As I discuss in Chapter 5, your internal thinking is done through your senses, in just the same way as you experience the external world. So when you're describing an outcome or goal more specifically, using sensory-specific language – describing what you see, hear, and feel – you bring the outcome to life right now, making it real and attractive. You know exactly what you're aiming for and how you know when you get there.

## Checking where, when, and how

Another important area to consider when developing a well-formed outcome is the context in which you want the achievement. The simple but essential questions to ask to define an outcome's context are:

- ✔ Where?
- ✔ When?
- ✔ With whom?

Imagine that you have an outcome that's expressed as 'I want to be more emotionally detached'. And then imagine achieving this outcome. What does 'emotionally detached' mean for you? Are you planning to be more emotionally detached in every aspect of your life? How may your family and friends relate to an emotionally detached you?

When you add context to this outcome – such as 'I want to be more emotionally detached when managing the redundancy meetings so that I can effectively support those affected' – the outcome becomes a whole lot more specific and clear.

Be careful what you wish for. Consider the potential results of achieving your outcomes. Make sure that you're clear about what you want, or else you may find that you achieve your goal in aspects of your life that you really didn't want it in!

## Accessing resources

If you want to achieve your outcomes, work out what you *need* in order to do so. What kind of resources does the outcome require? The *internal resources,* those directly under your control, that you may need to get started may include:

- ✔ Skills
- ✔ Knowledge

> ✔ Time
>
> ✔ A positive frame of mind
>
> ✔ Health or fitness

Whatever you decide you need, do you already have the internal resources? If not, you need to work out how you're going to get them. At this point, setting smaller outcomes to start you on your way to achieving your main outcome may be a good strategy. For example, you may have to get some specific knowledge or start a new exercise regime in order to meet your broader goals.

In addition to internal resources, you may need resources from the outside. These can be a whole host of things, including:

> ✔ Support from others
>
> ✔ Money
>
> ✔ Equipment
>
> ✔ Information
>
> ✔ Contacts

Again, you may need to set well-formed outcomes about how you get these resources working for you.

 For your outcome to be well formed, work out whether you can access all the resources you require along the way. As a result, you can establish at an early stage whether the goal's likely to be achievable, and what else has to happen to make it so.

## *Identifying the impact*

One issue people don't always pay attention to when defining their outcomes is the impact that achieving an outcome may have on other things or other people. In the NLP model of well-formed outcomes, this consideration is known as the *ecology* of the outcome.

Any outcome that you achieve inevitably has consequences for other areas of your life. These may be good or bad, so consider these before you get started. For example, if you set yourself an outcome of getting a particular new job yet this position means more time away from home, what effect may achieving your outcome have? Is it OK for you to see less of family or friends? Is it OK for them? Do you have to give up some studies, leisure activities, or exercise? If you need to spend a lot more time in a car, do you already have a back condition that may worsen?

## Impact and insights

Susan, a friend of mine, wanted a more senior job, ideally at board level. She'd wanted this outcome for some time, but feedback at interviews was that she needed either different experience or an MBA. Being the family's main breadwinner and with a very young child, Susan felt stuck. She wasn't able to work out feasible ways to find time away from her job and family to study.

Then Susan considered the entire ecology of the situation. She decided that if she didn't achieve her outcome, not only would she be frustrated in her work for years to come, but she would fail to earn the salary she wanted to support her family. Funding an MBA and losing income while she studied would be difficult, but she did have some savings. Spending time studying would take her away from her son and partner a little more than usual, but there were ways to minimise the impact. And achieving her goal would open up choices of where to work, where to live, and where to get the best schooling for her son.

By weighing up all the implications of her outcome, Susan went on to complete her MBA and build the career she wanted, while maintaining a positive family life.

Useful and challenging questions to ask about the potential impact of your outcome include:

- ✔ What will I gain when I have this outcome?
- ✔ What will I lose when I have this outcome?
- ✔ What will happen when I have this outcome?
- ✔ What won't happen when I have this outcome?
- ✔ What will happen if I don't have this outcome?
- ✔ What won't happen if I don't have this outcome?

In addition, if your achievement of this outcome may have a negative effect on other people, you may even want to check out their thoughts on the ecology of your goal.

Armed with the answers to all these ecology questions you can make an informed choice about your outcome. You will have weighed up the pros and cons, and be able to decide if this is the right outcome for you. If so, you can move on to ensure it has the other characteristics of a well-formed outcome outline din the following sections. If this is not the right outcome for you, ask yourself: 'What do I want instead?' Then review this new outcome against all the characteristics of a well-formed outcome.

# Making Your Outcomes Irresistible

After you craft a well-formed outcome (for the details go to the section 'Creating Well-Formed Outcomes', earlier in this chapter), you're on the road to success. Well-formed outcomes require you to work out exactly what you want and jump-start your conscious and unconscious minds to work on achieving your goals.

Now you have the opportunity to make your outcomes *irresistible,* so you just have to achieve them. You can make an outcome irresistible by:

✔ Actively experiencing the outcome

✔ Using anchors

✔ Getting the bigger picture

✔ Taking the first step

The following sections cover each of these techniques in detail.

## Acting as if you've achieved your goal

You can enrich your outcome and make it more achievable by spending time imagining achieving it and experiencing how things are going to be when you have it. After all, top athletes mentally rehearse their top performance. If you have watched top class sprinters as they prepare to start an important race, you may have noticed them staring into space. They are running the race in their minds before the event, looking towards the finish line -and being first over the line of course!

In a quiet space, take a few minutes to think about one of your outcomes as if you already have it. Notice what you see, hear, and feel. Really live the experience, making it vibrant and strong. Add in as many details as you can into what you see, hear and feel to make it rich and realistic.

The unconscious mind doesn't make a distinction between what's real and what isn't (see Chapter 10). When you act as if you already have the outcome, both your conscious and unconscious minds are thinking about it. It's a kind of mental rehearsal. As a result you:

✔ Notice opportunities and possibilities.

✔ Connect with relevant people, information, and things.

✔ Make a plan to get to the goal much more easily.

## *Anchoring an outcome*

In Chapter 8 I explore the benefits of setting anchors to help you achieve a particular emotional state. Setting an anchor for your outcome is very powerful as well, because it reminds your unconscious mind regularly of what you want to achieve.

Seek out something that represents your outcome. You may have:

- ✔ A picture (maybe a beautiful photograph of the holiday destination you wish to visit).

- ✔ An object (maybe a toy model of the sleek car you want to own).

- ✔ A set of words (perhaps your outcome – or just a key word or phrase such as 'financial freedom' or 'Director'.

- ✔ A piece of music (maybe a favourite song with lyrics that relate to your outcome).

Whatever you decide best reminds you of your outcome, make sure you can have it in a place where you see or hear it frequently, to continue to motivate you to go for the outcome.

1. Whilst looking or listening to your anchor, remember your outcome. Spend time thinking about it and imagining you already have it – as described in the previous section, 'Anchoring an Outcome'.

2. As you imagine what you see and hear, notice the feelings that you experience. Intensify those feelings as much as you can.

3. Do something different for a minute or so. For instance, move around and think about the last movie you saw.

4. Go back to your anchor. Look at it, or listen to it as appropriate. You'll notice that you start thinking about your outcome and getting that good feeling all over again. If that doesn't happen for you yet, repeat steps 1-3.

5. If you have a visual anchor, place it where you can see it regularly. Even if you stop noticing it, your unconscious mind won't! If you are using a word or phrase, make sure you can access it regularly (you might record it on something you listen to regularly). Make sure your favourite piece of music is readily available on your personal music devices, computer or home hi-fi system.

You now have a trigger that will be a regular reminder – sometimes to your conscious, and other times to your unconscious mind – of your goal.

To discover other techniques for setting anchors turn to Chapter 8.

# *Exploring the bigger benefits*

Getting a deeper understanding of what an outcome can do for you really improves your motivation towards achieving it. After you have a well-formed outcome, ask yourself:

Then what happens?

Ask this question a number of times, as Figure 16-2 indicates. Each iteration can help you discover the higher-level outcome that you're aiming to achieve. In NLP, this process is called *chunking up*.

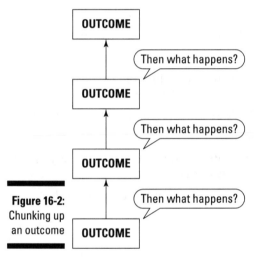

**Figure 16-2:**
Chunking up
an outcome

Connecting to the bigger chunk of gains you can have from achieving your outcome is likely to strengthen your motivation and determination to succeed.

Consider the following scenario. Neil has wanted to give up his job and start working for himself for some time. After years of trying various things, he's still no closer to doing so. Working with a coach, Neil chunks up his outcome to gain more information.

> NEIL: I want to start my own business this year, earning my current salary while having more spare time.
>
> COACH: *Then what happens?*
>
> NEIL: I have more work–life balance.
>
> COACH: *Then what happens?*

NEIL: I follow my passion and develop my photography skills.

COACH: *Then what happens?*

NEIL: I switch careers and become a photographer.

COACH: *Then what happens?*

NEIL: I look forward to work every day.

COACH: *Then what happens?*

NEIL: I'm fulfilled and content.

After Neil realises that starting his own business leads directly to his being fulfilled and content, this higher-level chunk of outcomes helps to motivate him into action.

You too can try this, with or without a coach. Just follow the steps in this simple exercise:

1. Find a space where you have time to think. This could be at work, at home, even when travelling as long as you're not driving.

2. Take a piece of paper and note down your outcome – what you want.

3. Ask yourself: 'Then what happens?'

4. Repeat the question from step 3 until you run out of answers or you find yourself giving answers that you have already given.

5. Reflect on what you've discovered. How motivated do you now feel to go for your goal?

## Getting started

If you've ever been involved in writing business plans, you probably followed the standard discipline of setting your goals and then defining all the steps of the plan needed to achieve the goal. Yet how many people do that for their own personal and work goals?

I've coached many people who procrastinate and stumble at the stage of creating a plan for an outcome. Sometimes creating a plan seems too big or difficult a job. Sometimes people just don't know yet what they need to do.

If you find yourself stuck at the planning stage, then set yourself the small outcome of doing *something*. Ideally you go through a planning process like the one I describe in Chapter 12. Some key questions of this process are:

✔ What needs to happen?

✔ Does anything else need to happen?

✔ What needs to happen first?

Whatever you do, do something. Getting started with a first step or two helps you gain the momentum you need to achieve that outcome!

# Developing Outcomes at Work

Profit-driven businesses are sometimes forced to work with short-term goals, pressured to supply income to shareholders. These businesses set outcomes and goals ahead of a trading year. If things fail to go to plan (and they often do, in my experience), then many people are tempted to move into problem solving and fire fighting. Some organisations engage in these reactive activities so much that they've become the natural way of working.

One problem with problem solving is that you have to think about a problem in order to solve it. So your attention's on what's wrong – or what you *don't* want – rather than what you *do* want. See the section 'Knowing what you want', earlier in this chapter, for more on this problematic way of thinking.

I frequently spend time with businesses that explore their problems thoroughly in order to fix them. They're good at finding solutions. However, today's solution may just lead to the next set of problems. After all, they are solving yesterday's problem, not looking forward to anticipating what kind of problems might arise in the future.

To concentrate on a problem, you use the same kind of thinking that created the problem. When you shift your approach to outcome thinking – what you want or desire – things change.

While the techniques in this chapter up to this point focus on using well-formed outcomes to set, work towards, and achieve your personal outcomes, you can extend this process to your interactions with others. Think about what opportunities you have to craft well-formed outcomes with:

- ✔ Others
- ✔ Teams
- ✔ Organisations

The following sections offer advice for extending the power of well-formed outcomes to all these other audiences.

## Helping individuals create outcomes

Leaders from all types of businesses attend the leadership development programmes I run. Just about all these directors and senior managers have one thing in common: they believe that solving problems that their team members push upwards is a key part of their leadership responsibility. After all, don't they have that job because of their superior knowledge, experience, or training?

So the managers advise on how to solve problems and the team members continue to present more problems. People work hard and believe they're doing their best job. Yet these managers get so caught up in problem solving, they just don't have time to think strategically and anticipate and plan for the future – often a key part of their role. And the people working for them don't get to develop their problem solving skills or get the fulfilment that comes from taking responsibility for, and making things happen, in their own area.

When leaders, or anyone in business, encourage and help people to address problems by developing well-formed outcomes, significant change happens. With well-formed outcomes in place, the people who have the problems start to think differently and work out what they want instead of what they *don't* want. They become more empowered to sort things out and not pass all difficulties upwards. Their job satisfaction increases and others can get on and do a more proactive job, such as strategic thinking.

Sabine, a good friend of mine, was frustrated in her work as a global HR director. Travelling, long hours, and internal politics were getting her down. She found a new job with a little less travel and a bit more independence, but the hours were long and the organisational structure made influencing others difficult. So she found another new employer and became a VP of HR, with a bigger salary and smarter car. Yes, she had to travel a lot more, but she figured that was OK because she was receiving an outstanding benefits package and lived extravagantly. But within six months, she was unhappy again. Finally, Sabine stopped 'solving' the problem (the things she didn't like about various jobs) and developed a well-formed outcome (a job with variety, working strategically, more time with her husband and enough money to live comfortably), she was able to become a happy, successful and respected HR consultant.

Next time someone brings you a problem at work, try this experiment. Listen, create rapport (turn to Chapter 6 for more), and then ask her: 'And what do you want instead?' After the other person expresses an outcome rather than the problem, ask her more questions from the well-formed outcome model (see the section 'Creating Well-Formed Outcomes', earlier in this chapter). Wrap things up by helping the person identify the first step and watch for her to make progress.

## Developing shared outcomes for teams

I work a lot with teams in organisations. Some of those teams believe that they have a shared outcome or goal. Some don't. What's constant, however, is the broad range of descriptions that team members give about what they're trying to achieve.

Team working is challenging for most people. The difference and diversity in maps of the world across a group of people (explore this in Chapter 4) make influencing and relating quite challenging – at least until you read this book and master NLP influencing techniques!

One of the simplest ways to transform team performance is to develop well-formed outcomes for the team. These outcomes may well have to be negotiated among team members. Negotiating outcomes becomes easier when you use a full range of sensory-specific language to describe the outcome and describe the evidence that lets people know when the outcome's achieved. Using such language not only creates a more vivid description of an outcome, but allows team members to understand and connect with the outcome using their preferred sensory system. (Find more on sensory systems in Chapter 5.)

## Empowering organisations with well-formed outcomes

Corporate executives set outcomes for their organisations, but these goals are rarely well formed. In my experience, business goals are often expressed in numerical form, very briefly, and with little if any sensory language. These are the shared goals of the whole organisation and depend on the combined efforts of all employees to achieve them, yet contain little to motivate individual effort.

Take a look at the current goals and targets expressed in your business. Evaluate these goals, asking yourself the well-formed outcome questions in this chapter. What types of information are still needed in order for these goals to meet the conditions of a well-formed outcome?

When goals cascade down from the top of an organisation, through divisions, departments, teams, and ultimately to individuals, little exists to motivate people to want to achieve them. If you have influence over the planning process, you may want to ensure that the business goals are well formed. If you currently don't have this opportunity, you can still ensure that the team and individual goals that affect you are well formed. Start to ask questions from the NLP outcome model and you find yourself influencing others around you to think about their goals in ways they've never considered before.

## Building success with well-formed outcomes

Businesses tend to be busy places with lots of activity. Getting things done is usually a high priority. If you were able to slow down your activity for a moment and stop for long enough to develop a well-formed outcome for everything you do, what longer-term benefits can you imagine?

You can set outcomes for just about everything you do. Situations in which using the well-formed outcome model can be useful include:

✔ **Selling:** Helping customers work out what they want.

✔ **Negotiating:** Ensuring you have a realistic outcome.

✔ **Influencing:** Getting what you want from a conversation or meeting.

✔ **Coaching:** Helping others to improve their performance.

✔ **Relating:** Building important relationships and networks.

✔ **Recruiting:** Knowing exactly what kind of people you need.

✔ **Setting targets:** Determining goals for sales, costs, productivity, or efficiency.

# Chapter 17

# Modelling Winning Performance

. . . . . . . . . . . . . . . . . . . . . . . . . . . . . . . . . . . . . . . . . . . .

## In This Chapter

▶ Discovering how to achieve excellence

▶ Looking at others' successes for inspiration

▶ Creating, refining, and sharing models

▶ Using models based on famous people

. . . . . . . . . . . . . . . . . . . . . . . . . . . . . . . . . . . . . . . . . . . .

*B*usinesses are continually looking to improve results and get people working more productively. The world is competitive, and to get ahead many businesses are trying to be leaner and meaner, getting the most effectiveness and efficiency out of their available resources, especially their people.

These days recruiting people is a sophisticated process. In-depth interviews, personality, and aptitude assessments all contribute to the goal of hiring the best. Yet so often, 20 people may be recruited for the same kind of job, go through the same skills training, and end up performing at 20 distinctly different levels.

This phenomenon has baffled and frustrated leaders for many years. With similar experience, the same training, and the same job, how can such marked variations in output result? In attempting to answer this question, executives often end up questioning the entire recruitment process or challenging the value or quality of training. To try to resolve the discrepancies, heavy performance management kicks in and the poorest performers leave the company and the cycle starts again. Meanwhile, management and training attention has been taken away from the strongest performers, leaving them less likely to reach their potential.

If only you were able to pinpoint what makes the difference between one person's excellent achievements and another's much lower level of performance. And perhaps you can also pick up the group in the middle – those workers who are getting adequate, but not exceptional, results – and take these individuals to higher performance levels.

This is where NLP comes in. With its roots in finding out how people achieve excellence, NLP has much to offer the business world by shaping and inspiring exceptional job performance. Find out more in this chapter about NLP modelling and how to use it with individuals, teams, and entire organisations.

# Patterning Yourself on Others' Successes

Every field has people whose outputs are superlative. Business, sports, drama, music, medicine, art, craftsmanship, and more all present highly talented people creating exceptional results.

When someone consistently achieves excellence, you often hear things like 'Oh, she's a natural' or 'It's in his blood'. Is it? Well, with NLP, where the skills come from isn't important. What matters is that you can understand and replicate the thinking and strategies of others to achieve your own exceptional performance.

 NLP *modelling* allows you to examine in fine detail exactly what someone does to achieve the results they do. Most modelling activities are described as intuitive. Modelling is certainly outside of people's conscious awareness much of the time, so they don't know *how* they're getting the results they do. What's more, people often just can't understand why everyone else can't do the same!

When you identify and break down the individual steps that a person goes through to do something, you create a *model* that you can use to help achieve the same yourself, as well as to use when working with others.

If you're concerned that you may become something of a clone of that person, rest assured! No matter how closely you model Tiger Woods, you can't become him – although you may develop some of his prowess on the golf course. You don't have – and never can have – his personal history, his physiology, or his personality. By modelling your golf technique on his, you're just taking on some of his capabilities.

The following sections explore specific techniques that you can use to create models for performance excellence.

## Remembering how you got started

When you think about babies and toddlers, that they develop by modelling is obvious. From a very young age, babies watch and listen to parents and siblings intensely. You may notice them attempting to match the movements of others as their motor control develops. They smile when someone smiles at them. As they grow a little older, they start to stand and then walk.

They also pick up language by listening to and then imitating others. As their language skills grow, they get to grips with rhythm, tonality, and increasingly complex words. Then these tiny humans start to link words together, eventually articulating full sentences, with grammar and syntax.

So how can an infant with a brain that's still quite underdeveloped embrace language for the first time, yet many adults struggle to learn another language fluently?

Unfortunately, beyond those early years, humans move further and further away from modelling as a development process and more towards teacher-led learning. Someone tells or shows you what to do – and corrects you if what you do or say is wrong. People become increasingly inhibited and concerned about making mistakes. Ultimately this natural tendency to model, and keep on practising, diminishes – but that latent capability to model is still there. NLP offers tools and approaches to enhance your ability to get an accurate model, as I explain in the section: 'Developing a Model of Excellence'.

## *Benchmarking*

Many businesses today use *benchmarking* to appraise their own internal processes against those of others within or outside the organisation. Like NLP modelling, benchmarking is an approach to studying excellence.

Benchmarking involves identifying the activities of other businesses, parts of your own business, or even individuals to identify and evaluate what executives often term 'best practice'. Studying others' processes and activities can be time consuming, but the rewards are good – particularly if as a result you discover better practices than those of your own business in order to boost your performance.

Current benchmarking techniques largely focus on reviewing and analysing effective business processes, such that once they are analysed and understood they can be replicated elsewhere. NLP modelling does something similar with the *internal* processes that take place for an individual achieving excellence. You may choose to use NLP modelling as a part of you formal benchmarking exercise, or as a stand alone technique when you just want to be able to do something as well as someone else.

Take some time to consider what aspects of your business you want to benchmark against others' to find different tools and processes to improve effectiveness. Now consider which particular skills you would like more of in some areas of you business, which you could model from people achieving excellence in your business or elsewhere.

The range of capabilities and skills that you can enhance by using modelling is almost endless. Whether something is seemingly small, like managing your diary better, or much larger, such as leading successfully, modelling has a part to play.

Some (of the many) business aspects for which you may find modelling a useful technique include:

✔ Negotiating successfully

✔ Being assertive

✔ Planning

✔ Innovating

✔ Selling

✔ Analysing data

✔ Leading

✔ Decision making

✔ Making powerful presentations

# Developing a Model of Excellence

NLP started with modelling (see Chapter 1). NLP founders first developed the Meta Model (Chapter 12), then the Milton Model (Chapter 10), and many more models after these.

Modelling is an extensive subject. In this book I introduce some of the most popular and effective models and modelling techniques. With the information in this book, you can begin to tackle some modelling projects yourself. If you want to discover even more about modelling, read *Modeling with NLP* by Robert Dilts (Meta Publications, 1998), in which he explains both the process of modelling and how it can be applied to various aspects of leadership, including problem solving, delegating, training and influencing.

One of the barriers to creating an effective model is to focus on amore than one capability. What I mean here is that if you want to model how someone achieves an excellent result, she may use a number of different capabilities to get there. For example, you want to model the sales person who generates consistently high new business sales. Bear in mind what steps this sales process takes, which may include:

✔ Identifying potential customers

✔ Contacting new prospects

> ✔ Getting a meeting with a prospect
>
> ✔ Putting together a proposal
>
> ✔ Closing the sale

Each of these processes require a distinct different approach and set of capabilities, so decide whether you need models for just one or two steps of the process to gain sales from new customers, or for each step in turn.

Developing a model of excellence has three key phases:

> ✔ Eliciting and devising the model.
>
> ✔ Removing the non-essential.
>
> ✔ Designing a way to train others in it.

The following section covers each of these phases in detail.

## Building a model

Working out *how* someone else gets the results they do is not as simple as asking them – unfortunately! So much of what humans do they do habitually – they don't know they're doing it, Modelling takes patience ands perseverance. You need to pay attention to a whole range of things that someone does in order to build your model. The following sections describe all the various aspects of behaviour and thinking that may be important to your model.

The sidebar 'Modelling a useful skill' showcases a series of observations gathered in the process of building a specific model.

### Physiology

Adopting the *physiology* (posture, breathing, movements, gestures, and facial expressions) of another person can be a useful part of modelling someone. This process may feel quite alien at first, but it goes quite some way towards stepping inside another person's world and having some of the same experiences.

Pretty obviously, to model someone with a distinct physical capability, like hitting a tennis ball, you need to attempt to do physically exactly what the model does. Physically mimicking another person may seem less obvious when you're modelling training skills or telesales capabilities.

Observe the person doing what it is that he does so well. You may wish to tell him what you're doing, if it's part of a whole modelling process that you'll need to question him about. If you're modelling someone from a distance, just watch him very carefully. Pay attention to his posture, movement, and expressions; you may well be amazed at what you discover. (Turn to Chapter 6 to find out about all the subtle variations of body movement and posture that people use.) Then try the same posture, movements and expressions on for yourself. If the physiology is very different to anything you're used to, you may need to practise it in a quiet place or even in front of a mirror, to be sure that you have the right kind of movement and that it works for you. As you take on a different physiology, notice what different thoughts and feelings you have.

Glen really admired his friend Peter. Whenever Peter entered a room, people turned to him, smiled, and opened up conversations. In contrast, Glen seemed to be able to enter a room unnoticed – and stay that way for some time. Glen suspected that Peter's height and not insubstantial build created these positive results in group situations. However, I persuaded Glen to model Peter's physiology. Glen observed that when entering a crowded room, Peter always stood straight and held his head high, with his shoulders back and down. Peter breathed deeply and smiled. He also looked around the room to catch someone's eye and made a movement towards this person as their eyes met. Glen tried on Peter's physiology and movements. Despite being of much smaller stature than Peter, even on the first time of trying Glen found someone to talk to, even if not quite as quickly as Peter. After further practise Glen became much more confident in adopting his new physiology and always found companions to chat with in any group situation.

### Thinking strategies

NLP modelling pays particular attention to the *strategies* people have, specifically the thoughts someone has and how these thoughts are structured and organised. These strategies are the many, sometimes tiny and rapid steps that happen unconsciously in your mind – and that result in the good performance you desire.

Strategies involve the use of your senses. A strategy for cooking a meal, for example, can easily involve all five senses, whereas only seeing, hearing and feeling activities are likely to come into play in a strategy for meeting a deadline. (Chapter 5 explains in some depth how you use your senses when you think, often unconsciously.)

As well as working out precisely what somebody's internal processes are in sensory terms, how you give some things more prominence than others is also important. The qualities of your internal representations of your thoughts are described in NLP as *submodalities*. I explain these submodalities in depth in Chapter 9. Submodalities identify distinctions in thinking such as:

✔ Is a picture large or small? Dull or bright? Still or moving?

✔ Are sounds loud or quiet? Near or far away?

✔ Are feelings strong or weak? Hot or cold?

To model which sense someone else uses when he runs through a process (and then use this sense yourself), you must first pay very close attention to him. Whether you are modelling chairing a meeting, making a cold sales call or any other skill, you need to watch and listen closely. Ideally, you will tell the other person what you admire in him and gaining his agreement to you building a model of his capability. Then move through the following steps:

1. **Pay attention to where the person's eyes are moving.**

   Eye movements are very informative. As I discuss in Chapter 5, the direction in which someone's eyes move tells you much about his thinking. Figure 17-1 summarises these eye movements and what they most commonly represent.

   Make sure you do this on a number of occasions so that you can spot the patterns.

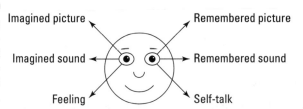

2. **Build on the model by interviewing the person to find out more about what he's doing or thinking when they are performing the skill that you are modelling.**

   You can ask:

   • What's the first thing you did or thought?

   • What was the next thing you did or thought?

   When you ask these questions, often you get a simple 'I don't know', which indicates that the other person may not know his own process. Target your question more specifically by asking something like:

   > I noticed that your first step seemed to be to see something in your mind's eye, something you remembered [or whatever action you noted earlier]. Can you tell me what you saw?

3. **Help your interviewee go backwards and forwards through the sequence to work out any missing steps.**

   Whenever you discover something new in the sequence, ask the person what the next step was. Because many activities are part of an unconscious process and they happen very fast, people being modelled often have difficulty telling you all the steps. Help the person access his strategies by asking:

   > What did you do or think just before [the last step described to you]?

   Then ask:

   > What was the *next* thing you did or thought?

4. **Write down a model of the individual strategies and their sequence.**

   Talk the other person through the steps. Ask him to try them out one by one as you read them to him. Does he notice anything missing, or anything extra that shouldn't be there? Are the steps in the right sequence? Update your model if necessary.

5. **Gather information from the other person about the submodalities at play during the sequence.**

   Ask the other person questions such as:

   - Is the picture bright? In colour?

   - Does the internal voice have a certain tone?

   - Where does a particular feeling seem to come from?

   Turn to Chapter 9 for more questions to ask about submodalities.

   Update your model with these qualities. When you have a step where an image is, for example, still rather than moving, note that into your model as that characteristic may be important. You are working to get the most accurate representation of what the other person does so that you can do the same when you test out the model for yourself.

Modelling another person's strategies can be challenging and time consuming but also very valuable. Strategy modelling gives you:

- ✔ Amazing insights into someone else's world.

- ✔ The opportunity to use another person's strategies to get the equally good results.

- ✔ The chance to build your own behavioural flexibility.

Find out how to test whether you have extracted all the key steps in another's strategies in the later section, 'Testing your model'.

### Metaprograms

*Metaprograms*, or patterns of motivation, can be a key part of the difference between average and exceptional performance. (Read all about metaprograms in Chapter 7.)

I've met just a few people who can review large quantities of numerical data very quickly and immediately identify which figures are worthy of extra attention. At least part of this success may come from these individuals' metaprogram patterns. For example, they may:

- ✔ Be able to move easily along the spectrum from big-picture thinking to specific-detail thinking and back again.

- ✔ Be motivated to notice difference and exception, rather than sameness. These individuals may even tell you that the figures they extract from the mass of data just 'seem to leap off the page'.

Spend some time investigating someone else's metaprograms when you're modelling using the approaches you find in Chapter 7. Make sure you check out each metaprogram in the context of what the other person is specifically doing well, as people may be operating different metaprogram patterns in different areas of life. When you find a metaprogram pattern that is quite different to yours, check out whether it's an essential part of the model (refer to the 'Testing your model' section). If you discover that adopting this metaprogram is critical to achieving the result you want, you need to act as if (pretend) that you work with this pattern.

### Beliefs and values

Often at play in excellent performance are various beliefs relevant to the capability that the successful person is demonstrating. These beliefs may be as straightforward as 'I believe I can do this' or 'I believe that doing my best is important'. Other beliefs may be more specific to the task at hand ('I believe that other people's time is as valuable as mine), but certainly indicate what someone thinks is true or important.

Similarly, people's values affect their performance. For example, a leader who generates commitment and trust in his people may have a strong value of honesty.

If the person you're modelling has very different beliefs and values to you, you may find that your resulting model contains things that are hard for you to believe or value. At this point, you have choices:

- ✔ **Remove the personally inconsistent belief or value from the model and see whether it's essential for success.** Try out all the other elements of the model that you have built, without using the belief or value in question. As long as the belief or value isn't essential, you'll still get the results you want.

✔ **Act *as if* you have the belief or value – just for the purposes of running the model.** This technique's particularly useful when you have to act as if you believe that you're capable of doing something well, something that you didn't previously believe. The unconscious mind is very powerful, and telling it that you can do something has an impact.

## Testing a model

Once you have devised a model for the capability that you want, you need to test it out. NLP offers a model for this, involving a series of simple steps, known as the TOTE (Test, Operate, Test, Exit) model. The TOTE model was first designed and presented by Miller, Ganter and Pribam in 1961. NLP originators (more on these in Chapter 1) enhanced the TOTE model and it's particularly useful in testing out the effectiveness of a model of excellence.

The TOTE model suggests that when you want something (have a goal), you behave in order to achieve that goal. You then test to see whether you achieved your goal. If you're successful, you stop the behaviour. If you're not, you change the behaviour. For example, you want to lift a box from the floor. You bend down to pick up the box. You quickly test – have I picked up the box? If you have, you move on to your *next* goal, which is to put the box somewhere else. If you find that the box didn't lift, you try again, this time with much greater effort. You quickly test – have I picked up the box? You have, so you move on to your next goal. These steps are outlined in Figure 17-2.

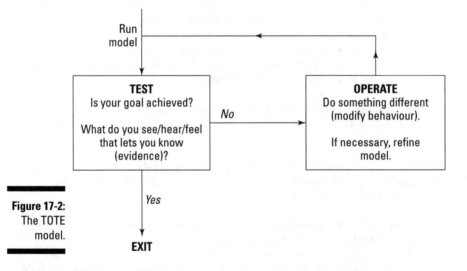

**Figure 17-2:**
The TOTE
model.

Run model

**TEST**
Is your goal achieved?

What do you see/hear/feel that lets you know (evidence)?

*No* →

**OPERATE**
Do something different (modify behaviour).

If necessary, refine model.

*Yes*

**EXIT**

Try out your model. For example, if you have modelled securing a meeting with a prospective customer, the steps you go through will be like this:

1. **Test.** Make a telephone call, using all the elements of your model.

   Review what happens using sensory evidence – what do you see, hear and feel?

   In this example, if you hear the prospect agree to a meeting, and see the appointment in your diary, you can reached your goal, in which case move to step 4.

   If you don't hear agreement or see an appointment in your diary, move to step 2.

2. **Operate.** You need to modify your behaviour – do or say something different. .

   Check that you completed all the steps of your model. If not, try again using *all* the elements.

   If you used all the components of your model, something is missing and you need to do some further work with the person you modelled.

3. **Test. Using your updated model, make a telephone call.**

   Review what happens using sensory evidence – what do you see, hear and feel?

   If you hear the prospect agree to a meeting, and see the appointment in your diary, you can reached your goal, in which case move to step 4.

   If you don't hear agreement or see an appointment in your diary, move back to step 2 again.

4. **Exit.** Your model is tested and works effectively.

## Modelling a useful skill

After you go through all the steps of gathering information for a model (see the section 'Building a model', earlier in this chapter), you probably have a lot of information to pull together – physiology, strategies, metaprograms, and beliefs and values.

The following explores an example of a real-life model that Chris, a colleague of mine, uncovered while observing Chelsea and seeking to model her successful way of *engaging a new audience within the first minute of a training presentation.*

✔ **Physiology.** For ten minutes before the presentation, Chelsea busies herself, shuffling papers, lining up all the things she needs, and getting her working space in order. She periodically scans the group with her eyes, smiling at anyone she makes eye contact with. Just before she's about to start, she stands up straight, leans back slightly, breathes very deeply, and speaks, smiling as she does so.

*(continued)*

*(continued)*

✔ **Strategies.** Chelsea asks herself what she's heard about the people attending. How far have they travelled? How keen are they to be at the workshop? How much pressure are they under? Anything else? This is an *auditory internal process.*

Chelsea then looks at the room of people and asks herself: do people appear to know each other? How much rapport exists? Are people rushing in late? Do people seem relaxed or frazzled? Are many having rushed calls on mobile phones? This is a *visual external process.*

She listens to any snatches of conversation she can hear. She puts her attention on discussions about busy-ness or the journey. What do these words and intonation suggest her audience may be feeling? This is an *auditory external process.*

Chelsea next remembers her own pictures and feelings on her journey. Did her journey feel easy or stressful? Was the venue easy to find? Was traffic free flowing? This is an *internal visual process followed by a kinaesthetic process.*

Finally, Chelsea quickly recalls her answers to all the questions she's asked herself. She then runs a short movie, with sound, to imagine what may be true for the people in the room right now. This is an *internal visual and auditory process.*

Chelsea runs the movie several times and asks herself, 'If I were in that movie, how would I feel?' She then has a feeling. This is an *internal kinaesthetic process.*

Chelsea looks at her watch, tells herself the time's right to start, and stands up straight. As she takes a deep breath and says 'Good morning' to the room, she remembers the feeling she imagined they may have from her movie and decides what to say. If the feeling is good, such as calm or optimistic, Chelsea says something positive about everyone being there and what a great day's ahead. If the feeling's less good, such as stressed or anxious, she paces the audience's feeling by talking humorously about the challenge of the traffic or finding time to be away from the work place – in order to change the audience's emotional state.

✔ **Metaprograms.** Personally, Chelsea has a high preference for options rather than procedures, hence her flexible approach to starting the meeting depending on what her last-minute assessments suggest. She also has a mixed toward and away from metaprogram. She wants the presentation to go well and she wants to move her audience away from any negative emotion they're holding at the start of the day.

✔ **Beliefs and values.** Chelsea believes that she can engage the audience in the first minute. She values the time they give up to attend the training. She believes that respecting their experiences is important.

Chris 'tried on' what he modelled from Chelsea. He found that organising his working space distracted him and he preferred to have that done before delegates arrived. But, Chris smiled at people and used the same physiology as Chelsea. Then he used Chelsea's strategies to evaluate how to start the presentation. Being less options oriented than Chelsea, Chris chose to act *as if* he was motivated by options, to get the benefit of her metaprogram pattern. Like Chelsea, Chris is equally toward and away from, and shared Chelsea's desire for things to go well and to ensure no bad experience for attendees. Finally, although Chris shared Chelsea's value and one of her beliefs, he still didn't believe that he can engage an audience in the first minute. So, Chris used the rest of his model to determine what results he got. He was delighted to find that he too was able to get people engaged really quickly and easily at the start of training sessions. Then he changed his belief about his ability to do it!

## *Taking away what you don't need*

After you outline and try out a model, you can move to the process often known as *the subtraction process*. As you see in the sidebar 'Modelling a useful skill', modelling can lead to a lot of information. All this information is relevant, but some aspects may be less critical to the success of the model.

After you gather as much information as you can, you then need to find out what you can afford to lose, while still getting the same results!

You need to take things out of the model systematically, just one thing at a time. For example, in the presentation skills modelling based on Chelsea's activities in the sidebar 'Modelling a useful skill', Chris found that he could take out the paper shuffling at the beginning, and the underlying belief that he could engage the audience in the first minute, and he still got the same results. If he tested removing Chelsea's strategy to run a movie, he may well find that the model doesn't work for him.

By removing specific bits of your model, you can determine which parts make a difference to the result and which don't. Keep what you need as a minimum to get the excellence you want. Feel free to throw the rest out!

## *Passing on a model*

Given the scale of a business and the many people and skills that you can apply in more than one discipline, the ultimate value of a model doesn't merely lie in being able to replicate great performance yourself, but in ensuring that others can too.

The final phase of modelling is passing on the model to anyone else that needs to develop excellence in this skill. You may take key individuals through the model one by one, train it to a group, or share it with a learning and development to teach it to people throughout the organisation.

Passing on your new model to others is an excellent final test of its effectiveness. Can others now use it and also get good results? If not, there's likely something missing – something that you are adding in that you aren't aware of. If so, go back to the modelling phase and start to model what *you* are doing, to check out the missing piece.

# *Discovering the Strategies of Genius*

Robert Dilts, a skilled and prolific modeller, has contributed much to the field of NLP modelling. He developed models based on some of the greatest talents of all time, making these processes for success accessible to everyone.

Dilts has modelled a wide array of people, many of them no longer alive, including:

- Leonardo da Vinci
- Wolfgang Amadeus Mozart
- Albert Einstein
- Aristotle
- Sigmund Freud
- Walt Disney

The test for the effectiveness of a model is whether someone else can try the strategies and get similar outcomes to the originator of the excellence. So the fact that a model was created posthumously (and that you can't check it out with the originator of the excellence) isn't a problem. The key is formulating a usable model that gets you the results you want.

The following sections briefly explore two models that Dilts created based on Einstein and Walt Disney. For more information on these models access the Encyclopaedia of NLP published by Dilts and DeLozier, which can be accessed via www.nlpu.com, or read Strategies of Genius Volumes 1 and 2 by Robert Dilts, Meta Publications, (1994 and 1995), which can be purchased from www.nlpu.com.

## Innovating like Einstein

Albert Einstein (1879–1955) is best known for his theory of relativity. His discoveries and contribution to theoretical physics are unparalleled.

Einstein's ability to question the beliefs and assumptions of his time – and to develop radical models of the world – was awe inspiring. In your own business, how may overturning conventional thinking and finding whole new perspectives on how things work be useful?

When Robert Dilts modelled Einstein, he made some interesting discoveries. For example, when you think of Einstein, you may imagine him surrounded by hugely complex mathematical equations, completely beyond your comprehension. I know I did! But in fact, Einstein's creativity didn't have its roots in maths, but in pictures – imagined visual images, to be precise. Einstein used his vivid imagination to see things in his mind. He knew that he rarely thought with words. After he had a concept really well developed in his mind, an internal feeling told him the concept was worth taking to the world. Only then did Einstein work to express this idea in words and mathematical symbols. So a brilliant visual imagination was the root of the kind of abstract thinking that led to the genius of Einstein.

Think about the areas of your work where being completely innovative may be helpful. Spend a little time every day trying Einstein's strategy. Let your imagination run wild in pictures. Pretend you have the imagination of a young child again. Enjoy the experience and don't attempt to make sense of it or put words to it – until you get the feeling that you want to. Who knows what fabulous ideas, innovations, or inventions may evolve?

# Problem solving the Disney way

In your business, do you need more creativity? More opportunities? More innovative problem solving? More effective planning? Well, Walt Disney's strategy, as modelled by Dilts, may be of great value to you.

Walt Disney (1901–1966) possessed creativity and inventiveness that many consider second to none. Disney, through his amazing animated characters, not only entertained the world but started a whole new genre of film making, contributing much to the field both technically and artistically. Beyond this, Disney established a successful and sustainable business empire that's gone from strength to strength since his death.

### A strategy for creative success

Through modelling the late Disney, Dilts discovered three facets to his creative strategy. To create any of his famous characters and concepts, from Mickey Mouse to Pluto to Disney World and Epcot Center, Disney took his creative idea through three phases of thinking:

- ✔ **Dreamer.** This is a stage of imagining and fantasising. You don't judge any ideas and you allow random thoughts and absurd combinations to flourish. The experience is rich, full of colour and sound and feeling.

- ✔ **Realist.** This is the pragmatic part of the process, where you consider the amazing and crazy ideas from the Dreamer stage in terms of what may be possible or achievable in the real world.

- ✔ **Critic.** Only at this third stage do you evaluate and judge an idea. Is it good enough to achieve what you want? Your reflections during the Critic stage lead to refinements and improvements to the idea and its eventual implementation.

Almost everyone has a Dreamer, Realist, and Critic inside him – but often one or two of these roles have more dominance than the others. One of the most common patterns is that the Dreamer and Critic come to the fore. The Critic can quickly tear apart an idea by deciding that something can't work and putting an end to a potentially fabulous new concept – without making a realistic appraisal of the idea.

Use the Disney creative strategy I outline in the following section, 'Planning with the Disney strategy' to practise working in all three roles, Dreamer, Realist and Critic. This helps you to build your skill in your least preferred role and enhance your ability to generate creative ideas that can be put into action.

### Planning with the Disney strategy

You can use the Disney strategy in many different ways. The following is just one of the approaches I've used to coach people who are planning and problem solving. You can take yourself through this process, and it also works well with groups.

The basic concept of the exercise is to get multiple perspectives on an idea. The exercise works best if you lay out three different positions or spaces, as Figure 17-3 indicates. Work through the exercise without stopping until you have a robust plan. This might take only a few minutes, but allow up to half an hour. Think of an idea, or goal, that you have and then move through the following steps:

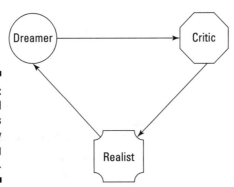

**Figure 17-3:**
Physical locations for a Disney planning exercise.

1. **Place three sheets of paper on the floor, as Figure 17-3 indicates.**

   Label the papers *Dreamer*, *Realist*, and *Critic*. Be sure you can stand on each piece of paper comfortably and move easily from one space to another.

2. **Step into the Dreamer or *want to* space.**

Stand with your head and eyes up, body balanced and relaxed. Thinking about your idea or goal, ask the following questions:

What do you want? (Be sure to state your answer in the positive – rather than what you *don't* want.)

What will you see, hear, and feel when you have it?

What are the benefits of this for you or for others?

When can you expect to get the benefits?

When you have this goal, then what happens?

Once you have considered your answers to the questions it may be useful to you to write them down.

3. **Step into the Realist or *how to* space.**

Stand with your head and eyes straight ahead, with your body leaning slightly forward. Ask the following questions:

How will you know when you have your goal?

Who needs to be involved?

What needs to happen?

When will the goal happen by?

When will each phase be completed by?

What's the first step?

Once you have thought through the questions, you may wish to write down your answers for future reference.

4. **Step into the Critic or *chance to* space.**

Stand with your eyes down, head down and tilted to one side (whichever side feels most comfortable to you). Tilt your body slightly as well. Ask the following questions:

Who does this affect?

What or who can make or break this idea?

Why may someone object?

What are the positives of *not* doing this (or staying the same)?

What's missing from the plan?

After you answer the preceding questions, think about any further questions you want to pose to the Dreamer. You may find it helpful to write down your answers and new questions for the Dreamer.

5. **Step back into the Dreamer space for the *second Dreamer phase*.**

   Stand with your head and eyes up and your body balanced and relaxed. Ask:

   > How can you take care of what's missing from the plan?

   Add any further insights to your notes.

6. **Move into the Realist space again for the *second Realist phase*.**

   Stand with your head and eyes straight ahead, and body slightly forward. Ask:

   > How specifically can I implement this?

   Add any further insights to your notes.

7. **Move on to the Critic space again for the *second Critic phase*.**

   Stand with your eyes and head down, and head and body tilted slightly. Ask:

   > Is anything else needed in or missing from the plan?

   Add any further insights to your notes.

   If the answer to the question at this point is yes, then loop through steps 5, 6, and 7 until you finally get a no.

   When you're able to answer no to this question, you know you have a creative, well-formulated idea or goal and a plan to achieve it.

# Modelling Yourself – For Yourself

One thing I come across again and again in coaching is people demonstrating amazing excellence in one area and struggling in another. You may well find that when you're looking for an approach to success at something, you already have a way of doing just that in another context. Some examples include:

- Someone with excellent problem-solving skills on projects but difficulty solving problems with work relationships

- A salesperson who sells services to customers really well but doesn't sell himself to his boss.

- A person who's very effective at speaking to a company conference but not at all confident when presenting to an external industry conference.

When you're looking for a particular capability for yourself, start by considering whether you get results doing something similar elsewhere in your life. Then examine what you can about your approach and develop a conscious model using the 'Building a Model' section earlier in this chapter as a guide. You may well be astonished by what you find you can do.

A client of mine, Neil, had great difficulty handling meetings with a particular customer. The customer had been let down, and Neil was working to rescue the relationship. Yet every time he prepared for a meeting with her, all he did was get anxious and stressed – and then went into the meeting in that state. Neil and I identified that his preparation strategies for customer meetings included imagining the meeting in his mind in advance. He ran a mental video of the situation (more on this in Chapter 5), saw the customer's upset face, and heard her tense voice. Neil then realised that he used a similar strategy for achieving well at his one of his hobbies, uphill cycling. Before a big ride he ran a mental video, but that video was of him reaching the top, easily and speedily. After he discovered that he was able to direct his own video and use the strategy of imagining things going well, his approach to the relationship with his customer improved dramatically. Neil rescued the relationship, and she became a very loyal customer.

# Part V
# The Part of Tens

"He's the only person I know who approaches team building like a do-it-yourself project."

## In this part . . .

The best things come in small parcels, and these chapters prove the rule. Every *For Dummies* book ends with an offering of bite-sized wisdom that's easy to assimilate.

In these chapters I spell out ten business benefits to using NLP, provide the inside track on using NLP principles in everyday situations, and run through the best in NLP resources and books.

# Chapter 18

# Ten Business Benefits of NLP

## In This Chapter

▶ Getting the best from your colleagues

▶ Reflecting on business improvement with NLP

▶ Becoming aware of the benefits

*T*his book covers a wide range of NLP approaches and techniques, and many ways to use NLP at work. You can gain masses of business benefits by using NLP, whether for yourself or more widely throughout the organisation. In fact, once you are familiar with NLP you may well wonder how you ever made any progress at work before!

In this chapter I've summarised just ten of the areas in which NLP makes a significant difference to business performance and results.

## Recruiting the Best

Hiring the right people for the job is crucial to companies replacing, expanding, or developing in new areas. Recruitment is time-consuming and often expensive, and of course leaving jobs unfilled means less work gets done and important targets get missed. Recruitment has become a far more sophisticated discipline over the years, with expertly trained interviewers, psychological, personality, and ability testing and other assessments. However employers still sometimes find that the person appointed does not live up to expectations.

Introducing NLP to the hiring process adds some valuable additional dimensions. Just because someone has a great CV and comes across well at interview, doesn't necessarily mean he is right for the job. By using metaprograms (more on these in Chapter 7) to determine the working preferences and motivations of the interviewee, and matching them to what the job requires, you can make a much more effective appointment. In addition, using precision and clean questions (find these in Chapter 12) to interview uncovers valuable information about the individual, and their more deeply-held beliefs, attitudes, and thinking patterns. These indicate how well someone is suited to a job, and to the culture of the company.

# Making Effective Change

The corporate world is forever faced with all kinds of pressures which require substantial change. Upsizing, downsizing, relocating, opening and closing in different international markets, and many other change situations all affect businesses. Mostly this change does not happen easily and quickly. It's a complex and demanding process.

Help is at hand with NLP. NLP helps leaders to communicate in different ways, and to support employees in making the necessary changes, overcoming both resistance and anxiety. Using NLP in business improves awareness of patterns of thinking, enhances flexibility and makes change smoother and easier.

# Achieving Goals

Achieving or exceeding specific goals is generally considered the most important measure of business success. Yet the unpredictability of market conditions can put a company off course from achieving its objectives – particularly its financial targets. Failing to cascade objectives through the organisation in a way that makes sense to, and motivates, staff, is another factor which can lead to goals being missed. Business activity which results from this sort of failure is untargeted and not necessarily aligned with company goals.

Using NLP to develop well-formed outcomes throughout an organisation, engages people with well-defined, meaningful goals. Once everyone in the organisation has a clear understanding of what they're aiming for, and know what it will look, sound and feel like, they'll be far more motivated to go for it. More can be found on well-formed outcomes in Chapter 16.

In addition, the more flexible the behaviour within an organisation, the easier that organisation will find attaining its goals. One of the NLP principles is that if you want a different result you need to do something different. This is as true for a group or organisation level as it is for you and me.

# *Enhancing Performance*

Doing more with less is the objective of many organisations. Getting people to work more effectively and efficiently helps to improve profitability. Most people look to do their best to have job satisfaction and get the reward and recognition that they desire.

Another NLP tool organisations use is modelling. Identifying the strategies of those who achieve exceptional results allows others to create similar results, increasing the all-round performance of a team or group within the business. Modelling is covered in depth in Chapter 17.

Most organisations these days invest significantly in performance reviews and development plans for their employees. NLP brings a new richness to giving feedback and building skills. When people receive evidence-based, actionable feedback, supported by coaching, they become more effective. The NLP approach to feedback and coaching helps people to develop more skills and achieve more in their jobs.

Finally, people don't work at their best when experiencing conflict, disagreement, or misunderstanding. They're much more productive when they relate well to others, feel listened to and respected, and communicate effectively. Good communications are at the heart of NLP. In many organisations they are the difference that makes the difference to business performance.

# *Enhancing Creativity and Innovation*

Innovating to create new business opportunities, more efficient processes, and better solutions to problems, keeps a business moving forward and staying competitive. Yet many organisations have a communications style and approach to management that actually blocks creativity.

When you empower and coach people you unleash their creativity and their willingness to take risks. Using NLP coaching tools you support others to solve problems by establishing positive outcomes and encouraging individuals to develop their own methods for achieving them. As people discover their own and others' patterns (see Chapters 5 and 7 for examples of patterns), they build flexibility and improve their relationships, leading to a supportive climate for innovation.

# Motivating and Energising People

Engaging people and igniting their interest and passion for the business, a change programme, or a future goal, is a regular challenge for businesses. When the pressure is on, things aren't going so well, or people feel anxious about the future, it's an even harder job to motivate and energise.

The powerful communications techniques offered by NLP provide the opportunity to influence groups of people successfully. Using sensory language to provide vivid descriptions, artfully vague language, which I explain in Chapter 10, to allow people to make their own sense of the messages given, or metaphor to convey complex ideas in a more comprehensible form, give communicators the tools to inspire and convince.

# Decreasing Response Times

The twenty-first century has brought us an increasingly dynamic and fast-changing business world. Political environments change dramatically, financial markets fluctuate widely, globalisation brings unexpected competitive pressures, and rapid communications create further pressures. Responding fast and well for some is an easy as turning round an ocean-liner on a sixpence.

By building great self awareness, NLP-style, and utilising NLP tools and techniques, business people develop much more flexible ways of thinking and working. Businesses employing people with this capability are much more fleet of foot and able to respond quickly and well to unexpected changes.

# Keeping Talented People

Retaining experienced and valuable people is a challenge businesses face. Employees move on for a number of reasons, including wanting to find new opportunities for development and career progression.

Many aspects of NLP help organisations to address the needs of their people. Coaching with NLP helps people to improve their influence, increase their flexibility, and achieve more. A coaching culture moves employees from a problem-thinking to an outcome-thinking frame of mind, giving them more autonomy and opportunity for growth. It's much easier to keep people when they're making a good contribution and progressing well.

In addition, businesses with well-defined values, a compelling vision and truly effective communications are much more likely to retain the employees that feel able to align with, and work hard to achieve, company goals. People are motivated by the opportunity to strive for and achieve great results, and consequently are much more likely to stay in the organisation.

# Communicating Effectively

Talking, discussing, writing, emailing, presenting, and more: Whatever the reason and whichever medium is used, enormous amounts of time and energy are devoted to communicating in business. Time after time, these communications don't achieve the desired effect. People don't understand, aren't persuaded, or just don't even notice the communication!

With its extensive models and tools for communication, NLP offers business people the opportunity to have much more constructive interactions. By spotting different patterns, influencing more flexibly, and building rapport, differences, conflicts and misunderstandings are reduced. NLP offers a step change in influencing capability which creates very different results.

# Improving Teamwork

Cooperation and collaboration between teams of people is essential in many areas of business. Achieving a particular goal often requires a range of specialisms, plus numerous 'pairs of hands' just to get all the work done. Some teams just don't seem to work well together. They might be in conflict, may not communicate well, or just simply don't get on!

Huge improvements in team working result when team members learn to notice their own patterns of thinking, and then those of each other,. As they recognise and respect their diversity, team members start to build the flexibility to work together well. When the team also has well-formed outcomes and a compelling vision, it aligns more fully to its aims and aspirations and moves towards the desired results.

# Chapter 19

# Ten Tips for Using NLP in Business

. . . . . . . . . . . . . . . . . . . . . . . . . . . . . . . . . . . . . . . . . . . . . . . . . . . . . .

### In This Chapter

▶ Making it easier to use NLP at work

▶ Avoiding the mistakes others have made

. . . . . . . . . . . . . . . . . . . . . . . . . . . . . . . . . . . . . . . . . . . . . . . . . . . . . .

*H*ow you use and benefit from NLP is a very personal thing. You may well know just where you want to start and how you're going to go about incorporating all you now know into the workplace. Alternatively, you may find it helpful to get a few pointers to make it easier, and to avoid some pitfalls that might be ahead.

This chapter has ten tips for using NLP in business. These tips are words of advice based on my experience of supporting people to integrate NLP into their lives and work. I hope you find them helpful.

## Practise, Practise, Practise

It's wonderful watching toddlers learn to walk. They stagger a few steps, fall over, then get straight back up and try again. Youngsters practise, practise, and then practise some more until they aren't just tottering but walking. And when they've started walking, then they practise running, then jumping, skipping and dancing.

Are you one of those adults who has lost the determination they had as a teeny tot? If you really want to integrate NLP into your working life and get all its benefits, then keep on practising. Be prepared to fall over occasionally and then just pick yourself up, and practise all over again!

# Make It Up Good

A key pillar of NLP is knowing what you want. Thinking about an outcome that you desire rather than getting away from a problem that you have. That unconscious mind of yours is really powerful. What ever you feed in, it takes on board. Think about the possibilities of something going wrong and guess what, it most likely will.

When you imagine what's going to happen later today, tomorrow, or in ten years' time, you're making up the future in your mind. That's the power of imagination. Imagine that interview going well, and it probably will. Think about tripping over your words in that presentation, and you just might. So when you consider what you want, and what's coming up, and you think about what may happen, what you'll see, hear and feel, be sure to make it up good!

# Be in Rapport

Discovering new ways of thinking, and opening up possibilities, are the joys of NLP. It's a bit like being a kid at Christmas and getting masses of exciting new toys. I have witnessed many newcomers to NLP rush out into the world with their new toys with rampant enthusiasm, only to find they didn't put the batteries in. In this case, the batteries are rapport. You kow you ahevrapport when there is a connection between you and another person. Conversation is easy and trust exits. If you don't have rapport, you might find yourself doing NLP 'at' people. It might be very tempting to use those precision questions to challenge a colleague each and every time they say 'always', 'nobody', 'should', and the like. Believe me, if you're not in rapport this is a sure way to lose friends!

# Do a Bit at a Time

There's a whole feast of ideas and tools in this book for you to try out at work. You might feel overwhelmed and unsure as to where to start. Using NLP well is a skill, developed by trying things out, practising, and noticing what happens. If you take on too much too soon you may not know what it is that you're doing that's working and what isn't. Or, you might even procrastinate and do nothing at all as you just don't know where to start. Try out different facets of NLP at your own pace. Just get started and do it a bit at a time.

# *Avoid the Jargon*

Once you've experienced the benefits of using NLP and your enthusiasm grows, beware of becoming an NLP bore. I have met quite a few of them in my time! I've heard things like 'You and I have similar metaprograms', or 'We need to write that poster for all rep systems.' Be assured, this is not a great way to win friends and influence people!

I have visited businesses whose introduction to NLP has been jargon-fuelled. Did those people embrace NLP and get the benefits? No. They got pretty turned off. You may be tempted to share all your new-found knowledge with others. If you do, steer clear of the jargon and technical descriptions, avoid overwhelming people, and at all times make sure you have rapport.

# *Try Out New Techniques*

One of the NLP principles states that there is no failure, only feedback. Whatever you do, you're not failing, just getting more information about what isn't working. So what have you got to be afraid of? Try out the various techniques you come across in this book. Watch out and listen for the results you get. Experiment and try new things. If what you're doing isn't working, do something else until you reach your outcome. You'll become really good at using NLP and be building your flexibility as you do it.

# *Change Yourself Not Others*

Oh, how I'd like to change some of the people I work with at times. If only they thought more like me! Now that you've got all these wonderful insights and methods for changing people, wouldn't it be great to start to sort some of your colleagues out? Sorry, but it doesn't work like that.

The person to work on is yourself. Only you can change you. The incredible thing is that once you begin to do things differently, others will adapt and change their responses to you. So once you build rapport with that grumpy colleague and talk to him using his language patterns, not your own, hey presto! He's compelled to respond to you differently, and funnily enough, that was what you wanted.

Of course you may well ask what about coaching and training others with all these wonderful tools. Well, yes, that's just a wonderful thing to do, and really beneficial to those you do it with and yourself. Remember you're not changing them. You give feedback, you coach, and you support, but all the change comes from within.

# Stay Curious

Being curious about what you can accomplish through NLP is a really valuable state to be in. It gives you an open mind, and stops you making judgements before you try things out. Curiosity about your own unconscious mind and the patterns you run is a sure-fire way to find out more and widen your choices of how you act and react to things. It's not easy to give yourself a hard time when you' re constantly curious!

Being curious about other people also changes your outlook. When a colleague does something that seems crazy to you, or talks in a way you just don't get, be curious. Not only do you find out much more about that person and how to communicate with them more usefully, you stop yourself getting angry, frustrated, irritated or generally upset by their behaviour. Now that's got to be worth doing!

# Notice Your Successes

Now that you've spent time thinking about using NLP at work, you may want to get on and get some big wins, and fast. As you motor on to your destination, don't forget to stop and admire the scenery! The things you do with NLP along the way are important and you'll be achieving things all the time. Notice what effect you are having with your new way of thinking, the techniques you use, your questions and your different words and phrases (not forgetting your self-talk). Pay attention to your successes, however small, and be encouraged that you' can go on to achieve more and more.

# Have Fun

There's an awful lot to think about with NLP. With your new skills, you can make sure it doesn't weigh you down. You're now taking charge of your life to meet your dreams and aspirations. Enjoy. Have some laughs, and look for fun wherever you can as you travel on your journey.

# Chapter 20

# Ten Online NLP Resources

*T*he Internet offers a wealth of information on NLP, and continues to play an important part in the spread of NLP worldwide. If you wish to expand your knowledge of NLP, you can now visit hundreds of Web sites. (And if hundreds of options sound a bit overwhelming, don't worry, I highlight ten of my top choices in this chapter).

When you extend your NLP research online, you can connect with other people using NLP. You can locate groups which meet regularly in different regions to practise their NLP skills. And you can join in with discussion forums to share experiences. If you're interested in NLP training you'll find a wide choice of training organisations offering their (offline) courses. Maybe you have experience in NLP but want to keep up to date with latest developments by attending conferences. If so, you'll find these promoted on the Internet. And of course there is much to learn about NLP online – articles, case studies, research papers and more are available to read online, and increasingly mp3 podcasts are being made available for free too. Finally, books, CDs and DVDs, and magazine subscriptions can be bought online.

The ten sites featured in this chapter all offer valuable and helpful information, as well as providing links to many more online – and real-world – resources.

## NLP University

The NLP University Web site (www. nlpu.com) is a must-visit site. You can find information on the NLP University which is a training organisation that offers summer residential NLP training camps at the University of California in Santa Cruz, where NLP originated (more on the origins of NLP in Chapter 1).

The jewel in the crown of this Web site is the *Encyclopedia of Systemic NLP and NLP New Coding*, written by long term NLP developers Judith DeLozier and Robert Dilts. This book is the most comprehensive reference work on NLP in existence at over 1500 pages. Formatted as a traditional encyclopaedia, this publication is available to purchase (NLP University Press, 2000), yet is also offered online, free of charge, demonstrating the generosity of spirit and strong desire to share NLP knowledge by its authors. If you want to find out more about any particular NLP tool or techniques, aspects of its history, or just to get a deeper understanding of some of the unusual names (some call them NLP jargon!) that aspects of NLP have , you can view up to 25 pages of the encyclopaedia online a day.

# Association for Neuro Linguistic Programming

The UK-based Association for Neuro Linguistic Programming, or ANLP (www.anlp.org) is a not-for-profit membership organisation, supporting the NLP and coaching communities. Through its Web site you can identify and connect to practitioners and master practitioners if you want to work one-to-one on a personal issue. The onsite directory also lists its trainer members should you want to pursue NLP training.

The ANLP Web site also offers research information and case studies online, and links to books, CDs and DVDs You can also access a directory of UK-based NLP networks, in the form of practice groups, locally organised groups offering regular meetings in which NLP skill scan be practised or guest speakers heard. These groups all focus on explaining NLP skills and knowledge. Two excellent business NLP practice groups are promoted, based in London and Manchester. All details can be found on the site.

The ANLP also publishes *Rapport* magazine, a quarterly publication that's available free to members but can be subscribed to on-line by non-members. This magazine offers articles and case studies on the use of NLP in many areas, including business and coaching. Selected articles are reprinted on the site and back issues can also be ordered through the site.

# The NLP Conference

You can keep up with the details of the leading UK NLP conferences held at www.nlpconference.co.uk. Two conferences annually bring together leading international NLP innovators , trainers and experienced users of NLP, offering a broad range of workshops to select from, depending on your field of interest, including the application of NLP in business.

Additionally, the site offers articles, links to resources, and information on practice groups.

# Anchor Point

The Web site www.nlpanchorpoint.com is a valuable source of articles from leading developers and users of NLP in a range of situations, including business. The articles have all been published previously in the leading NLP magazine, *Anchor Point*. This site also offers a variety of NLP-based items for purchase, including books, audio and video, and other NLP tools.

# The Professional Guild of NLP

The Professional Guild of NLP is an independent association of professional training organisations and individual, trained NLP practitioners – mostly UK-based. If your appetite for NLP has been whetted and you'd like to attend an NLP training in the UK, you can identify a suitable training provider amongst Guild members, by searching the site: www.professionalguild-ofnlp.com. Alternatively, if you want to find a practitioner to work with on a personal issue, again you can search amongst Guild members on the site. In addition, you'll find some articles and other information on this Web site that may be of interest.

# Resource Magazine

Resource Magazine (www.resourcemagazine.co.uk) is a quarterly magazine of articles and insights on personal and business development. Published by Porto Publishing, the magazine is available, on subscription only, from the Web site and is delivered through the mail. The site offers a selection of free articles, including some excellent business articles and a free online sample of the magazine before you buy, so you can check out if it's for you.

# NLP Events

NLP Events (www.nlpevents.co.uk) lists a calendar of NLP events on offer all over the UK. Workshops, seminars, conferences, training programmes, and more are advertised on a month-by-month basis and continually updated, so you can discover relevant events near you at a glance. You can search by location, organisation and other criteria, and click through to each event organiser for more information and to book.

# The Clean Collection

The Clean Collection (www.cleanlanguage.co.uk) is a Web site owned by James Lawley and Penny Tompkins of The Developing Company. On this site you can access a prolific array of articles on Clean Language, Clean Space, metaphor ands other aspects of NLP. Written by Lawley and Tompkins, and many others, the articles cover a number of uses of these techniques in business and coaching, including case studies of specific applications. You can also find a number of techniques outlined and explained in some of the articles. You'll also find an online discussion forum, free to join for anyone using clean techniques to create change in organisations or elsewhere.

# NLP Weekly

NLP Weekly (www.nlpweekly.com) is an online magazine and blog. It contains a range of free articles and online videos. Edited by Slomo Vaknin, this networking and communications forum is now a large and active online NLP community. The online forum contains discussions on many threads, including NLP in business. Well worth a visit.

# Success Strategies

Success Strategies (www.successstrategies.com) is the Web site of Shelle Rose Charvet. Charvet is the author of *Words that Change Minds,* a highly practical book about using metaprograms at work (see Chapter 21 for more on this book.), and is an internationally-renowned trainer of the Language and Behaviour Profile (more on this in Chapter 7).

The Success Strategies site contains many articles – written by Charvet and others – that are full of practical tips and examples of using NLP to get results in business situations. You can get some useful ideas, free f charge, fro these articles, on how to to approach specific problems you currently face – in sales, communications or employee motivation.

# Chapter 21

# Ten Great Reads to Build Your Business NLP Library

. . . . . . . . . . . . . . . . . . . . . . . . . . . . . . . . . . . . . . . . . . . . . . . . . . . . .

### In This Chapter

▶ Targeting NLP principles to business specialisms

▶ Expanding your NLP knowledge and resources

▶ Introducing new NLP perspectives in your work

. . . . . . . . . . . . . . . . . . . . . . . . . . . . . . . . . . . . . . . . . . . . . . . . . . . . .

*A*mong the amazingly wide range of NLP books available, a smaller (but still impressive) number focus on using NLP tools and techniques in particular business disciplines. To help you build your business NLP library and expand your understanding of NLP techniques, this chapter lists ten of my favourite books, covering subjects from selling to creativity.

## Visionary Leadership Skills

If you're a leader, an aspiring leader, or just looking for a new way of thinking about leadership, then *Visionary Leadership Skills* (Meta Publication, 1996) is worth reading. Author Robert Dilts is one of the long-term developers and innovators in the field of NLP, as well as being an astounding trainer and prolific author. In this book, Dilts talks about *visionary leadership*, which he defines as the desire to enrich or change your life or your world. He explores the NLP skills and tools needed to lead change, including creating a vision, maintaining a good emotional state, managing beliefs and enhancing communications and influence. I like the fact that many of the skills covered have been studied and modelled from effective leaders – some business leaders, others not.

# Successful Selling with NLP

Joseph O'Connor, a talented NLP trainer and probably the most prolific British author of accessible NLP books, teamed up with Robin Prior, an experienced NLP executive coach and business consultant, to write *Successful Selling with NLP* (Thorsens, 2000). In this book the authors show how NLP can support the sales process by building strong customer relationships focused on meeting customer needs.

I found this book easy to read and follow, breaking the sales process down into each component part and identifying how to maximise your chance of success at each part of the sale. If you need to sell, your products, services or ideas, this entertaining book may be just what you're looking for.

# Words that Change Minds

The popularity of *Words that Change Minds* by Shelle Rose Charvet (Kendall/Hunt Publishing Company, 2nd edition, 1997) comes from its engaging and entertaining style combined with its useful and matter-of-fact advice. The book is full of humorous anecdotes and useful illustrations of how to understand others through their language and behaviour, based on NLP metaprograms (more on these in Chapter 7).

Charvet outlines the benefits of understanding and working with metaprograms in various business areas – including selling, advertising, recruiting, negotiating, and motivating. Charvet's practical, down to earth style gives very clear tips on how to spot people's metaprogram patterns and how to adapt to work with them. A very practical book indeed.

# Presenting Magically

If you want to add something powerful to your presentations, *Presenting Magically* (Crown House Publishing, 2001) is sure to hold something useful and enlightening for you. Authors Tad James and David Shephard, highly experienced NLP trainers, share the secrets of great presenters – how they think and what they do to captivate their audiences.

Using NLP tools and approaches, this book is full of tips, techniques, and useful exercises to help you enhance your next presentation and become a masterful presenter. You can try out the author's recommendations just one at a time, and notice the increased successes you get in engaging and motivating your audience. You can even learn to entertain and handle hecklers if you need to!

# Self-Coaching Leadership

*Self-Coaching Leadership* (John Wiley & Sons, 2007), by Angus McLeod, is a book which offers interesting and useful insights into leadership. This pragmatic and enjoyable book focuses on making the shift from managing to leading. Leaders at all levels – and indeed executive coaches – find this a worthwhile read.

McLeod is a very experienced performance coach who has coached at Board level in numerous organisations. He has a good reputation amongst the coaching world internationally, and is a founder of the Coaching Foundation.

This accessible book, much of which is informed by NLP, provides lots of exercises, which you can use to help you to know when and how to lead (rather than manage). Along the way, you discover tools to help you do a better job, reduce stress, and develop new leadership skills. In fact, working through the book is somewhat like having McLeod there coaching you!

# Tools for Dreamers

If you want to be more creative and innovative in business, *Tools for Dreamers* (Meta Publications, 1991) by NLP developers Robert Dilts and Todd Epstein has a world of ideas and inspiration. The book's premises are all based on the experience of NLP modelling of highly creative people, such that the structure of creative thinking can be understood and used by others.

*Tools for Dreamers* explores the strategies and steps involved in improving creativity at an individual level (day to day creativity and personal flexibility), group level (managing group creativity and stimulating innovation) and organisational level (promoting entrepreneurial beliefs and attitudes). A useful reference for any leader or trainer wishing to maximise creativity an innovation in business – or elsewhere.

# Training with NLP

In *Training with NLP* (Thorsens, 2002), Joseph O'Connor and John Seymour use their extensive experience and success as trainers and authors in the field of NLP to produce an excellent guide to training others. Whether you're a full-time trainer or only spend a portion of your time developing people's skills and abilities, this highly practical book has something for you. In addition to building confidence, presentation skills, and communication techniques, the book introduces ways to enable others to learn faster.

# The Unfair Advantage

*The Unfair Advantage* by Duane Larkin (Lakin Associates, 2001) is a workbook version of the NLP tools and techniques that Larkin has used for many years while training sales and marketing personnel to significantly improve their results. The book is full of practical exercises and covers a wide range of sales and marketing challenges, including telemarketing, direct mail, face-to-face selling, and more.

# Consult Yourself

If you're interested in applying NLP insights to good effect in management consultancy, then *Consult Yourself* (Crown House Publishing, 2005) by UK-based Carol Harris is a must-read book. The book covers problem solving, planning and analysis, information technology, networking, coaching, marketing, and more. It's particularly useful if you're an independent consultant or if you're new to consultancy, exploring the whole range of issues to consider to effectively manage your business, your clients, and your work.

# Communicating Strategy

One of the concerns held by many business leaders I work with is how to gain understanding and buy in to the business strategy throughout their organisation. *Communicating Strategy* (Gower, 2008), by Phil Jones, provides a well-thought through approach to both communicating, and engaging people, with organisational strategy.

With its roots firmly in NLP this book is pragmatic, easy-to read, and instructive. It deals not only with how to ensure others hear, understand and connect with a strategy, but what you need to do to stimulate action and motivate people to make changes to achieve the plan. A must-read for any reader wanting to overcome the obstacles which get in the way of implementing a new strategy to get significantly improved business results.

# Index

• *N* •

## • *O* •

## • *P* •

### • W •

# Notes

# Notes

# FOR DUMMIES®

## Do Anything. Just Add Dummies

## UK editions

### BUSINESS

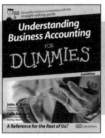

978-0-470-51806-9

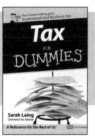

978-0-470-99245-6

978-0-470-75626-3

### FINANCE

978-0-470-99280-7

978-0-470-99811-3

978-0-470-69515-9

### PROPERTY

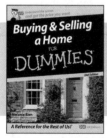

978-0-470-99448-1

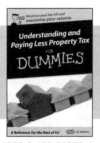

978-0-470-75872-4

978-0-7645-7054-4

Backgammon For Dummies
978-0-470-77085-6

Body Language For Dummies
978-0-470-51291-3

British Sign Language
For Dummies
978-0-470-69477-0

Children's Health For Dummies
978-0-470-02735-6

Cognitive Behavioural Coaching
For Dummies
978-0-470-71379-2

Counselling Skills For Dummies
978-0-470-51190-9

Digital Marketing For Dummies
978-0-470-05793-3

Divorce for Dummies
978-0-7645-7030-8

eBay.co.uk For Dummies,
2nd Edition
978-0-470-51807-6

English Grammar For Dummies
978-0-470-05752-0

Fertility & Infertility For Dummies
978-0-470-05750-6

Genealogy Online For Dummies
978-0-7645-7061-2

Golf For Dummies
978-0-470-01811-8

Green Living For Dummies
978-0-470-06038-4

Hypnotherapy For Dummies
978-0-470-01930-6

# FOR DUMMIES

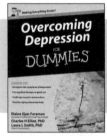

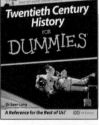
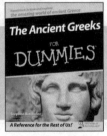

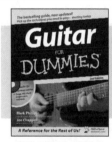

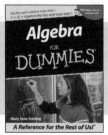

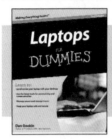

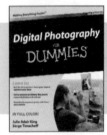

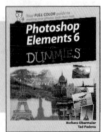